Japan Transformed

Japan Transformed

POLITICAL CHANGE AND ECONOMIC
RESTRUCTURING

Frances McCall Rosenbluth
and
Michael F. Thies

PRINCETON UNIVERSITY PRESS

PRINCETON AND OXFORD

Published by Princeton University Press, 41 William Street, Princeton, New Jersey 08540
In the United Kingdom: Princeton University Press, 6 Oxford Street, Woodstock,
Oxfordshire OX20 1TW

Library of Congress Cataloging-in-Publication Data
Rosenbluth, Frances McCall.
  Japan transformed : political change and economic restructuring / Frances McCall
Rosenbluth and Michael F. Thies.
    p. cm.
  Includes bibliographical references and index.
  ISBN 978-0-691-13591-5 (hardcover : alk. paper) — ISBN 978-0-691-13592-2 (pbk. :
alk. paper) 1. Japan—Politics and government. 2. Japan—Economic policy. I. Thies,
Michael F. II. Title.
  JQ1631.R67 2010
  320.952—dc22

                                                                        2009030845

British Library Cataloging-in-Publication Data is available

This book has been composed in Sabon

Printed on acid-free paper. ∞

press.princeton.edu

Printed in the United States of America

10 9 8 7 6 5 4 3 2 1

Contents

Tables and Figures

Preface

The midst of the most severe global financial crisis since the Great Depression might seem an odd time to be writing a book about Japan's new political economy. So much is up in the air in Japan and in the world economy that a book aiming at enduring explanation might appear foolhardy. In the most stable of times, unforeseen contingencies can have dramatic effects on the flow of events, and such uncertainty is even greater when the global financial system is shaken to its core. Like other countries, Japan will be forced to adjust to skittish international investors and lackluster consumer markets at home and abroad, and it will employ a wide array of policy measures to do so. Add to this the fact that the Liberal Democratic Party that has ruled Japan for so much of the postwar period faced its greatest electoral challenge ever in 2009, and the present surely seems like a less than propitious moment to launch a book about Japan's political system. But this book is about deeper structural changes that shape the ways in which political parties compete with each other, how they fashion their party platforms, and who will be the winners and losers in the Japanese political economy in today's "hard times," and in years to come.

The pivot of our analysis is a momentous change in electoral rules in 1994, when Japan abandoned its personalistic Single Nontransferable Vote system in favor of new rules with a more partisan and more majoritarian cast. Under the old system, three to five candidates were elected from each district. Multimember districts sound innocuous enough, as long as voters vote for parties, and each party receives its "fair share" of legislative seats. But in the old Japanese system, voters could cast only a single vote for an individual candidate, and since any party seeking to win a legislative majority had to field multiple candidates in most districts, electoral competition was dominated by "blood feuds" between members of the same parties.

The Liberal Democratic Party formed a legislative majority in 1955 when two smaller parties merged. Gaining control of the budget and policy making gave the majority party a huge advantage, but it now had to mitigate the potentially fratricidal combat among party members who were running against one another in each district. Following the path of least resistance, the party sought to distribute votes across multiple candidates by giving individual politicians the resources with which to cultivate personal followings. The LDP "sold" targetable favors in the form of tax breaks, budget subsidies, and regulatory and trade protection to corporate and agricultural constituents. With the coffers of campaign contributions raised from these "sales," LDP politicians ingratiated themselves with voters. LDP politicians and their minions showed up at weddings and funerals with money in their pockets. They sponsored flower-arranging classes, local festivals, trips to hot springs, and all sorts of other activities that connected name recognition with goodwill in their districts.

Money-intensive electoral politics and politicized market regulation introduced huge inefficiencies into the economy. These were largely invisible during the 1960s and 1970s, when export revenues were pouring in and the economy was growing rapidly. To be sure, Japanese voters as consumers were paying exceedingly high prices because politicians were selling protectionist regulation to industry. And protectionist regulation dampened the motivation to innovate in many areas. But for Japanese voters enjoying rising incomes and high employment, the occasional glimpses of government-business corruption were not alarming.

Many Japanese voters and foreign admirers thought that the postwar "economic miracle" would last forever. The Japanese system seemed a smarter variant of capitalism that took seriously the value of government-business cooperation, long-term corporate planning, and worker loyalty. Japan enjoyed superhigh economic growth and rapid urbanization for decades without experiencing the ill effects that often attend social dislocation, such as income inequality or crime. In the world outside, Japan's buying spree of American and European real estate and corporate assets set off waves of awe, self-doubt, and xenophobia.

Despite appearances of stability, however, tectonic plates were shifting under Japan's postwar political economy that eventually set off a succession of political earthquakes. First, Japan metamorphosed from a poor agrarian society into a rich urban one. Not only are wealthier voters less easily impressed by pork and patronage, but urban, middle-class voters were ill served by the barriers to food imports and the "bullet trains to nowhere" with which the LDP had consolidated its rural base. As the interests of a dwindling rural population diverged from those of a burgeoning urban one, the LDP's electoral machine became less efficient in generating electoral majorities. Electoral costs soared, and politicians' need for ever more campaign finance led to an accelerating drumbeat of scandals.

Second, as Japan's economy grew, it became inextricably intertwined with the world economy. However much the LDP may have tried to help Japanese exporters and protect importers, Japan's growth intensified foreign demands that it open its markets to foreign competition. Sectors of the economy that depended less on government protection, including automobiles and consumer electronics, came to see the LDP's dependence on the agricultural vote, and on campaign contributions from weak sectors of the economy, as a liability. Foreign governments, angry about Japan's agricultural protection, had no means of retaliating directly against Japanese farmers, but they could pressure Japan by imposing tariffs on Japanese cars or electronics. Economic globalization thus exposed the internal contradictions of the LDP's winning coalition of "steel and rice," and the party split and lost power for the first time.

New electoral rules adopted in 1994 ushered in a system of 300 plurality-rule single seat districts and 180 seats allocated to parties proportionally, with voters casting two separate votes—one for a district candidate and the other for a party list. This is a complex electoral system with some subtle effects that we describe, but the upshot of it is that it eliminates intraparty competition and strengthens parties' ability to put forward competing platforms that aim at the average voter—urban and middle-class. Institutions matter, but they themselves are shaped by political choices. We pay careful attention to the reasons why the politicians adopted these new rules, so as not to confuse the effects of the underlying reasons for change with the effects of the rule change per se.

Sweeping demographic and economic changes doomed the old coalition of steel and rice producers, rendering the electoral system for which it had been constructed an anachronistic burden. But there is more than one way in which rich democracies can come to terms with their largely urban populations and "globalized" economies, and Japan's particular choice of electoral rules has sweeping consequences that we document in this book. By moving in a majoritarian direction, Japan's political leaders chose electoral rules that would produce policies with a strong neoliberal center of gravity. A political party seeking a legislative majority under these new rules needs a broad coalition of voter support, the most efficient strategy being a set of policies that appeals to many voters without imposing unnecessary costs. Parties competing under majoritarian rules tend to emphasize low taxes and consumer protections over redistribution and protection. The contrast with proportional electoral systems—the road not taken in Japan—is striking. Where parties get legislative representation in proportion to their actual popularity (especially when districts are large and even small parties can win a few seats), a single majority party is unlikely and governments are formed by coalitions of parties. But because each individual party remains separately accountable to its particular constituency base, coalition governments often logroll to give each party something that its constituents care about intensely. Governments in proportional representation countries are more likely than governments in majoritarian countries to establish strong social security systems and regulations protective of labor and other groups that might be disadvantaged by trade openness.

The current financial crisis that erupted in the autumn of 2008 will loom large in discussions of policy and politics for some time to come. Governments everywhere must focus on the immediate threats to banking systems, employment, and consumer confidence. This might make a theoretical approach such as ours, which emphasizes the importance of institutions and the rules for political competition for explaining long-run patterns in politics and economic policy making, seem hopelessly academic.

But the current crisis will end at some point. While we cannot predict precisely what Japanese political economy will look like as the country grapples with emergency measures—which party or coalition will hold power, or how soon Japan will return to the path of economic liberalization—we are more sanguine about predicting the medium-term future. Unless the current crisis generates a strong enough sense of economic insecurity to cause Japan to abandon its new majoritarian electoral rules in favor of more proportional rules, the eventual policy response will be consistent with maintaining free markets internationally and domestically.

As we elaborate in this book, however, Japan faces a larger challenge than "merely" climbing out of the current economic malaise. In a society that is aging more rapidly than any in history, whose working-age population is shrinking precipitously, and whose welfare model has until now depended on employment protection for male breadwinners, the increased volatility brought by globalization and liberalization will send shockwaves through Japanese society for decades after the financial crisis has subsided. Inequality will rise to levels unknown since the 1950s. Japanese governments will have to build a new welfare model that can withstand the "creative destruction" of more unfettered capitalism and the inevitable expansion of economic immigration. Our reading of the New Japanese Political Economy suggests that the outcome will resemble the liberal market economies, such as the United States and the United Kingdom, much more closely than they will the more comprehensive social welfare systems of continental Europe.

Acknowledgments

Writing a book is rarely a solitary experience, and ours has been enriched with help from many quarters. In some ways our collaboration began almost twenty years ago at the University of California, San Diego, where Gary Cox and Mat McCubbins inspired us to learn more about American politics as a vantage point from which to think about Japan, and where we benefited enormously from their interest in Japan. In subsequent years we have gained insights and received corrections from conversations with many colleagues on both sides of the Pacific. In particular, we wish to thank Masahiko Asano, Kathy Bawn, Barry Burden, John Campbell, Peter Cowhey, Gerry Curtis, Margarita Estévez-Abe, John Ferejohn, Alan Gerber, Carol Gluck, Keizo Goto, Peter Gourevitch, Bernie Grofman, Koichi Hamada, Yasushi Hamao, Yusaku Horiuchi, Takeo Hoshi, Ikuo Kabashima, Junko Kato, Masaru Kohno, Ellis Krauss, Ikuo Kume, Arend Lijphart, Kenneth McElwain, Meg McKean, Michio Muramatsu, Megumi Naoi, Greg Noble, Roger Noll, Hugh Patrick, Robert Pekkanen, T. J. Pempel, Sam Popkin, Mark Ramseyer, Steve Reed, Ron Rogowski, Jun Saito, Rob Salmond, Dick Samuels, Hiroshi Sasaki, Ross Schaap, Ethan Scheiner, Len Schoppa, Susan Shirk, Matthew Shugart, Jack Snyder, Steve Vogel, Rob Weiner, Barry Weingast, and David Weinstein. Jun Saito and Annalisa Zinn had a great deal to do with the research and analysis behind chapter 8, for which we thank them. Margarita Estévez-Abe's and Len Schoppa's suggestions made for a much better book, and their factual corrections spared us grave embarrassment. Carles Boix suggested links to the literature on democratic transitions, Torben Iversen insisted on relevance to comparative political economy, and Ian Shapiro cleared away more jargon from the manuscript than we like to admit. For excellent research assistance, we would like to thank Linda Hasunuma, Andrea Katz, Natsu Matsuda, Shoki Omori, Adam Scharfman, Sakina Shibuya, Kyohei Yamada, and Yuki Yanai—Japan scholars of the future.

We are fortunate to have been the recipients of generous funding from a variety of sources including the Council on Foreign Relations, the Abe Fund, and the MacMillan Center for International and Area Studies at Yale, as well as UCLA's Terasaki Center for Japanese Studies and Academic Senate Committee on Research. For masterful editorial help and suggestions, we thank Chuck Myers at Princeton University Press.

Abbreviations and Stylistic Conventions

ABBREVIATIONS

Electoral Systems, Political Parties, Politics

CGP	Clean Government Party (usually called by its Japanese name, *Komeito*)
CP	Conservative Party
DPJ	Democratic Party of Japan
DSP	Democratic Socialist Party
JCP	Japan Communist Party
JSP	Japan Socialist Party (later changed its name to Social Democratic Party)
LDP	Liberal Democratic Party
LP	Liberal Party
MM(M)	Mixed-Member (Majoritarian) electoral system (Lower House, 1996–present)
NFP	New Frontier Party
NLC	New Liberal Club
NPH	New Party Harbinger (*Sakigake*)
NPN	New Party Nippon
PNP	People's New Party
PR	proportional representation electoral rule
SMD	single-member district
SNTV	Single Nontransferable Vote electoral system (Lower House, 1947–1993)

Bureaucratic Agencies and Programs

BOJ	Bank of Japan
FILP	Fiscal Investment and Loan Program
FSA	Financial Services Agency
MITI	Ministry of International Trade and Industry (became METI—Ministry of Economy, Trade, and Industry)
MOF	Ministry of Finance
SDF	Self Defense Forces
SIA	Social Insurance Agency

CONVENTIONS

For Japanese names, we follow Japanese practice and write the surname first, followed by the given name.

Romanization of Japanese words is not completely standardized, especially as regards long vowel sounds, as with the "o" sounds in "Tokyo." In some works, long vowels are presented with a macron over the vowel, or as "oh" or "ou." Except in the case of names whose owners prefer another style, we eschew all such guides to pronunciation, and do not distinguish between long and short vowel sounds. We are hoping that if the text is ever performed onstage or reproduced as an audio book, a fluent speaker of Japanese will be hired for the job and will know what to do.

Japan Transformed

CHAPTER 1

Why Study Japanese Political Economy?

INTRODUCTION

Japan limped into the twenty-first century with an economy in deep malaise. Following the collapse of the Tokyo stock and real estate markets that began in 1990, the Japanese economy failed to regain its stride, languishing at near-zero growth for a decade and a half. Saddled with a large fiscal deficit, the government was hard pressed to stimulate the economy in the wake of the 2008–2009 financial tsunami originating in New York.[1] The prolonged slump that had been called "Japan's lost decade" began to look more like a chronic affliction.

Despite appearances, Japan is not an economic has-been on its last legs but a country in the throes of a transformation from a corrupt, managed economy to an economy shaped by a more open and scrappier political process. Japan's political system is healthier than ever before, though it will be tested heavily by new global pressures, rising inequality, and a rapidly aging population. This book seeks to explain what happened to create Japan's new political economy, how it matters, and what it means for Japan's future.

Japan's twenty-first-century metamorphosis into a "normal democracy" has not gripped the attention of the West as did its earlier phase as a voracious conqueror of export markets seemingly on the verge of global economic dominance. The subject of hysterical movies, xenophobic rhetoric, and countless university courses, the once-defeated Japan had turned the tables and was now the Godzilla invading American shores.[2] In 1988 a group of U.S. congressmen, protesting what they felt were Japan's unfair trading practices, smashed a Toshiba boom box with sledgehammers on the steps of the Capitol. Historian Paul Kennedy declared that Japan was poised to replace the United States as the world's leading economy.[3]

---

[1] Japan's debt, at 170 percent of GDP in January 2009, was the largest among industrialized countries.

[2] Crichton 1992; Burstein 1988; Friedman and LeBard 1991; Vogel 1979; Choate 1990; von Wolferen 1990; Prestowitz 1988; Fallows 1989.

[3] Kennedy 1989.

Japan deserves more attention today than it received in its false glory days. As subsequent events made clear, much of the earlier fanfare about, and fear of, Japan was misplaced. Japan's economic model was not nearly as powerful as it looked. Large market shares masked thin profits and low productivity, signaling trouble for the economy's endurance. Government protection let inefficient industries survive for too long, hampering what Joseph Schumpeter once described as capitalism's innovative "creative destruction." Essential postwar industries became national and global laggards, compounding inherited problems in the financial and public sectors of the economy.

Though with little domestic fanfare and even less notice from the rest of the world, Japan began reinventing itself in the 1990s in ways that evoke parallels with the Meiji Restoration of 1868. As with the Meiji overthrow of the Tokugawa regime, Japan's political economy in the twenty-first century replaces a failed attempt to close its borders with one that accepts integration with the world economy as inevitable. Also as occurred in the Meiji Restoration, the old political structure that rested on uncompetitive domestic forces collapsed, to be supplanted by new institutions more compatible with global integration. Japan's new electoral rules, established in 1994, create noticeably different incentives influencing how politicians regulate the economy and how they approach foreign policy. Because Japan remains the world's third largest economy,[4] it is important to understand how its domestic politics will shape its engagement with the world in years to come.

Transformations like those Japan is undergoing tell us about how politics works in a more general sense. When do political institutions change, and do they matter apart from the forces that brought about their change in the first place? How powerful are institutional incentives in shaping the political and economic landscape? How do they interact with inherited political culture and the interests of entrenched elites?

Most theories of politics of the developed world are based on the experiences of the United States and Europe. Despite being one of the world's richest countries, Japan is often the "odd man out," not only because language barriers impede the full integration of Japan's experience into the Western canon, but also because the policies Japan has adopted have seemed anomalous in the context of either Anglo-American laissez-faire or continental European welfare states. Now that Japan is moving in an

---

[4]Japan is number three when measured according to purchasing-power-parity (PPP), having recently been surpassed by China. In nominal terms (at current exchange rates) Japan's economy is second only to that of the United States.

Anglo-American direction, should we interpret these changes as harbingers of global economic convergence? The key to understanding the economic system to which Japan is moving, we will argue, lies both in pressures from the world economy and in how they are filtered through domestic political institutions.

JAPAN IN THE WORLD

Despite nearly two decades of economic stagnation, Japan remains a colossal power. Its economy is enormous, and although it has been surpassed in absolute size by China's (with China's ten-times-as-large population), Japan is economically still more than a third larger than fifth-ranked Germany and twice as large as the United Kingdom or France. Although Japan officially has no army, navy, or air force, owing to its constitutional renunciation of war, the Japan Self Defense Forces (SDF) are in fact a formidable military by another name. By many other measures as well, Japan is an extremely influential player whose actions have bearing for world peace, prosperity, and health. Understanding why the Japanese do what they do on the world stage requires knowledge of how Japan's democracy translates the preferences of its citizens, interest groups, bureaucrats, and politicians into national policy and action.

Table 1.1 compares Japan with other OECD countries, plus China, in terms of territory, population, and economic size. Japan's millions are densely nestled in the valleys and narrow plains of a mostly dormant volcanic mountain range, forming the four major islands and countless small ones that make up the Japanese archipelago. The total land mass is smaller than the state of California and only 4 percent of the size of the United States, and only 12 percent of Japan's land is arable. Japan is also physically smaller than France and marginally larger than Germany and the United Kingdom. Metropolitan Tokyo, with over 35 million residents, is the world's largest city, dwarfing Mexico City (19 million) and New York City (18.5 million).

With few stores of natural resources but considerable ingenuity, occasional predation, and institutionalized economizing, Japan built a powerful industrial economy to rival the world's greatest. Japan's 2008 GDP per capita was $35,300, well behind Luxembourg's $85,100 and the United States' $48,000, but above Germany's $34,800 and far, far ahead of China's $6,100. Japan's weight is felt in visible industrial exports, as well as in its less visible purchases of raw materials from around the

TABLE 1.1
Japan's Place in World Rankings, 2008: Size and Wealth

Area ('000 sq. km)†	Population (millions)	GDP ($ billions)‡	Per Capita GDP (US $)‡
2. Canada (9,984.7)	1. China (1,338.6)	* EU (14,960)	3. Luxembourg (85,100)
3. United States (9,826.6)	* EU (491.6)	1. USA (14,580)	6. Norway (57,500)
4. China (9,597.0)	3. USA (307.2)	2. China (7,800)	10. USA (48,000)
6. Australia (7,686.9)	10. Japan (127.1)	3. Japan (4,487)	11. Ireland (47,800)
* EU (4,324.8)	11. Mexico (111.2)	5. Germany (2,863)	15. Iceland (42,600)
14. Mexico (1,972.6)	16. Germany (82.3)	6. UK (2,281)	18. Netherlands (41,300)
36. Turkey (780.6)	17. Turkey (76.8)	8. France (2,097)	19. Switzerland (40,900)
41. France (643.4)	21. France (64.1)	10. Italy (1,801)	21. Canada (40,200)
50. Spain (504.8)	22. UK (61.1)	11. Mexico (1,578)	22. Sweden (39,600)
54. Sweden (450.0)	23. Italy (58.1)	12. Spain (1,378)	23. Australia (39,300)
60. Japan (377.8)	25. South Korea (48.5)	13. Canada (1,336)	24. Austria (39,200)
61. Germany (357.0)	31. Spain (40.5)	14. South Korea (1,278)	25. Denmark (38,900)
63. Finland (338.1)	34. Poland (38.5)	16. Turkey (931)	27. Finland (38,400)
66. Norway (323.8)	38. Canada (33.5)	18. Australia (825)	28. Belgium (38,300)
68. Poland (312.7)	54. Australia (21.3)	20. Netherlands (688)	30. UK (37,400)
69. Italy (301.2)	59. Netherlands (16.7)	21. Poland (685)	32. Spain (36,500)
73. New Zealand (268.7)	74. Greece (10.7)	29. Belgium (399)	34. Japan (35,300)
76. UK (244.8)	75. Portugal (10.7)	33. Sweden (358)	36. Germany (34,800)

94. Greece (131.9)	78. Belgium (10.4)	34. Greece (351)	* EU (34,000)
105. Iceland (103.0)	80. Czech Republic (10.2)	37. Austria (325)	37. Greece (32,800)
106. South Korea (98.5)	83. Hungary (9.9)	39. Switzerland (310)	38. France (32,700)
107. Hungary (93.0)	88. Sweden (9.1)	41. Czech Republic (274)	41. Italy (31,000)
108. Portugal (92.4)	93. Austria (8.2)	42. Norway (267)	49. New Zealand (28,500)
111. Austria (83.9)	95. Switzerland (7.6)	45. Portugal (245)	50. Czech Republic (26,800)
113. Czech Rep (78.9)	110. Denmark (5.5)	50. Denmark (214)	51. South Korea (26,000)
117. Ireland (70.3)	111. Slovakia (5.5)	51. Hungary (206)	53. Slovakia (22,600)
127. Slovakia (48.8)	113. Finland (5.3)	53. Finland (201)	54. Portugal (22,000)
131. Denmark (43.1)	116. Norway (4.7)	54. Ireland (199)	58. Hungary (20,500)
132. Netherlands (41.5)	124. New Zealand (4.2)	60. Slovakia (123)	70. Poland (17,800)
133. Switzerland (41.3)	125. Ireland (4.2)	61. New Zealand (119)	83. Mexico (14,400)
137. Belgium (30.5)	169. Luxembourg (0.5)	95. Luxembourg (41)	88. Turkey (12,900)
170. Luxembourg (2.6)	178. Iceland (0.3)	138. Iceland (13)	130. China (6,100)

Source: Central Intelligence Agency. 2009. *The 2008 World Factbook*. https://www.cia.gov/library/publications/the-world-factbook/.
Note: The numerical rankings are for all countries of the world, but these lists include only the thirty OECD member countries, plus China and an entry for the European Union as a whole.

†Area includes both land and water, which explains why the United States is ranked as larger than China.

‡GDP and GDP per capita are measured at Purchasing Power Parity. Measured instead at current exchange rates, Japan's economy is still somewhat larger than China's.

world. Japan exported $566 billion worth of industrial and other products in 2007, 22.4 percent of that to the United States and 13 percent to China. Japan's imports lean toward fuel and raw materials rather than finished manufactured products, a pattern that has gotten it in trouble with its trading partners that covet greater access to Japanese consumers. Toyota, Mitsubishi, and Sony have long been in greater evidence around the world than are American or European counterparts in Japan. In more recent decades, Japanese games and animation have also captured worldwide audiences as the Japanese economy shifts into software and services.

The Japanese government has spent considerable sums in support of its diplomatic aims to maintain peace and prosperity. Japan is the number two foreign aid donor in the world behind the United States, and also second to the United States in terms of support for the United Nations, the World Bank, and the International Monetary Fund. As a fraction of GDP, Japan pays the UN twice what the United States contributes (and more than Germany or the United Kingdom), and its contributions to the World Bank and the IMF, respectively, are greater than, and on par with, those of the United States.[5]

Evidence of Japan's financial muscle is consistent with its typical description as an economic giant, but Japan's military strength is less widely understood. After World War II, the Japanese public was not only disillusioned with the militarism of its own government but also horrified by the devastation visited upon Hiroshima and Nagasaki by American atomic bombs. Japan's low military profile, though initially imposed via the 1947 constitution by the U.S.-led Occupation, retains widespread popular support. As the economy prospered, however, the small percentage of Japan's GNP allocated to military expenditures grew to enormous sums. Although Japan's $42 billion spent on defense in 2007 is still less than 10 percent of the U.S. defense budget, the striking feature of contemporary military spending is not how little Japan spends but how far ahead of the rest of the world are U.S. military expenditures. The United States accounts for about two-fifths of the world's military expenditures, which is as much as the fourteen closest-ranking military spenders combined, and seven times more than China.[6] Japan's military budget in 2007 ranked seventh in the world, after the United States, China, Russia, France, and the United Kingdom, but ahead of Germany.

[5]Philip Lipscy (2005) argues that Japan has greater influence in the World Bank than in the IMF because Japan could, if it wanted, bypass the World Bank in offering aid but it could not create a substitute for the IMF's provision of international financial stability.

[6]U.S. Office of the Secretary of Defense 2007.

By whatever measure, Japan is one of the world's greatest powers. Understanding how Japan became powerful and how it uses its might is important, if for no other reason, for grasping the prospects for world peace. General theories and approaches of politics, suitably modified, are useful in enabling us to understand Japanese politics and policy making. At the same time, the Japanese example can help us understand what is idiosyncratic about theories developed in the American or European contexts, and can contribute to more general theories of politics.

THEORIES

We build the case here that Japan's policy choices are politically shaped rather than culturally or economically determined, and that politics in Japan follows a logic similar to that of politics elsewhere. There are numerous examples of existing theories that explain aspects of Japanese political economy quite well. As we discuss in the following chapters, materialist and institutionalist theories of democracy receive validation in explaining when representative government took root in Japan. A classic materialist account of Japan's current democratic stability would credit relative income equality after World War II with limiting leftist demands for redistribution. Institutionalists would point to constitutional provisions that regularized political competition and sustained among the electorate stable expectations of peaceful contestation for power. Theories of strategic competition predicted accurately both the number of factions in the LDP and the number of political parties that survived.[7] For the reforms of the 1990s, materialist theories help account for the collapse of Japan's electoral rules in terms of changes in the distribution of economic resources. Institutionalist theories, which shift the focus to the electoral underpinnings of policy making, are important for elucidating how electoral incentives buffered and channeled economic pressures for several decades prior to the collapse.

While Japan nicely showcases the usefulness of some theories of politics, it sits uneasily with others. It would be a pity if our understanding of the politics of advanced democracies were to leave Japan out simply because it is hard to find theories that can explain the conspicuous mismatch between Japan's experiences and those of others. But what is one to make of Japan's small welfare state on an American scale, combined

[7]Reed 1990; Kohno 1997; Cox 1997.

with income equality, heavily interventionist economic policies, and sticky labor markets that more closely resemble those in many European states?

Political sociologist Gøsta Esping-Andersen classified rich democracies into "three worlds" of welfare capitalism: "social democracies" such as in Scandinavia where governments underwrite equal outcomes to a substantial degree through wage coordination and progressive taxation; "Christian democracies" such as Germany and Italy that protect organized labor (though without the thoroughgoing commitment to societal equality of the Scandinavians); and Anglo-American "liberal" market economies that privilege economic growth over either equality or employment.[8] This typology describes Western Europe and the United States relatively well, but Esping-Andersen himself admits to being stumped by Japan.[9]

Our approach focuses on the interplay between political institutions and material forces. The institutional arrangements governing political competition shape the economy in discernible ways. But politicians can never completely control the distribution of resources. Wealth has a way of growing where innovation is most active, with or without government sponsorship. The Japanese government did slow the effects of globalization on politics by promoting exports ahead of the imports that would have introduced a wider range of competitors to Japanese markets. But export businesses that were winners on the global stage eventually sought to cut loose from the domestic-market-bound laggards—the farmers and small businesses—that could survive only with government protection. In time, the acquisition of resources by new groups and the collapse of formerly powerful groups threw Japan's political institutions into disarray. This, in a nutshell, is the story behind the boom and bust of the 1980s and 1990s and the electoral reform that followed. The existing rules of political competition proved unworkable, and the changed electoral rules put into place a new regulatory structure with vast consequences for the shape of Japan's political economy.

PLAN OF THE BOOK

An interest in politics is not the most common pathway to the study of Japan. More typically, people are drawn to Japanese aesthetics, animation, or—before the bubble burst—the Japanese "economic miracle."

[8]Esping-Andersen 1990, 1999.
[9]Estévez-Abe 2008.

Politics was the poor relation of this ancient and exotic society that had been transformed into an economic powerhouse in a few short years after the Second World War. Time was, not long ago, when the Japanese themselves spoke disparagingly of their "first-rate economy and third-rate politics (*keizai ichiryu, seiji sanryu*)." The postwar electoral system did indeed establish a bad set of incentives for Japan's political leaders, leading to corruption on a massive scale from which the "first-rate economy" was ultimately not immune. Japan's changed political system, following the electoral reform of 1994, gets higher marks on a normative scale of democratic governance, but its economic consequences are mixed. As is true everywhere, Japanese politics is key to its policies, including those that structure the economy.

In chapter 2, we explore the view that Japan's polity and economy have been shaped decisively by a unique cultural heritage. In contrast to this, we provide a view of culture as politically shaped and often in flux. We do not deny that cultural repertoires make some political strategies more likely than others, but they do this by supplying the materials for political entrepreneurship rather than by blinding actors to alternative choices. Japanese political behavior and Japanese culture more generally respond to broader incentives. Factions come and go, depending on what political candidates gain from factional affiliation; citizens' respect for bureaucrats waxes and wanes depending on bureaucrats' policy-making discretion; voters heed party platforms, or not, depending on whether the party platform is a likely to be translated into policies, and whether it provides a useful cue for voting behavior. The variation in these and other attributes of Japanese politics over time is considerable.

Our brief sketch of Japanese history from prehistoric times demonstrates the stark changes in Japanese values that have accompanied changes in circumstances. Any notion that Japanese culture is an immutable force operating on the minds of modern Japanese is belied by the variety of cultures in Japan's own past. On inspection, "culture" turns out to result from historical changes that themselves stand in need of explanation. Otherwise the appeal to "culture" is no more enlightening than is the description of Japan's early postwar economic success as a "miracle."

Chapter 3 recounts several Japanese experiments with democracy, beginning with the Meiji oligarchs who attempted but failed to insulate Japan's new constitutional monarchy from party competition. What are the conditions under which democracy emerges and is sustainable? Was Japan's democratic interlude during the 1920s a genuine expression of government "by the people," or was it doomed to fail? Did Japan's late industrialization (as compared to that of the United States and the United Kingdom) consign it to a pattern of economic organization that required a "strong state," militating against pluralist democracy? Was Japanese military expansionism into Asia an inevitable outgrowth of its political and economic structure, or was Japan playing, perhaps a little too late, the realist game of power politics that the European nations had pursued during the nineteenth century?[10] Our evidence reveals the inadequacy of approaches that rely on such economic factors as income levels, income distribution, or the timing of industrialization. We show that the strategic behavior of actors was crucial to choices over economic and military policy, as were the rules governing political competition among those actors.

Chapter 4 tells the story of Japan's postwar political system, characterized by long-term dominance by the Liberal Democratic Party. Japan's multimember-district electoral rules required any party wishing to win or maintain a majority to field multiple candidates in head-to-head battles. This created a vote allocation problem: how, in a democracy, could a party persuade voters to allocate their votes across candidates to maximize the party's electoral fortunes? Given that voters could be expected to resist control from the top, one might suppose that the resulting internal competition would destabilize large parties. Indeed, the LDP was highly factionalized and looked prone to splits along multiple lines. Because the benefit of the party label suffered under the pressure of copartisans campaigning against one another, the LDP's long-term command of a legislative majority has always posed something of a puzzle.

This chapter unravels the puzzle by examining how the LDP managed to overcome the joint product-differentiation and vote-division problems that the electoral system created. In short, the LDP traded its control over government policy for campaign finance from corporations and votes from heavily subsidized backward sectors of the economy. This advantage was sufficiently large to keep party factions loyal to the majority party and to preclude party splits.

The Japanese experience sheds light on the debate in comparative and American politics as to conditions under which parties appeal to core or swing voters,[11] showing that electoral rules that introduce intraparty competition enhance the electoral importance of core voters. This, in

---

[10]Iriye 1972.

[11]Cox and McCubbins 1986; Lindbeck and Weibull 1987; Dixit and Londregan 1996; Levitt and Snyder 1995; McGillivray 2004; Golden and Picci 2008. On Japan, see Horiuchi and Saito 2003.

turn, vanquishes the old saw that the Japanese political system is sui generis. Japanese politicians respond to electoral incentives just as politicians do in other democracies. By obliging each incumbent to create a core group of loyal voters, the electoral rules generated enormous collective action costs for voters who might otherwise have supported redistribution to the median on a simple left-right continuum.

Japan's postwar political economy, which we take up in chapter 5, has been likened to a phoenix rising from ashes. Within a few decades after total defeat and the utter devastation of its industrial cities, Japan turned itself into an economic juggernaut, poised, some thought, to take over the world economy with commercial power in lieu of military force. Standard accounts of Japan's postwar economic success center on the prescience of the Japanese bureaucracy, or on market institutions such as main banks and cross-shareholding that improved on laissez-faire capitalism by building in a "long-term perspective."

The argument put forward here is rather that the Japanese heavy industrialists, who came through the war with large sunk costs in munitions, steel, and shipbuilding, lobbied the LDP to back their investments with a development strategy privileging heavy industries. The result was protectionist regulation, budget subsidies, and tax deals that set Japan on a development plan that supported exports while discouraging competing imports. The plan meshed well with the LDP's electoral strategy: in exchange for policy favors, industry funneled enormous campaign contributions into the LDP's electoral campaign coffers. All was well while the economy grew, for voters gave the LDP credit for the phenomenal success. But eventually the economy faltered under the weight of accumulated inefficiencies, and the LDP found itself with decades of economic mismanagement to pay for.[12]

Chapter 6 considers why the LDP in 1994 abandoned the electoral system that it had mastered for so long, in favor of a new system that mixed single-member districts and proportional representation. This chapter explains the political causes and consequences of electoral reform. Japan's demographic transformation from a largely rural nation of farmers and small shopkeepers to one of urban workers undermined the effectiveness and raised the costs of the LDP's vote allocation strategy described in chapters 4 and 5. By the early 1990s, some in the LDP's leadership

---

[12]Understanding this reality is of particular comparative importance in view of the claims currently being made about China's economic miracle. Investment misallocations analogous to those experienced in Japan are likely to have comparable deleterious effects for the Chinese economy not too far down the road.

reckoned that the "floating" urban voters were harder to allocate efficiently across multiple candidates in multimember districts, and it would be better for the party's fortunes to adopt plurality electoral rules that would advantage the largest party, in combination with proportionality rules that would keep the Opposition divided into smaller parties.

This finding is buttressed by our analysis of the changes in Japanese politics since electoral reform. Although out of office for only a brief time, the LDP has undergone an unmistakable transformation. LDP factions have atrophied, for much diminished is the need for LDP politicians to raise resources to differentiate themselves from copartisans. Electoral campaigns have become more programmatic and less personalistic, as the new electoral rules give the advantage to campaigns that can appeal efficiently to broad swaths of voters. Voters appealed to in this way take greater interest in, and have greater influence over, national policy.

We argue that economic policy and the market institutions to which they give rise are politically driven. The electoral rule change of 1994 provides a rare opportunity to test this claim. Chapter 7 investigates economic policy after electoral reform for evidence of stasis or change, and finds that banking and stock market regulation have shifted toward the interests of the average consumers and taxpayers, as we would expect. Japan's version of neoliberalism is the result, as the government unwinds protection of economically inefficient sectors, including agriculture and parts of the service sector such as distribution.

Although the Japanese government is tackling the problems of low productivity by allowing fiercer domestic and international competition in Japanese markets, Japan's troubles are far from over. Income inequality looms large because Japan's protected sectors harbored millions of workers who were "underemployed" and paid wages beyond their economic contribution. Electoral competition has put the spotlight on Japan's weak welfare protections, a problem that the rapidly aging population and economic swings put in high relief.

Japan's electoral rules, which pit two large parties against one another in competition for the median voter, weaken the political power of labor unions and minimize the possibility that Japan will grapple with income inequality through employment guarantees and unemployment compensation in European fashion. But median voter preferences have begun to push the dominant parties to support more generous public funding of pensions and other forms of social security than was the case in the past. Japan's political economy has shifted from the postwar equilibrium—of economic protection of politically favored groups—to a freer market that produces losers whose only hope of policy attention is their proximity to the median voter.

Chapter 8 examines the effects of changes in domestic political incentives on foreign policy. In recent years, Japan's Asian neighbors have sounded alarm bells about signs of rising Japanese nationalism. Textbook censorship continues to downplay Japan's history as an imperialist power in Asia. Japanese opinion polls show growing public support for an assertive Japanese foreign policy and for amending the "peace constitution" to permit rearmament.

Several explanations for Japan's new nationalism are on offer, primarily having to do with geopolitical changes. China continues to grow in strength as a regional and global power, while the end of the Cold War casts doubt on the depth of American commitment to protect Japan's interests. North Korea has become more dangerous and threatening. And the Iraq War is likely to stoke fears of a new era of American isolationism.

A closer look at Japanese public opinion data, however, reveals a more subtle pattern that defies explanation by exclusive reference to changes in Japan's external environment. Whereas the Japanese public increasingly supports an assertive foreign policy, opinion polls show no growth in national pride, or in a willingness to "follow the government, right or wrong." As we saw with domestic policy in chapter 7, we show here that parties now have an incentive to make broad appeals to the average voter with public-goods-oriented policies. Under the old electoral rules, politicians appealed to voters on narrow, personalistic grounds, but with more centrism built into the system, appealing to voters on issues of national policy makes electoral sense.

Some people wrote off Japan's political reforms of the early 1990s when they failed to usher in a new era of two-party competition with regular alternation in government. We take up this subject in chapter 9. It is true that Japan has not moved all the way to a Westminster system. It is also true that there is little hope for judicial independence while one party continues to appoint all the members of the Supreme Court. But it would be a mistake to underestimate the far-reaching effects of the electoral reform. Although the LDP has remained in government for all but a few months since 1994, the electoral strategy by which it does so has changed discernibly. In single-member districts, each LDP candidate must aim for a plurality of votes, in competition with other parties' candidates pursuing the same goal. The old "divide and conquer" electoral strategy of carving out and cultivating a niche of loyal voters with personalistic appeals is now both inefficient and insufficient. Programmatic party competition, on national and foreign policy issues, increasingly shapes the debates in which voters take part. The prospects for regular partisan alternation in government are higher than ever, as is the possibility that the LDP will collapse, leading to a dramatic realignment of the party system.

Whatever the ultimate fate of the LDP and the rival Democratic Party of Japan, the fundamental reorganization of Japan's political system that began with electoral reform in the early 1990s will continue to work its way through Japan's economic, social, and national security policies. Under the new electoral rules, propping up cartels in exchange for campaign funds is no longer a key to victory, and politicians are debating each other and taking positions on competing visions of the public interest. This is the good news. Although policy change is halting and uneven, changes in financial regulation, labor market institutions, and foreign policy follow a striking pattern: the cozy deals of the postwar period are under siege, and voters are being drawn into public debate over Japan's future.

CHAPTER 2

Japanese History and Culture

INTRODUCTION

Tourists visiting a country for the first time can be overwhelmed by cultural differences, large and small. To an American setting foot on Japanese soil, the cars drive on the wrong side of the road; mass transport and street commerce seem somehow to be highly sterile and automated, and yet nearly chaotic owing to the sheer number of people moving about; and strangers seem at once extremely polite and emotionally remote. The social choreography that organizes human life, ordinarily invisible and taken for granted, is unnervingly unfamiliar. It is often when visiting another country that people become aware for the first time of their own cultural baggage masquerading as common sense.

Japanese politics looks unusual as well. If one were to arrive in Japan during an election campaign, one would notice that candidates do not engage in house-to-house canvassing, but instead set up temporary soapboxes at train stations, grasp as many as a dozen microphones in white-gloved hands, and proceed to shout at commuters as they hurry to or from their trains. One's ears would be assaulted as well by the voices of candidates or their assistants blasted from the loudspeakers atop trucks circulating through the streets beginning at eight in the morning. The candidate would be stating his or her name and party affiliation over and over again, saying nothing about policy, but pleading to be remembered at the polls on the upcoming election day. Someone examining old election results would also notice that Japanese voters tended to give "sympathy votes" to candidates who lost in previous elections. What deeper meanings can be deciphered from these and other clues?

Japanese culture, and hence Japanese political culture, is different in many interesting ways from what might be found in other advanced democracies including the United States, Canada, and Western Europe. Of course, every democracy is unique in some ways, but the fundamental premise of comparative politics is that they are not so different as to be incomparable. The basics of democracy—voters, parties, elections, legislatures—are ubiquitous, and the individual country cases are variations on a theme. Beyond the formal rules enshrined in constitutions and electoral laws, there are norms, what Douglass North referred to as "informal institutions." Norms are the cultural glue that help members of a society to fill in the gaps left by the formal rules; they are based on a template of shared beliefs and serve as internalized guides to action. Norms develop over generations and may go unquestioned even when formal rules break down as a society undergoes some form of political transition.

But when circumstances change dramatically enough, even long-standing norms can be overturned by new beliefs about how the world works. Sometimes shifts from one organizational scheme to another are imposed exogenously, by invasion or occupation. Sometimes they may be local responses to external events, a sort of preemptive revolution designed to forestall encroachment by outsiders. Other times, they are internally driven by the failings of an old equilibrium, and can lead to regime collapse, internal warfare, or anarchy. A historical view reveals that the Japanese political economy and Japanese culture have experienced each of these types of transition, some more than once, and proved to be highly adaptive to new constraints and opportunities. People might fall back on well-established norms as they struggle to adapt to new circumstances, but the norms themselves can change over time as well. Like cultural values anywhere else, the Japanese "folk psychology" that informs the countless unspoken assumptions about the conduct of normal life is sticky but not permanent, for the capacity to adapt to changing circumstances is a universal human trait.[1]

The main focus of this book is the upheaval of the 1990s when the economy broke down and political stability collapsed temporarily. We argue that the wrenching transition that has proceeded since 1990 can be explained by a political and economic structure that was inherently vulnerable to external interventions and ultimately incompatible with a globalized economy. Attempts by government leaders and private actors to shore up the system only exacerbated the problems that arose as symptoms of that incompatibility, and both politics and the economy have undergone fundamental and often painful reconstruction as a result.

Just as it would be incorrect to presume that Japanese culture and society have remained largely unchanged over centuries, it would be equally misguided to overestimate Japan's cultural homogeneity at any given time. To observers from North America or Europe, Japan might appear to be homogenous, and, to be sure, the Japanese government frequently

---

[1]Ferejohn and Satz (2001) introduce the concept of "folk psychology" to capture the way normative structures straddle objective circumstances and choice.

takes pains to cultivate that image. As Gavan McCormack has written, "[a]n ideology rooted in the myths of uniqueness and the 'pure' blood tradition is still proclaimed, often stridently, by representatives of the tradition of centralized authority." But McCormack rightly points out that "[f]or most of its history, Japan has been a highly decentralized state and society" and one whose centralizing myths are once again in serious question.[2] However ardently Japan's leaders may wish the country's citizens to sing in unison in support of the status quo, one need not strain one's ears to hear a complex set of melodies, shot through with not a few discordant voices: the native populations that were pushed aside by new immigrants in the third century AD; villages and religious groups that resisted centralized control in medieval Japan; working women today who challenge the "good-wife-wise-mother" model of womanhood, to name a few. Changes under way in Japan's political economy today do not advantage all dissenting groups equally, but they are assuredly undermining many of the preserves of privilege.

So Japanese culture matters for Japanese political economy, but that culture is complex and variegated and malleable. While some cultural norms can survive and even supersede the formal rules of politics or commerce, sometimes old beliefs and old ways of doing things fall by the wayside, and new norms and understandings arise in their place. Japanese politics and culture have changed profoundly and repeatedly over time, and in this chapter we provide a brief sketch of those changes as historical context for our subsequent discussion of the most recent break with the past.[3]

JAPANESE HISTORY AND JAPANESE CULTURES

Contemporary Japanese culture is viewed by the outside world, and for that matter by many Japanese themselves, as distinct in important respects from both neighboring Asia and the Judeo-Christian West. In Japan, this perception is called *Nihonjinron*, or "the theory of Japaneseness." Although Japanese culture was greatly influenced by proximity to

---

[2]McCormack 2001: 12.

[3]What follows does not aim to be comprehensive. Our purpose is merely to highlight some of the dramatic shifts that have occurred over time. There are countless outstanding textbooks on Japanese history. For readers interested in more complete introductions to the various periods in Japanese history that we only touch upon, we recommend Totman 1981; Schirokauer 1993; Souryi 2001; and Gordon 2002.

China's glittering civilization—and was later transformed by explicit emulation of the West—the Japanese have a self-image of cultural uniqueness.

That self-image is accentuated by the island nation's physical isolation, which impeded human migratory patterns for well over a millennium. Not until 1945, when the U.S. and Allied forces occupied Japan after World War II, was Japan conquered by a foreign power. Compare this to central Asia[4] or Europe,[5] where marauding armies often brought swift changes in overlordship, or to the New World, where conquest resettled ancient lands with new amalgams of cultures.

What are the characteristics of Japanese culture that are said to have been nurtured in relative isolation on Japanese soil? Many Japanese think of themselves as a society that values the group over the needs and wants of individuals. They value hard work, particularly when directed to the common cause, and are leery of people who seek to display extraordinary talent or native ability. They view themselves as being hierarchically organized and status conscious. They believe they are unlike westerners in seeking to avoid conflict whenever possible, and in their preference for settling disputes through intermediaries rather than directly or adversarially through courts of law. Unlike the Chinese love of excitement (*renao*) and the color red, Japanese aesthetics are spare and understated (*sabi*), matched by the value they place on quiet dignity, self-control, patience, and the ability to intuit the needs of others.

Taken as a snapshot of modern Japan, these stereotypes and self-perceptions manifest considerable accuracy. But Japanese political behavior, and Japanese culture more generally, are responsive to broader structural incentives that can be identified through comparative analysis. They have changed enormously, and countless times.

The First Japanese: Egalitarian Hunter-Gatherers

The origins of the Japanese people are shrouded in prehistoric mystery, but paleontologists and archaeologists are able to piece together some broad contours. During the last ice age, between 120,000 and 12,000 years ago, such a great quantity of the earth's water was frozen at the

---

[4]Kublai Kahn's conquest of Asia was repelled at Japan's shores in 1274 and again in 1281, not by fierce defending Japanese armies but by *kamikaze*, or divine winds (really big storms) that broke up the Mongolian fleets before they landed.

[5]Even England, which was relatively off the beaten path for most of the wars that engulfed early Europe, was taken in turn by the Romans, Angles, Saxons, and Jutes, and was then overrun by the Norman invaders shortly before Kublai Kahn failed to take Japan.

poles and elsewhere that Japan was not a series of islands at all but a large strip of land enclosing the Japan Sea. Japan was attached to the mainland from the north, through what is today's Sakhalin and Hokkaido, all the way to today's Korea in the south through Kyushu. Fossilized remains of large mammals, including giant deerlike animals and large elephants, have been found in Japan,[6] along with evidence of humans, dating back to about 30,000 BC, who must have followed migrating herds there from the mainland. There is also evidence of migrations thousands of years ago up through the Ryukyu Islands from Polynesia far in the south, though no one knows when these migrations took place, or how they contributed to the first-known Japanese civilization, called *Jomon*.[7]

As is typical of hunter-gatherer societies, the Jomon people seem to have lived in small, relatively egalitarian tribal communities eking out a subsistence living by hunting, fishing, and gathering food from surrounding forests.[8] Females in such societies tend to be of similar status to males, and the Jomon society evidently was no exception. Hunter-gatherer families are characterized by a gendered division of labor: while males are off hunting, females are busy gathering food from forests and waterways that account for as much as three-quarters of the caloric intake of the community.[9] Thus females are economically viable on their own if necessary, which puts them in a relatively strong position within families and

[6]The Naumann elephant, named after the German scientist who identified the fossils, was a southern relative of the woolly mammoth and once roamed present-day Nagano prefecture and elsewhere. It was hunted to extinction in Paleolithic Japan.

[7]Archaeologists are divided on the question of whether or not the Ryukyu chain of islands (including Okinawa) was part of Jomon. Imamura 1996.

[8]There is some interesting human osteological evidence that also suggests a comparatively egalitarian community. The relative bone sizes of adults is useful evidence concerning the organization of past societies about which we have few other sources of information, because the allocation of scarce nutrients during childhood and adolescence can have lasting influence on adult height. If some families were socially and politically privileged, their children would tend to be taller than the children of disadvantaged families. Osteological evidence can also tell us about the status of women in the same way. Societies that elevate the role of males might ration food to female children, producing an accentuated size differential between adult males and females. In contrast to the findings for subsequent Japanese societies, Jomon bones are similar in size, both among males and between males and females (Boix and Rosenbluth 2004).

[9]Dahlberg 1981; Boserup 1970; Kuhn and Stiner 2006. One might imagine that hunting skill could have been useful to males in gaining access to women who would appreciate the extra protein, but status differentiation probably did not get very far. Material success was as much a function of cooperation and chance as of individual skill. Furthermore, an animal begins to rot once it is killed, so there is little value in trying to hoard it; indeed, sharing every kill within the band appears to be typical of the few remaining hunter-gatherer societies in the world today.

gives families little reason to teach their daughters that marrying well is their only hope for a good life.[10] Indeed, artifacts suggest that Jomon religion centered on a goddess of fertility, vestiges of which may have been incorporated into Japanese folklore in the form of Amaterasu Omikami, the sun goddess who is said to have been the mother of Japan's first emperor.[11]

The Yayoi: Japan's Neolithic Revolution

In the third century BC, the Jomon society began to be displaced by a culture of sedentary agriculture known as the *Yayoi*. The best scholarly guess based on circumstantial evidence is that the Yayoi culture of rice farming was brought from the mainland, by way of Korea, through large-scale immigration in the third century BC. It seems that there were waves of population movements out of northern China during the first millennium BC as climate and usage destroyed China's northern forests, producing the Gobi Desert. Judging from the linguistic links across the Turkish, Mongolian, Manchurian, Korean, and Japanese languages, groups from central or northern Asia may have moved westward through modern Turkey and Hungary and eastward as far as Japan to find new arable land.[12] The Jomon people were considered barbarians and many were killed by the conquering Yayoi, but the wide range of facial morphology in Japanese people of today is living testimony to some degree of assimilation. The *Ainu* people of Hokkaido, who are shorter than average Japanese and have more facial hair, as well as Okinawans in the south, bear more resemblance to the Jomon population than do modern Japanese, who look more like people on the Northeast Asian continent.[13]

---

[10]Hrdy 1999; Iversen and Rosenbluth 2010. Physical anthropologists point out other reasons for the male-female size differential, both of which no doubt operated on the Jomon as elsewhere. (1) If males compete for females, we expect larger male size to be at a premium. But insofar as hunting required cooperation, there would be limited opportunities for competition of this sort. (2) If neighboring tribes fight each other and steal each other's women as spoils of battle, females may select larger and stronger males for mates. The osteological evidence for this proposition is mixed (Divale and Harris 1976); either the Jomon were spread out and not particularly warlike, or this effect is muted by other factors.

[11]Takayanagi 1975; Kirkland 1997. Smits (2000: 122) notes that Japanese subjugation of Okinawa in the medieval period removed female religious officials from power but did not eliminate their roles altogether.

[12]Yoshitake 1930. Japanese may be a "mixed language" with an Austronesian (Jomon) substratum and an Altaic (Yayoi) superstratum (Lewin 1988: 99), or it may be principally Altaic (Yayoi) (Vovin 1994; Unger 2000). The debate is over where to put the emphasis.

[13]Imamura notes that several genetic markers, such as types of blood proteins, ances-

The Yayoi civilization was organized around groups of hamlets governed by chieftains. The chieftains, who may have gained their positions from leadership in battle, passed along titled, stipend-carrying lineages known as *uji* to sons or retainers.[14] Folklore has the Japanese imperial family originating in 660 BC from the sun goddess, but evidence points to roots in *uji* politics imported from the Korean peninsula.[15] Indeed, cultural influences continued to flow from the continent into Japan through the Korean peninsula for centuries to follow.

The Yayoi people must have brought new ways of thinking with them, but an explanation for the shift in social organization from the Jomon's egalitarian to the Yayoi's hierarchical model must consider material conditions: sedentary agriculture allows for the possibility of accumulating and storing wealth in the form of food. In hunter-gatherer societies, there is little reward to those who can steal or defend perishable animal carcasses from others, but stores of rice and the land that produces them are another matter; they retain their value with time. Rice cultivation also made possible dense human settlements, for now land could be worked intensively and more people could be fed. Not only in Japan, but everywhere it occurred, the Neolithic revolution brought political hierarchies and wealth inequality in tandem.[16]

Sedentary agriculture also brought inequality between the sexes. Labor-intensive agriculture placed a premium on male brawn that had not existed in the foraging and gathering activities that had been a woman's domain. Females were put out of the business of producing food and instead began to specialize in the family-specific activities of child rearing. Women also worked extremely hard processing food and making clothes, and helped in the fields on a part-time basis, but were unthinkable as heads of households. A household division of labor emerged, typical of

---

trally link the Ainu and Okinawans (1997: 209; Hudson 1999: 151). Any Japanese on the street can also tell you another interesting fact: "Jomon" Japanese have wet earwax, whereas most Japanese—with Yayoi traits dominant—have dry earwax, which is also common on the East Asian continent.

[14]Hall 1966: 34–44; Piggott 1997: 55.

[15]The Korean origin of the Yayoi civilization is not a popular idea in Japan and perhaps will not be widely accepted until either Japanese attitudes toward Korea significantly improve, or definitive genetic studies are done, whichever comes first. Edwards 2000.

[16]We see evidence of this in the increased dispersion of male height in Yayoi populations compared to the Jomon. According to one calculation, families at the bottom of the socioeconomic ladder would often have had enough rice, after taxes, to "keep hunger away from the household for only three-fifths of the year." Takigawa 1969: 79, quoted in Yamamura 1974: 11.

agrarian societies, in which the woman belongs to the male head of the household.[17]

Yamato Political Consolidation and the Classical Period

Over the course of the first few centuries AD, *uji*-based hierarchy expanded to encompass not just intravillage society, but cross-village relations as well. Centralized control was never complete, but the most powerful chieftains, called the Yamato and centered on present-day Osaka and Kyoto, did dominate weaker leaders. Inequalities between elites and ordinary peasants increased. Variations in military prowess partly explain these differences, as horses, weapons, and improved technology of all sorts were imported from the mainland. Opponents were either defeated in battle or co-opted through kinship arrangements. As Conrad Totman tells us, Shinto was manipulated as a source of power and hierarchy as well, as vanquished groups saw their gods incorporated "into the Yamato pantheon at prudently subordinate levels."[18] Eventually, most of southern and central Japan, up to the area around present-day Tokyo, came under Yamato influence. A relatively uniform system of heredity and title developed by around the year 500,[19] the precursor of the Heian dynasty to follow, in what is commonly called the "classical" period of Japanese history.

Chinese influence permeated elite Yamato society in earnest by the sixth century. Probably the three most important and far-reaching aspects of this influence were Buddhism, writing and literacy, and Confucian-influenced bureaucracy and hierarchy. By the mid-seventh century, the leaders of the most powerful *uji* assumed Chinese-style imperial titles, which dovetailed easily with their indigenous beliefs about descent from the sun goddess and, therefore, their divine right to rule. The Taika Reform of 646 formalized this notion of imperial power, and established the ruling family as the arbiters of landholding and political power. It took

---

[17]Iversen and Rosenbluth 2010. Under the land reform of the mid-seventh century, women were also allocated land, but as junior members of extended families. Yamamura 1974: 7. Although male-dominated family arrangements have typified Japanese farm life for centuries, an interesting variation exists from the court society of the Heian period (794–1185), in which females of noble families tended to live with their parents or with their brothers even upon marriage. The freewheeling sex among the nobility described in Lady Murasaki Shikibu's *Tale of Genji* of the early eleventh century (often referred to as the world's first novel) must have given these men sufficient doubt about the paternity of their offspring that it made more sense to undertake the upbringing of sisters' children, where the genetic link was certain.

[18]Totman 1981: 11.

[19]Totman 1981: 11–12.

decades to implement, and there were coups and countercoups that transferred power from one family to another, but by 700, the aristocracy was well entrenched atop the social and political structure of Japan.

Politically and economically, the classical period can be characterized as one of huge and increasing inequality. A tiny, but highly accomplished and highly privileged aristocracy dominated an illiterate, atomized peasantry and a small, but growing urban population. Chinese influence over its neighbors was at its peak between the T'ang (618–907) and Song (960–1279) dynasties when Chinese prosperity spawned official diplomatic missions, unofficial trading expeditions, and Buddhist proselytizing efforts, as well as the introduction of writing and literacy[20] to Japan. The Japanese political elite were awestruck by Chinese imperial power and cultural grandeur, and sought to adopt Chinese top-down management and organization wherever possible.[21] Temples and shrines built in Japan's capital city of Kyoto (then called Heian) in the tenth century were splendid displays of architectural emulation. Over the centuries, the bright red paint faded into the browns and blacks we see today, a visible marker of how much Japanese aesthetic sensibilities have changed over time.[22]

An eighth-century experiment with a national conscription army on the Chinese model was short-lived, partly because there was no external threat to galvanize a centralizing response. The result was an imperial family that rested on a fairly loose coalition of related warrior clans, traced to the *uji* system, that pledged fealty in exchange for a share of power but whose members were not always in balance. Within the ruling class, the power of the imperial family was always tenuous, for it was merely one noble family among many. The rest of the nobility not only ensured that their land was exempt from some taxes, but also hired ordinary farmers to clear new lands from forests and swamps, thereby increasing noble holdings at the expense of the emperor's tax base.[23]

Medieval Japan: Tumult and Bottom-Up Politics

The relatively peaceful years of centralized imperial rule and a flowering court culture that celebrated the refinement and superiority of the aristocratic caste came to an end in the late twelfth century. This was when the

[20]Both Buddhism and *kanji* were first introduced to Japan in the middle of the sixth century.

[21]Totman referred to this as "aristocratic bureaucracy" (Totman 1981: 18–69).

[22]One exception is the enormous and dazzlingly red Heian Shrine built by the Meiji oligarchs in 1895. Intended as a memorial to the heyday of the Japanese imperial court, it is also a reminder of Japan's massive importation of things Chinese.

[23]Yamamura 1974: 13.

Minamoto and the Taira clans, both members of the extended imperial family and armed to the teeth, battled each other for control of the imperial court.[24] They were struggling to fill a vacuum, for by this time the emperor could not afford to keep a national army. So weakened was the imperial court that it had come to rely on warrior families for control of the provinces.

The Minamoto family defeated the Taira family in a series of battles between 1180 and 1185 that came to be memorialized in Japanese history and legend as *The Tale of the Heike* (Heike was another name for the Taira).[25] The Minamoto family eventually established a military government in Kamakura, far to the east of Kyoto, where the Minamoto had their largest landholdings. In 1333 another warrior clan, the Ashikaga, overthrew the Minamoto and ruled (from the Muromachi district of Kyoto) until 1573, but with diminishing territorial control as a growing number of warrior families carved out more or less autonomous domains.[26] Until a coalition led by the Tokugawa clan took decisive control over the entire nation in 1600, rule by a succession of warrior families was frequently and extensively contested.

Medieval Japan was a time and place of great foment where status and wealth were up for grabs in some fundamental ways. During the Kamakura period (1185–1333) before the military government was strong enough to usurp power from the imperial court completely, the basis for property rights became confused and multilayered because military governors gave their partisans grants of land without first establishing a new system of land tenure.[27] Japanese litigiousness seems to have reached its historical high when Kamakura courts of law were kept busy with disputes over land ownership and use, as recorded amusingly in Kyogen plays.[28]

---

[24]Actually, both clans were ex–imperial family members. The Taiho Code of 702, cognizant that too big an imperial family could easily descend into factional power struggles, mandated that "descendants six generations removed from their imperial sire would lose their princely status. Upon declassment, these ex–imperial family members were granted one of two family names, Taira or Minamoto." Many became militia leaders (*bushi*) who were hired by nobles to protect their property and press claims for more. Noble dependence on them eventually led to more and more *bushi* influence at court (Totman 1981: 64–69).

[25]Maas 1995. Even if the tales are only half true, the account of the Battle of Ichi no Tani of 1184, in which Minamoto no Yoshitsune led a cavalry charge down a cliff against the unsuspecting Taira army, must be one of the most spectacular battle stories in human history (Varley 1994: 129–130).

[26]Ishii 1995; Hall 1995.

[27]Conlan 2004; Asakawa 1911; Adolphson and Ramseyer 2007 point out that monasteries were often the chosen protectors of land because of their tax-free status and because their militias could repel marauders.

[28]Ramseyer 1994. The use of courts requires at least two conditions: an expectation that

The civil war that broke out in 1467, known as the Onin War, marked the beginning of the particularly violent Warring States period (*sengoku jidai*), when larger proportions of the Japanese populace were recruited to fight in one army or another than had ever been mobilized before. In exchange for peasants' willingness to fight, the commanding lords were forced to make economic concessions in the form of tax breaks and land grants.[29] When the men called to arms felt the concessions were insufficient, they sometimes rebelled and formed their own communal defense known as *ikki*, as when a local militia in Yamashiro Province forced the clan armies to leave the province in 1485.[30] Bottom-up rebellions also occurred in the Kyoto region and elsewhere, giving rise to a phrase of the day, *gekokujo*, which means "the lower conquers the higher."[31]

Tokugawa and the Way of the (Redundant) Warrior

Loyalty is today a prized Japanese virtue, but it was in short supply during the medieval period because it was potentially so costly. Medieval warriors frequently changed sides, even in midbattle, rather than risk forfeiting their land to the victors. Interestingly, unquestioning loyalty to one's lord and other attributes of "the way of the warrior" (*bushido*) became a guide for living only after Tokugawa hegemony made loyalty redundant, for within the rigid social structure established after 1600 there was little possibility that abandoning one's social station would result in personal gain.[32] Those who made up the Tokugawa coalition might not have crushed

---

their judgments will be enforced, and uncertainty about how the case will be decided. Otherwise the disputants would spare themselves the hassle and expense of a court case. Japanese litigiousness declined in the fifteenth century, not to recover for centuries to come because neither of these conditions was present. The civil war years of the late medieval period offered no certainty of enforcement, and the military hegemony of the Tokugawa government left little room for doubt about the outcomes of many kinds of cases.

[29]Inaba forthcoming; Ike forthcoming. The concessions to mobilized farmers may account for the continued economic and population growth despite famine and war (Farris 2006: 7, 189).

[30]In 1488, the Ikko Ikki formed by a sect of Amida Buddhists in Kaga Province forced the warlord Togashi Masachika out of the province (Tsang 2007; Adolphson 2000). Not until 1575, when Oda Nobunaga's armies razed the last holdout villages and forts, did these areas of Japan come under centralized rule.

[31]The *ninja* of the Iga and Koga valleys were farmer-warriors who resorted to stealth and skill to protect lands from invading armies (Souyri 2001; Adolphson 2000; Tsang 2007; Adolphson and Ramseyer 2007).

[32]Berry (2005: 842) points out that Yamamoto Tsunetomo, the author of the samurai classic *Hagakure*, invented a code of abject loyalty during the Tokugawa peace when this loyalty would never be tested. "To speak of loyalty in these circumstances is deceptive silliness."

their enemies in the Battle of Sekigahara in 1600 had they not convinced many of their enemies to switch sides at the last minute. Once in power, Tokugawa Ieyasu and his descendants laid the framework for 250 years of stable rule by making disloyalty unprofitable.

The Tokugawa established political order with the use of some impressive strategic thinking. First, they stripped the vanquished warrior clans of their lands and relocated them to the provinces in the far reaches of southern Japan. Samurai were allowed to keep their swords while all others were disarmed, but far from the new capital of Edo (Tokyo), the warrior families could prosper and develop a stake in the new regime without the possibility of mounting a serious military threat.[33] The Tokugawa gave the lands encircling Edo to members of the extended Tokugawa family, and allies were given lands in the concentric circles beyond that.

A second stratagem was to hold the domain lord's (*daimyo's*) wife and heir hostage in Edo under the pretense of wanting to populate the capital with provincial families. The daimyo himself was required to spend alternate years in Edo, expending enormous resources on these biennial processions from the provinces to the capital (*sankin kotai*) that might otherwise have been used in more threatening ways. The Tokugawa further drained outsider domains of resources by requiring them to pay for expensive public works, such as dams, dikes, and bridges, in various parts of Japan. The third step of closing Japan off from international trade was a risk-averse move that prevented domains from flourishing at the expense of the central government, but that had the long-run self-defeating effect of limiting Japan's economic development while the rest of the world surged forward with the benefit of gains from international trade.[34]

Japanese Politics and Culture, Then and Now

Even our cursory excursion into Japan's history reveals a variety of cultural pasts with equal claim to being Japanese. The ancient Jomon people,

---

[33]The policy of dividing labor between warriors and farmers (*heino bunri*) actually began earlier, and was the innovation that allowed some leaders, such as Oda Nobunaga, to create highly trained armies and feed them (Inaba forthcoming). The Tokugawa developed this division of labor into a sort of caste system, with artisans and merchants below samurai and farmers. Below all of these were "nonpeople" (*hinin*) who took on jobs considered unclean in Buddhist doctrine, such as butchery and undertaking.

[34]Hall 1966; Hall and Mass 1974; Bolitho 1974; Totman 1967, 1975, 1993. In practice, the bilateral bargaining power between individual domains and the Tokugawa overlords varied considerably. Brown (1993) has called the Tokugawa regime a "flamboyant state"

though embattled, outcompeted, and assimilated to near extinction by the Yayoi over two thousand years ago, were typical of hunter-gatherers in their relatively egalitarian social organization. The Yayoi, who brought rice cultivation with them from the mainland, were hierarchical in a way that is typical of densely populated agricultural societies that organize to protect their stores and seek to take land from others. As population density increased, it became more important to eke out as much as possible from available land, giving an advantage to those with entrepreneurial talent as well as to those who had a knack for grabbing from others. The possibilities for wealth and political inequality far exceeded anything in hunter-gatherer societies. The Yamato and classical periods saw that inequality taken to an extreme level. Militarily powerful, highly cultured, wealthy elites, gathered around an imperial institution, used the administrative techniques and Confucian justification of hierarchy to separate themselves almost completely from the masses of poor, illiterate farmers. Buddhism, poetry, and music all flourished in service of and to celebrate the aristocracy, but left the masses untouched.

The turmoil of the medieval period disrupted both politics and culture in important ways. The need for each local baron to raise an army opened the path to career advancement for lower-class individuals who could master martial skills. The demise of centralized political control also freed up religious entrepreneurs, and various sects of Buddhism competed for the adherence of warriors of all stations.[35] Since the ability to read texts was key to some forms of Buddhist teaching, and also because it facilitated commerce and record keeping among the growing merchant class, literacy spread. At no point, of course, did Japanese society morph into some sort of egalitarian paradise, but the rigid divisions of the classical period disappeared. Merchants could buy samurai status, and common people could rise to prominence by virtue of their individual talents— something unheard-of in the previous era, and again suppressed in the early modern period that began in the seventeenth century.

Warrior culture left a strong mark on Japanese aesthetic sensibilities as well, one that survives to the present day, even if the political organization of the time lives on only in history books. Cherry blossoms took on

---

for claiming much but controlling little. Mitsubayashi (1975) thinks of the Tokugawa as a "domain state," emphasizing the resistance of domains to central Tokugawa control. This theme is echoed in Ravina 1999 and Roberts 1998, among others. See Toby 2001 for a summary of the debate among historians of Japan as to the effectiveness of central control.

[35]Totman 1981: 93–106.

special meaning as poignant reminders to medieval soldiers of the evanescence of life (*mono no aware*). Although they loved life and were often fighting for family and for the land that represented their livelihood (*issho kenmei*), they sought a way to steel themselves for battle. The tea ceremony, adapted from China, was a way to cultivate spiritual and mental discipline for soldiers who wanted to prepare themselves for death, should it be necessary. Zen Buddhism, with its emphasis on meditative practice to clear the mind of desire and worldly attachments, became the favored religion among warriors.[36] Along with the warrior's attempt to transcend earthly desires came an aesthetic appreciation for artistic representations of life's imperfections. The concepts of *wabi* and *sabi*—simplicity and imperfection—have their origin in Mahayana Buddhism imported into Japan centuries earlier, but in the fourteenth century they took on positive meaning and found their expression in the high value placed on asymmetry and irregularity in pottery, flower arrangements (*ikebana*), poetry, music, and calligraphy. The deliberate use of drab colors and spare lines in architecture dates from this period.[37]

Harder to find in contemporary Japanese culture are remnants of the rowdy medieval social arrangements, when neighbors sued each other over conflicting property claims, and when entire villages rose up in violent defiance of overlords if they thought they could get away with it. The medieval maxim that the "lower orders conquer the higher" (*gekokujo*) has been displaced by considerable deference to authority and respect for the status quo. Strongly visible in Japanese society are the comparatively recent influences of the Tokugawa regime, which consciously reengineered a vertical society. To shore up its place at the top of the social and political hierarchy, the Tokugawa once again propagated the patriarchal philosophy of Confucianism imported from China, which made a virtue of playing well one's given role in the system.[38] Servants were to serve their masters with devotion and loyalty, and rulers were to show benevolence to the weak. Political inequality and social rigidity thus reemerged,

---

[36]Varley (1973: 73) points out, however, that most medieval samurai were rough, unlettered men who sought their solace in salvationist sects of Buddhism, while Zen was favored by the ruling elite.

[37]Souyri 2001.

[38]While the Tokugawa placed themselves (warrior-administrators) at the top of the caste system, they never eliminated the imperial household or challenged the myths of its divine lineage. Since at least the classical period, when the Fujiwara clan was first among aristocratic equals and acted as the power behind the throne, all Japanese political leaders, of whatever stripe, claimed to rule on behalf of the emperor.

although it is important to realize the economic gains were fairly wide-spread. Indeed, by the end of the Tokugawa period, in the mid-nineteenth century, the lofty samurai often found themselves economically beholden to the lowly merchants, whatever their formal roles. Needless to say, this unofficial, unintended effect of the caste system (sort of a creeping, surreptitious version of *gekokujo*) spawned a wealth of irreverent, satirical books, plays, and woodblock prints that are still celebrated today.

CONCLUSION

What, if anything, is the legacy of Japanese history to Japanese political culture today? The biggest single lesson is that Japanese political culture can change dramatically with circumstances. But should modern-day Japanese draw on their own history, either consciously or unconsciously, they have a variety of often contradictory examples from which to learn. It is probably impossible to understand today's Japan without knowing what came before, but Japan's history includes so many different sorts of political and economic experiments that the idea of the present's being constrained to resemble the past is actually nonsensical. Which past?

Japan has seen periods of both social rigidity and stark hierarchy, but also periods of tremendous social churning, upward mobility, and relative egalitarianism. Political arrangements have ranged from atomized to highly centralized, and everywhere in between. Similarly, the role of women has changed considerably. Women fell from relative equality in the Jomon to subordinate appendages in the Neolithic Yayoi period. Aristocratic women during the classical period could inherit wealth and had the freedom to establish themselves as the arbiters of social status.[39] But Japanese women today are still fighting the more recent cultural inheritance from the Meiji Restoration, when women were asked to limit their aspirations to being "good wives and wise mothers."

Viewed from a distance, then, Japanese political history is far from monolithic. Almost any imaginable future arrangement can be sure to recall at least some parts of Japanese "tradition." Moreover, as modern

[39]In the first years of the twenty-first century, when the imperial institution is merely ceremonial (not just de facto, but de jure as well), the Japanese government has considered but rejected a proposal that imperial succession could pass to a female heir, the opponents of the bill citing tradition. Well, had they looked a little more closely (and further back), they would have seen plenty of precedents for female succession.

cultural historians tell us, competing ideas even vie for preeminence *at any given time*.[40] Deviation from the government's line depends on the degree of centralized information and control, and on the expectations of citizens about the potential costs of deviancy.[41] There is no doubt that during Japan's medieval period when everything was up for grabs, the clash of ideologies and interests was a dominant theme. Even during the national mobilization campaigns of the Tokugawa, Meiji, and prewar militarist governments, many people found room to define the contours of national myths for themselves.[42] Nonetheless, since the Meiji regime began in the mid-nineteenth century, the central Japanese government has managed rather well to "conjure up a public transcript of shared characteristics"—the myth of consensus and unity—that reduces the temptation to resist central leadership.[43]

The often noted Japanese inclination to avoid conflict is another way to describe a strongly bolstered status quo in which conflictual approaches are likely to fail.[44] In postwar politics dominated by a hegemonic party, finding a way to get on the inside had obvious payoffs. In the marketplace, consensualism was a useful strategy for both employers and employees once they had committed to lifetime employment contracts. With the upheavals of the 1990s, however, the Japanese have shown themselves to be as capable as anyone of savvy and self-serving political and economic conflict. Now that Japan has entered a new period of rapid change, the tumultuous medieval era might provide a repertoire of experiences from which to draw inspiration after all.

[40]Historians feel they are correcting overgeneralizations based on grand theories and top-down accounts of government achievement. Carol Gluck (1998: 451) takes heart in this change of emphasis, attributing it to a "heightened sense of historicity, a greater epistemological sensitivity, and [access to] an array of new methodological options.... The grand narratives of the nineteenth century have finally whispered out."

[41]Foucault 1977.

[42]On the Meiji construction of Japanese nationalism, see Maruyama 1958; but Gluck (1985) finds undercurrents of unassimilation everywhere. Ohnuki-Tierney (2002) reports that among the brave young men chosen to give their lives in *kamikaze* missions during World War II, some wrote in their personal diaries of their willingness to die for the emperor and nation, in keeping with the official propaganda, while others spoke more about their desire to be a tribute to their families.

[43]The language is from Scott 1990. On Japan, see Toby 2001: 198.

[44]Sheldon Garon (1997) documents the active participation of groups in society, including those in the middle class, in informal enforcement of social norms. Partly because they valued the resulting social harmony, and partly because it is often more comfortable to be an enforcer than to be a deviant, Garon notes that the government had no shortage of complicitors.

A second lesson we glean from this brief sweep through Japan's cultural history is that, as Gramsci noticed in Mussolini's Italy, dominant social norms confer rewards and punishments across society in ways that can be even more pernicious than overt repression because they are harder to challenge.[45] Because cultures consist of internalized normative orders, people outside the norm pay social costs for deviating (hence the Japanese proverb that "the nail that sticks up gets hammered down"—*deru kugi wa utareru*). To the extent that a country's culture is dominated by its mainstream current, the recourse to alternative norms may be cut off, raising the costs still further. If there is a silver lining to the collapse of Japan's "homogeneous" middle-class culture at the turn of the twenty-first century, it may be that in the future there will be a larger number of acceptable ways to "be Japanese" than at any time since the medieval period.

[45]Long before Gramsci, David Hume noticed the power of social norms and unspoken rules.

CHAPTER 3

Japan's Political Experiments

INTRODUCTION

From a country wracked by chronic civil war in the medieval period, Japan lurched to a static autocracy from 1600 to 1868 and then to a constitutional monarchy that evolved toward democracy in the late nineteenth and early twentieth centuries. A military coup in 1932 brought a halt to democratic reforms until American-led occupation forces set about installing a peaceful democracy in the aftermath of World War II. The period from roughly 1853 to 1952 was another century of turmoil that began and ended with both foreign intrusion and selective reinvention of what it meant to be Japanese.

Japan's prewar experiments with political arrangements speak to several enduring questions about the causes and effects of democracy. As students of political economy, our understanding of the conditions for successful democratic transition and consolidation remains incomplete, and Japan's experiences in the early twentieth century provide insight into some of the most pressing issues facing emerging democracies today. Why did Japanese democracy fail in the 1920s, despite pressures from below for greater government accountability? Some scholars blame Japan's late industrialization for a political and economic structure that led inevitably to military expansionism into Asia. Others suggest that Japan was seeking to play the nineteenth-century European game of power politics, half a century too late.

The events described in this chapter show that politicians' best efforts to discourage challenges to governmental authority notwithstanding, economic growth disperses resources in society in ways that make it hard for autocratic governments to maintain a lock on power. The Tokugawa regime lasted nearly three hundred years in part because the lid on international trade reduced the private wealth and social dislocations that result from economic growth. As the Tokugawa regime learned too late, however, foreclosing trade curtails only domestic threats, while foreign rivals might be gaining in strength. The Meiji leaders who overthrew the Tokugawa regime created a different set of institutions to keep themselves in power, but their task was complicated by their having to play against op-

position both at home and abroad. Though the ensuing military government of the 1930s succeeded in squelching domestic opposition in a way
the Meiji oligarchs never managed, sustaining military strength in the absence of democratic accountability proved harder than they imagined.

THE END OF TOKUGAWA JAPAN

In 1853 when U.S. naval ships steamed into Shimoda Bay near Edo
(Tokyo) seeking refueling ports and access to Japanese markets, the
Tokugawa government held to its centuries-old policy of refusing foreign
entry. One can hardly fault the Japanese for distrusting the West. Under
the Treaty of Nanjing following the First Opium War (1839–1842), Britain had seized Hong Kong and forced China to allow the sale of opium
that the British brought from Afghanistan in exchange for Chinese goods.
Other Western powers seemed to be moving into Asia to snatch what
they could, and the Tokugawa regime preferred to stay out of harm's
way. When the U.S. navy returned a year later with twice the fleet, however, the government relented and Japan was thrown into turmoil.

At first, the outer domains held to a strongly anti-Western posture,
criticizing the Tokugawa government for caving in so quickly to Western
demands. Daimyo Mori Takachika of the Choshu domain in southern
Honshu took matters into his own hands in 1863 when he ordered his
troops to open fire on all foreign ships in the waters around Shimonoseki
harbor. Choshu forces managed to damage several ships belonging to the
Americans, British, Dutch, and French before succumbing to overpower-
ing retaliation that destroyed Choshu's fleet along with some coastal
towns.[1] While Choshu and the other outer domains continued to resent
foreign intrusion, their new passion was to get rid of the Tokugawa regime that had failed to protect them.[2] Recognizing that the Tokugawa
regime had accommodated Western demands out of weakness rather than
from conviction, opponents of the regime saw an opportunity to overthrow the Tokugawa.

[1] Satow 1983. Ernest Satow was a diplomat assigned to the British legation in Yokohama
in 1862. The journal he kept during his two decades in Japan provides a lively account of
this period in Japanese history.

[2] Satow recounts with wide-eyed horror how daimyo retainers hacked to pieces with
samurai swords a British merchant visiting from Shanghai in 1862, ostensibly for the
"crime" of insufficient deference to a passing daimyo entourage. Satow 1983: 51. It took
some years for the leaders of the Meiji Restoration to construct a theme of nation building
out of hatred for foreigner and Tokugawa alike.

In the Meiji Restoration of 1868, a group of political entrepreneurs replaced the Tokugawa shogunate with a government that restored the emperor to the throne. It was a remarkably swift coup.[3] The overthrow was led by samurai from the outer domains, including Choshu, that had endured the brunt of Tokugawa repression. Many of the merchant class were happy to fund the venture, eager as they were to end a regime in which trade was suppressed and merchants were accorded low status.[4]

So both samurai and merchants had reasons to be unhappy: samurai because they had no money to go with their status, and merchants because they had money without status, and not as much money as they might make in a less heavily regulated regime. This odd coalition put together armies that, under the banner of national unity and imperial restoration, made easy work of a revolution. The Meiji forces defeated the Tokugawa's last stand decisively, at Hakodate in June 1869, and set upon the mission of strengthening Japan against external forces.[5]

THE MEIJI GOVERNMENT

The Meiji government, named after the emperor Meiji, who docilely went along with the construction of a new government around his person,[6]

---

[3]It could also be called a civil war, because some domains, particularly in northeastern Japan, remained allied to the Tokugawa government.

[4]Shively 1964–1965. Merchants had managed to make enough money to be considerably wealthier than the now largely unemployed samurai "warriors" who lived on rice pensions guaranteed by the government. Under Tokugawa sumptuary laws, merchants were forbidden to display their wealth in their clothing, so it became customary for merchants to wear jackets that hid brocaded designs, often in gold thread, under an austere black exterior. Merchants also underwrote the bawdy cultural life of castle towns, patronizing kabuki theater and *ukiyo-e* art that samurai could seldom afford.

[5]The Battle of Hakodate involved some of the most modern armaments of its time, paid for by Japanese merchant backers as well as members of the French navy of Napoleon III who offered their services and those of the ironclad *La Gloire*. In a letter to Napoleon III, French military officer Jules Brunet explained his reason for remaining in Japan to help the Tokugawa against the Meiji: "A revolution is forcing the Military Mission to return to France. Alone I stay, alone I wish to continue, under new conditions, the results obtained by the Mission, together with the Party of the North, which is the party favorable to France in Japan. Soon a reaction will take place, and the Daimyos of the North have offered me to be its soul. I have accepted, because with the help of one thousand Japanese officers and non-commissioned officers, our students, I can direct the 50,000 men of the Confederation." The 50,000 men never materialized (Sims 1998; Totman 1982: 73). Even with French help, the Tokugawa forces were no match for the Meiji army. By the last battle, the Tokugawa soldiers had dwindled to 800 against a Meiji force ten times larger.

[6]Emperor Meiji was born in 1852, the year before Admiral Perry appeared, and was

became in due course a constitutional monarchy. It is an intriguing counterfactual question whether, or under what conditions, this might have evolved into a sustainable democracy. Did Japanese society provide infertile soil on which democratic seeds were planted but failed to thrive? If Japan was hostile to democracy, was the hostility the result of cultural predispositions, bad economic fortune, or the strategic maneuverings of insiders who had much to lose from a democratic transition? This, in fact, was the question that consumed the U.S. government officials during World War II who were charged with planning the postwar occupation. Before reviewing the answers at which they arrived, we consider the evidence.

The Meiji Oligarchs

The people who overthrew the Tokugawa shogunate—the Meiji oligarchs, they are called—set about strengthening Japan's military and the public finances that supported it. A new national tax system based on land replaced the largely decentralized Tokugawa system in which each domain had been largely responsible for raising and administering its own budget. The Meiji oligarchs intended to rule Japan through a strong central government, on both domestic and foreign policy matters. To establish a national conscription army, the Meiji government eliminated the rules by which only samurai were allowed to carry weapons and received a regular rice stipend to support their livelihood, despite the fact that war-free Japan had not fielded an army for centuries. In the place of the Tokugawa hereditary social hierarchy, which had frozen families in their status since about 1600, the Meiji government established a peerage system to reward "service to the country." The highest titles (prince and count) they reserved for themselves and members of the imperial family. Other titles (viscount, marquis, and baron) they bestowed on various supporters and allies, as well as on former *daimyo* of the Tokugawa regime in exchange for their willingness to support the regime change.

Imperial symbolism, however, masked countless differences among the oligarchs over foreign and domestic policy. The oligarchs resolved most of their conflicts quietly with logrolls or compromises, but occasional controversies were fierce enough to show that the emperor was not a dictator who could force others to do his bidding. The most famous

---

coronated upon his father's death in 1867, the year before the start of the war that overthrew the Tokugawa regime.

example is the story dramatized in *The Last Samurai*, in which the oligarch Saigo Takamori led 40,000 samurai warriors in a doomed rebellion against the 300,000-strong Meiji conscript army. Saigo was, by Japanese standards, a bear of a man nearly six feet tall and of brawny build. He had a personality to match his physique, and his charisma made him the center of bitter opposition to the government's policy to disband the warrior class. Saigo had advocated a full-scale attack on Korea in 1873 for which the other oligarchs accused him of reckless warmongering to keep samurai employed. His bloody eight-month rebellion was brought to an end in Kumamoto on September 24, 1877, in a decisive victory by the Meiji conscript army, under the military command of Saigo's fellow Satsuma oligarch Okubo Toshimichi.[7] Contrary to the Hollywood version, *both* armies were equipped with all of the latest guns and artillery they could afford.[8] Saigo's samurai fought desperately, not to preserve swordsmanship and "the way of the warrior,"[9] but for full employment and for the preservation of their hereditary class.

The remaining oligarchs supported centralized government, but another point of difference was how much ground to concede to the general public in the new constitution. The most powerful oligarchs, Ito Hirobumi and Yamagata Aritomo, sought to rule Japan with a firm, authoritarian hand, while less powerful oligarchs including Okuma Shigenobu and Itagaki Taisuke favored a wider conception of popular liberties. Whether the weaker oligarchs resorted to the "populist card" to break into the center of power, or were kept in the periphery for their dangerous ideas, unresolved divisions within the oligarchy eventually brought party competition to Japan.[10]

Ito (1841–1909), an adopted son of a low-ranking samurai from Choshu, was a leader of the pro-imperial movement in his domain and rose to power among the oligarchs on a platform of top-down government. As head of the team chosen to draft the Meiji Constitution, Ito traveled

---

[7]Okubo was assassinated in May 1878 by six samurai from Satsuma seeking revenge. Iwata 1983.

[8]Saigo was in fact dressed in Western military uniform when he was injured, and committed suicide in the final charge at the Battle of Shiroyama in 1877. Something closer to Hollywood's *Last Samurai* had taken place long before, in the Battle of Nagashino in 1575, when Oda Nobunaga successfully used guns and rotating volleys of fire against Takeda's cavalry charge. Akira Kurosawa's classic 1980 movie *Kagemusha* memorialized this battle.

[9]The term *bushido* (the way of the warrior) was coined only in 1905, by Nitobe Inazo. Inazo was from a samurai family associated with the domainal government of Nambu (Iwate), which had arranged Nambu's peaceful accommodation with the Meiji government.

[10]For an extended discussion of the idea of a failed oligarchic cartel, see Ramseyer and Rosenbluth 1995.

to Europe in 1882 and returned to Japan with a Prussian model of constitutional monarchy in mind for Japan.[11] Yamagata Aritomo (1838–1922) also came from a low-ranking samurai family in Choshu, and cut his teeth in the pro-imperial movement in his domain,[12] but he became a military rather than civilian leader. In 1869 he traveled through Europe studying military organization, and he was the architect of the Meiji conscription army (also on the Prussian model) that defeated Saigo in 1877.

Itagaki Taisuke, from a middle-ranking samurai family in Tosa (now Kochi, on the island of Shikoku), was an early supporter of the Restoration movement who joined the Meiji government in 1869 as a councillor of state. But he came to resent the closed, inner circle surrounding Ito and Yamagata, and in 1874 he resigned from government and denounced its top leaders for hoarding power. He formed a rival political group, the Patriotic Party (*Aikoku to*), based on a manifesto that borrowed heavily from the U.S. Founding Fathers and from John Stuart Mill: "We, the thirty millions of people in Japan, are all equally endowed with certain rights, among which are the enjoying and defending of life and liberty, acquiring and possessing property, and obtaining a livelihood and pursuing happiness. These rights are by Nature bestowed upon all men, and, therefore, cannot be taken away by the power of any man."[13]

In later years, Itagaki would join with another leading voice in the oligarchy for wider popular participation, Okuma Shigenobu (1838–1922). Although he was the son of a military officer from the Hizen domain, Okuma had immersed himself in "Dutch studies" and English as a youth.[14] Following the final Meiji victory in 1869, Okuma became the chief foreign negotiator and later finance minister. After a series of clashes with Ito, Okuma was dismissed from government in 1881. In 1882, he founded the Constitutional Progressive Party (*Rikken Kaishinto*), a platform from which he accused the "Choshu clique" of opposing a meaningful role in government for the citizens of Japan. In 1898, Okuma and

---

[11]He remained a central oligarch until his assassination in 1909 by a Korean nationalist during Ito's stint as colonial governor of Korea.

[12]Both Ito and Yamagata were involved, in their youth, in attacks on foreigners and foreign property. In 1862, Ito was involved in burning down the British legation in Edo.

[13]Itagaki 1933. Our translation.

[14]"Dutch studies," or *rangaku*, was the Japanese term for the study of foreign ideas, many of which were introduced by Dutch traders in the eighteenth century. Japan was formally closed to trade, but a steady trickle of foreign goods, as well as books and ideas, was permitted through the port on the island of Deshima in Kyushu where the Tokugawa authorities could keep an eye on things. "Dutch studies" became synonymous with the study of Western medicine, biology, and astronomy.

Itagaki joined forces to form the Constitutional Rule Party (*Kenseito*) to challenge oligarchic rule. Okuma's resistance to Ito's narrower conception of constitutional monarchy provided the central tension built into Ito's Meiji Constitution.

Itagaki's and Okuma's populist moves sent shivers down the spines of the more authoritarian-minded oligarchs, who were determined to avoid a Japanese version of the political upheavals in Europe.[15] Ito would eventually pay Okuma and Itagaki the greatest possible compliment, by forming his own political party, the Political Friends Party (*Seiyukai*), in 1900. But he did not resort to party politics before trying to undermine the populist threat through meticulous constitutional engineering.

The Meiji Constitution

The Meiji government sent delegations all over the Western world to study institutions, organizations, and policy, with the goal of emulating what they considered to be "best practices" in order to catch up with the West. The oligarchs looked to Prussia for lessons in constitutional design, but this included learning from Prussia's mistakes as well as from its successes. In what has come to be known as the "Prussian constitutional conflict of 1864–1866," the Prussian Landtag (lower house) refused for several years to grant Kaiser Wilhelm his military budget despite the monarch's insistence that military affairs were entirely within his prerogative as sovereign. In 1866, Prime Minister Otto von Bismarck worked out an agreement that secured for the Prussian army "the dangerous freedom from parliamentary control."[16] Rather than use force against popularly elected representatives, the Prussian government agreed by way of the Indemnity Law of 1866 to acknowledge that it had violated the law in proceeding without a budget, in exchange for the assembly's willingness to vote retroactively all of the funds withheld.

The Meiji leaders took several precautions to avoid the Prussian problem. Article 1 of the constitution proclaimed that the government was accountable only to "the supreme will of the monarch" rather than to the voting public or their representatives.[17] The fundamental order of the state, the *kokutai* (literally, the "state body"), resided outside of the constitution in the person of the emperor. Although Article 4 of the Meiji Constitution goes on to speak about the emperor's governing "according

[15]Fujita 1959.
[16]Craig 1951.
[17]Fujita 1959.

to the provisions of the Constitution," the oligarchs seemed to feel certain that they would be in a position, as advisers to the emperor, to interpret the constitution in their favor as necessary.

In the way that Bismarck was the power behind Kaiser Wilhelm's regime, the Meiji oligarchs decided to govern through the emperor rather than let him rule in fact. The oligarchs constrained the emperor rather tightly through the Privy Council, an advisory body to the emperor on the British model. The oligarchs had little thought of vesting real authority in the emperor, intending instead to use him as a rallying point for national sentiment and support in the face of foreign threats. It was useful to the oligarchs that the imperial household, though eclipsed for centuries by de facto military rulers, remained the focal institution of national history for most Japanese people.[18]

The oligarchs elevated the Privy Council to an advisory status on legislation and imperial ordinances, and took care to fill it with close allies. The oligarchs also made the military accountable directly to the emperor, rather than to the legislature or the cabinet, for matters of "grave importance."[19] An imperial ordinance of 1894 further stipulated that the ministers of the army and navy should always be appointed from the ranks of the army and navy command, respectively. It seems clear that the oligarchs intended to keep the military directly under their own control, via their control of the emperor.[20]

Whether because they were confident in their constitutional and extraconstitutional powers, or because they took seriously the threat of recalcitrant oligarchs such as Okuma to arouse greater public antipathy, the antipopulist oligarchs agreed to grant to the legislature the power of the purse. According to Article 64 of the Meiji Constitution, "The expenditure and revenue of the State require the consent of the Imperial Diet by means of an annual budget"; and, under Article 71, the preceding year's budget became the default budget in the event that the Diet should fail to pass a new one. By these provisions, the government tied its hands, preventing itself from increasing military or any other spending without approval from the elected branches.[21] The historical record does not provide clear guidance as to whether the oligarchs granted the Diet budgetary

[18]Hall 1968.

[19]According to the 1889 imperial notification regarding the cabinet, "With the exception of military or naval affairs of grave importance, which having been reported directly to the Emperor by the Chief of Staff... the Ministers of War and Navy shall report to the Prime Minister." In Beckmann 1957: 92.

[20]Quigley 1947; Ienaga 1963: 190.

[21]Beckmann 1957: 71.

power because they expected to emulate Bismarck's masterful handling of the Prussian legislature. Alternatively, they may have felt that Japan could become a powerful nation only if citizens were involved in the decision making and would therefore be willing to contribute more resources as necessary, as Bismarck seems to have thought.[22]

Whatever their rationale in giving the public a voice in politics, the oligarchs nevertheless approached the issue with obvious hesitation. The institutional apparatus of representative government included two legislative chambers, a House of Peers and a House of Representatives, but all legislation was to be promulgated by the emperor upon the advice of the Privy Council. Similarly, the cabinet and the prime minister were not to be chosen by the legislature but appointed by the emperor upon advice from the Privy Council. The House of Representatives would be elected by the people, albeit only men who paid a high enough level of tax. The House of Peers was an even more conservative body, originally comprising all princes and marquises over the age of thirty, 15 elected representatives of the counts, viscounts, and barons, 150 additional members nominated by the emperor (read, Privy Council), and 66 elected representatives of the 6,000 highest taxpayers. During the first session of the Imperial Diet (1889–1890) there were 145 hereditary members and 106 new appointees and high taxpayers, but the oligarchs kept stacking the deck with new peers until the membership reached 403 in 1925.

Another reason that the oligarchs admired Prussia was for its military prowess. The oligarchs had noticed the dispatch with which Bismarck's government took Schleswig and Holstein from the Danes in 1864, unified Germany under Prussian rule in 1867, and defeated the famed French army in 1871. To the Meiji government, whose claim to legitimacy rested substantially on providing stronger resistance to foreign threats than the feeble Tokugawa government had been able to muster, a government that could generate military prowess had powerful appeal. The British and American models, though also associated with military might, were rejected by most of the oligarchs as too liberal, particularly in granting extensive powers to the legislature.[23] For the oligarchs, the value of surviving potential international threats would have been much diminished if they had been forced to give up power domestically in the process.

Also like the Prussians, the Meiji government wanted a strong industrial base to sustain the military, but it never developed tight control over

[22]Palmer 1959.

[23]There was some difference of opinion among the oligarchs on this and other points, as we discuss below, but the majority of oligarchs favored Prussian-style authoritarian rule.

the economy.[24] Either because their coercive powers were less extensive, or because the potential military threats to Japan were more distant than was the case for Germany, the oligarchs did not centralize the private financial system in order to transfer small savings into units large enough for heavy capital investment.[25] Finance and corporate governance in prewar Japan were quite decentralized and more resembled the small-scale bond and equity-based financial development that characterized the United States and England. Not until the advent of the military government of the 1930s would the Japanese banking system become a highly concentrated apparatus for funneling small savings into finance for the munitions industry.

The Imperial Diet

The House of Representatives got off to an inauspicious start in 1890, elected by a tiny percentage of the population and dominated by oligarchic power. Only 1 percent of Japan's population satisfied the property tax requirement to be eligible to vote in the first election, and the oligarchs rigged the electoral rules to make it hard for parties to cohere around policy platforms. The electoral rules, which gave each voter multiple votes to distribute among party lists, engendered intraparty competition that undermined party leadership. Nonetheless, the political parties proved hard to control. As in Prussia, the Diet's control of the budget gave representatives crucial leverage in bargaining for policies they favored, showing the name of the emperor to be an insufficient tool of authoritarian rule. It was at this point that Ito Hirobumi established his own political party, the Seiyukai, and in the process was drawn into competition for electoral support.

[24]It is often assumed, because of the influential work of Alexander Gerschenkron (1966), that the Meiji government created a well-organized financial system that could channel private savings into state-led industrial development. Gerschenkron argued that "late developers" like Germany and Japan needed a bank-based financial system to pool savings into capital-intensive development in order to catch up economically with early industrializers such as the United States and England. Economists have since cast doubt on the notion that capital-intensive development makes economic sense for countries with a comparative advantage in land-intensive agriculture or labor-intensive light manufacturing. But if Bismarck's goal was to build a military capable of defeating France and Russia, it is unlikely that economic efficiency is what he had in mind. The famous "iron and rye" coalition unifying Prussia with the rest of Germany in a protectionist union served well Bismarck's unification strategy even if it involved some misallocation of resources from their best possible economic use.

[25]The Meiji government settled for creating a large steel firm capable of supplying the nation's growing navy and the network of railroads to carry materials quickly where needed.

Thus two main parties, Okuma's Kenseito, and Ito's Seiyukai, competed for legislative majorities in fiercely contested elections. Adapting to the circumstances, both parties appealed to big business for money and to commoners for votes, rather than base their appeals on their historical roots as anti- and pro-oligarchy, respectively. Such was the force of the legislature that the Privy Council felt compelled to appoint as prime minister the leader of the Diet's legislative majority party by the early twentieth century.[26] The two parties alternated in government as elections dictated.[27] The fierceness of electoral competition precluded the parties from conspiring with each other against the growing working class, and by 1925 the legislature voted to grant universal male suffrage.[28]

A mere seven years later, Prime Minister Inukai Tsuyoshi, president of the Seiyukai, was assassinated in his official residence by military officers under his command.[29] Understanding how democratic forces emerged from inauspicious circumstances by the 1920s in Japan, and why, in 1932, democracy fell prey to violent overthrow, provides a glimpse into the fragile dynamics of democratic transitions more generally.[30] What went wrong in Japan? We will return to this question after viewing it from the vantage point of the American victors of World War II.

The Occupation of Japan

The postwar American interest in Japanese democracy was primarily geopolitical: Americans were convinced that a democracy would be less threatening. During World War II, the Roosevelt administration assembled an all-star group of bureaucrats and academic consultants to address the

[26]Harold Quigley, writing just before the military coup in 1932, was quite sure that the major parties had a secure footing and were steering Japan toward fuller democracy. The prime minister from 1918 to 1921, the Seiyukai's Hara Takashi, had come into politics as an outsider, from the Morioka domain in north-central Japan that had remained loyal to the Tokugawa regime, no less (Najita 1967; Duus 1968). Hara seems to have had a strategy designed to establish civilian control of the military by weakening the institutional power bases of the oligarchs, especially those of Yamagata Aritomo. But Hara was assassinated three months before Yamagata died, in 1921 (Ito 2004; Kawada 1998).

[27]Najita 1967; Scalapino 1968.

[28]Both parties would have preferred to limit suffrage to the propertied classes, but each feared the other would stage an electoral coup by appealing directly to the masses. Ramseyer and Rosenbluth 1995.

[29]Inukai had tried to stop the Japanese army from embroiling Japan in a war with China.

[30]Wartime politics in Japan is an interesting subject in itself because of the subtle differ-

question of what went wrong in Japan, in anticipation of the day when victorious Allied forces would occupy Japan and prepare it for reemergence in world affairs as a peace-loving nation.[31] Some in the U.S. government wanted the American military to "gut the heart of Japan with fire," and President Roosevelt himself is said to have shown interest in a plan to crossbreed the Japanese with docile Pacific islanders to "eradicate the barbarism of the enemy race."[32] On this view, Japan's problems were so deep-seated, maybe even genetic, that only a wholesale change in Japanese society would enable a real democracy to take root. On the other side of the argument were the academics and diplomats who had lived and studied in Japan. Joseph Grew, who had served as ambassador to Japan from 1932 to 1942, was convinced that the Japanese people were as innately peace-loving as any other, and that Japan needed only a change in political institutions to become a full-fledged democracy.[33] He knew that the uniform voice with which the Japanese government spoke during the 1930s masked considerable diversity of opinion that was silenced and suppressed.[34]

This disagreement within the U.S. government was never fully worked out, as evidenced by the Occupation's wide-ranging measures that seemed to buy into every possible theory of what went wrong in Japan. The Occupation government, often referred to as SCAP[35] imposed a new constitution with better institutional incentives, as Grew recommended.[36]

---

ences among the different branches of the military, the underground opposition on the left, and a constant drumbeat of criticism from groups on the right that wanted populist fascism in the mode of Hitler and Mussolini. See Shillony 1981: chapter 2.

[31]In February 1941, the State Department established the Division of Special Research to begin planning for postwar Japan. An advisory committee, under the chairmanship of the secretary of state, was assembled of experts inside and out of government, including George Blakeslee, an authority on law in East Asia; Cabot Coville, a foreign service officer formerly assigned to the American Embassy in Tokyo; Robert Fearey, a former assistant to Joseph Grew in the U.S. Embassy in Japan; and Hugh Borton, a professor of Japanese history at Columbia University. In 1944 the new State, War, Navy Coordinating Committee took responsibility for this work, but the State Department's benign view of the Japanese people—aside from militarist leaders—prevailed. Mr. Grew himself became assistant secretary of state in 1944 and gave his strong support to the argument that the Occupation should rule Japan indirectly, through Japanese government personnel, rather than directly as in Germany. Grew also favored preserving the imperial institution while transferring sovereignty to the voting public. See Borton 1967.

[32]Dower 1986.

[33]Grew 1944.

[34]Shillony 1981.

[35]SCAP, the acronym for Supreme Commander of the Allied Powers, was the official title held by General Douglas MacArthur, but it has come to be used to refer to the Occupation's governing apparatus as a whole.

[36]The Occupation charged constitutional reform to a Japanese committee headed by

Sovereignty was lodged in the people rather than in the emperor, the legislature was solely responsible for all laws, and the military was made accountable to the people's elected representatives. But taking no chances, SCAP also undertook to change as many parts of society as it could manage. The enormous business conglomerates (*zaibatsu*) were broken up and corporate shares were sold cheaply to the general public, in case monopoly capitalism was behind Japan's militarist expansionism. Land was seized from big landholders and sold to tenant farmers at fire-sale prices, in case rural poverty had fueled virulent nationalism and xenophobia. Education was decentralized and made open to the public, in case government propaganda was to blame for Japan's ills. The list is long, and at least in the first few years of the Occupation, New Deal idealists did their best to transform Japanese society into an idyllic civic culture.

By 1947, however, when the U.S. geopolitical priority had changed from demilitarizing and democratizing Japan and Germany to containing world communism, the Occupation underwent a "Reverse Course" as well.[37] New Deal reformism took a backseat to getting Japan's economy up and running to serve as a bulwark against communism in Asia. The Antimonopoly Law of 1947 was not overturned, but SCAP bureaucrats looked the other way as former zaibatsu companies began to forge the cross-shareholding ties known as *keiretsu*. Labor unions, previously the darlings of the Occupation authorities because of their antimilitarism, came to be viewed as a potential fifth column for Communist infiltration. General MacArthur forbade the unions to go through with their planned general strike of February 1, 1947, undermining the credibility of leftist union organizers who had staked their reputations on using the strike to achieve better working conditions for their members.[38]

---

constitutional legal scholar Matsumoto Joji. But the Americans thought the changes to the Meiji Constitution insufficient and took it upon themselves to draft a new constitution for Japan in the span of a few days. Dower 1999; Williams 1979; Gordon 1997.

[37]In July 1947 following his trip to Japan, George Kennan, who directed the State Department's Policy Planning Staff, wrote an article in *Foreign Affairs* under the alias "Mr. X" outlining a strategy of global containment. In October 1948 the National Security Council called on the Occupation to begin ceding more authority to the Japanese government, and a growing consensus in Congress was willing to relinquish demands for war reparations from Japan so that Japan could become, in the words of Army Secretary Kenneth Royall, a "bulwark against Communism" in Asia (Kennan 1947).

[38]As Hans Baerwald recalls from his years in the Government Section of the Occupation, the climate change operated through a shift in the balance of power among factions within the U.S. Occupation, as New Dealers were thwarted in their reform efforts (Baerwald 2002).

Prime beneficiaries of the U.S. government's new strategic priorities in Japan were the conservative parties, the Liberals and the Democrats, which together commanded a legislative majority in a coalition led by Liberal prime minister Yoshida Shigeru. With SCAP's blessing, in 1947 Yoshida resuscitated the prewar electoral rules, about which we will have much more to say in later chapters. The postwar "reformist" proportional representation electoral rules that SCAP had introduced in 1946 were deemed, in retrospect, too permissive of small, radical parties opposed to the U.S. government's new policy goals.[39] Bringing back the medium-sized district system of 1925 gave the Liberals and Democrats together a stronger legislative majority than they had commanded before. Two years later, in a move that foreshadowed McCarthyism in the United States, the Occupation government undertook a massive "Red Purge" that stripped thousands of suspected Communists of their jobs in government and business. The newly legalized, but embattled Japan Communist Party became a staunch opponent of the Occupation, and the Japan Socialist Party, which had briefly led a coalition government in 1946, hunkered down into what would become its habitual position as leader of the legislative opposition.

By the time the Occupation ended in 1952, Japan's economic recovery was well under way, thanks largely to the enormous procurement boom fueled by the Korean War. More momentously, democracy took root in Japan as well. Scholars and practitioners alike want to know why Japan's transition to democracy proved to be so secure. After all, some countries, such as Russia, have slid back from democracy into more authoritarian forms of government, while others, like Argentina, oscillate between populism and elitism. The Japanese case is not an ideal natural experiment, because despite some backsliding in reformist policies throughout the Reverse Course, SCAP tinkered with Japanese government, society, and economy at multiple levels. In that we are unable to examine the effects of one piece of the puzzle at a time—political institutions, economic deconcentration, and widespread access to information—we do not have a strong empirical basis from which to judge which interventions Japanese democracy could have done without. Deductively, however, we have reason to think that each of these reforms nurtured a hospitable environment in which democracy could thrive.

[39]In a letter to President Truman in 1947, Kenneth Coleman, a political scientist at the University of Wisconsin, noted wryly that Sanzo Nosaka, the leader of the Communist Party who had self-exiled in China during the war, was unfortunately one of the ablest politicians in Japan.

Political Institutions

Japan's new constitution relegated the emperor to a symbolic role, placing sovereignty instead in the hands of a popularly elected legislature.[40] This was undoubtedly the single most important reform of the Occupation, for it forced the politically ambitious to compete with one another openly in democratic elections for control of government instead of finding ways to procure the emperor's approval behind the scenes. Japan was re-created as a parliamentary democracy, in which the prime minister and his cabinet would be accountable to the legislative majority, rather than being appointed from the outside. No Privy Council gave a favored group extraparliamentary control, and the military was abolished. This effectively channeled all political ambition into electoral competition. Japan's pulsing moves toward democracy in the 1920s would have been far steadier, we surmise, if the elected legislature had been unimpeded by other centers of power unaccountable to the voting public.

Good institutions may be insufficient to cement a commitment to democracy, however, judging from the varying experiences of countries transitioning to democracy. In the moment when a governing party has lost a fairly contested election, whether it concedes to the winning party or chooses to barricade itself in office depends at least in part on whether the losing party expects to be able to get away with flouting the law. That, in turn, depends on how strongly the public supports the law, and whether they have the collective action capacity to enforce their wishes.[41] Institutional stability undoubtedly contributes to these social conditions, because voters are more likely to express strong support for the democratic rule of law when they have come to value the process and policies it produces. In prewar Japan, political institutions were seriously flawed from the standpoint of democratic transition because political parties were corrupt and unpopular.

Back in 1925, the three largest parties had struck a compromise in adopting multimember-district electoral rules that gave each party a chance to win a seat in each district. For reasons that we will explain in chapter 4, these electoral rules generated corruption as an unintended consequence.

---

[40]Even before the war, constitutional law professor Minobe Tatsukichi's "organ theory of the emperor," by which the emperor was part of the constitutional structure rather than a sacred power beyond the state itself, was overwhelmingly accepted until the military coup of 1932.

[41]Weingast 1997 calls this the "Przeworskian Moment" after Adam Przeworski, who drew attention to this scenario.

Political parties failed to develop party platforms on the basis of the public's interests and instead busied themselves selling regulation to corporate conglomerates (*zaibatsu*) in exchange for campaign money with which to woo voters. So great was public disgust with prewar political parties that the military coup in 1932 did not arouse public fury so much as sympathy for the elderly Prime Minister Inukai, who was assassinated.[42] It seems clear that fixing the electoral and legislative institutions alone would have gone a long way to putting Japan back on a course toward solid democracy, as Grew thought. But it also seems possible, as the New Dealers thought, that extreme income inequality would have undermined support for democratic rule of law, no matter what the political institutions.

Economic Resources and Distribution

As a broad generalization, societies with higher levels of per capita income are more likely to be democratic. "Modernization theory" claims that higher levels of societal wealth and education are likely to generate effective demands for political voice.[43] The mechanics of this relationship are contested, and some have argued that the relationship is spurious: any regime is more likely to be stable at high levels of income, so the clustering of democracies at the rich end of the continuum could be an artifact of democracies remaining democratic as they rise in income.[44]

The distribution of wealth may be at least as important for democratic stability as is the overall level of wealth, at least at lower aggregate levels of income. Democracy seems to be more stable when there is a strong middle class, presumably because the middle class represents a genuine dispersion of power away from a small elite.[45] Highly unequal wealth may threaten democratic stability by tempting the elite to protect their assets behind the walls of dictatorship.[46] In prewar Japan, wealth was indeed highly unequal. Three-quarters of farmland was tilled by tenant farmers for wealthy landlords, and vast wealth was concentrated in the

---

[42]Duus 1968: 24. Najita (1968: 510) wonders whether Inukai's problem, and that of prewar politicians generally, was that they were unsuccessful in explaining to the broad public "the deceptively simple truism that politics is power and that the framework of party government for the pursuit of power is valid and perhaps desirable in a modern society."

[43]Lipset 1959; Huntington 1987; Boix and Stokes 2003.

[44]Przeworski and Limongi 1993; Milanovic 2005; but see also Boix and Stokes 2003 for some countervailing evidence.

[45]Moore 1966.

[46]Acemoglu and Robinson 2002, 2006.

hands of a few families (*zaibatsu*), while urban and rural poverty were endemic.[47]

One reason the zaibatsu gained ground during the 1920s was that electoral competition in multimember districts was so expensive that politicians "sold" favorable regulation to zaibatsu firms in exchange for campaign contributions. Under conditions of extreme rationing of available capital, companies forged ties with a "main bank" to get preferential, if expensive, access to capital. Whether postwar democracy would have failed to take root under conditions of capital concentration is a question the Japanese case does not allow us to answer, because the Occupation officials took no chances. Infused with New Deal ardor to promote economic equality along with political freedom, SCAP undertook massive land reform and economic deconcentration in Japan.[48]

Efforts at deconcentration served a geopolitical goal, along with the ideological one, stemming from concern that concentrated economic wealth was one of the engines of Japanese imperialism.[49] In the Japanese case, however, the logic missed its mark, for the Mitsui and Mitsubishi zaibatsu opposed the war with China in the 1930s on grounds that seizing Chinese territory would ruin sales. The views of Mitsui and Mitsubishi were not unanimously held, and when they withdrew their part of the joint investment with the Japanese army in the South Manchurian Railway Company as the Japanese military became more aggressive in Manchuria,[50] the Nissan "new zaibatsu" was willing to take their place. The point is only that the Japanese zaibatsu were not champing at the bit to take Chinese territory to make up for shortfalls in the Japanese market—their investment with the army seems to have been an effect, not a cause, of Japanese imperialism.[51] Economic equality is probably good for democratic stability, and possibly good for markets as well, but Japan's

[47]Japan historians from Richard Smethurst (1986) to Tetsuji Okazaki (2007) document that economic growth was improving the lives of farm households throughout the 1868–1940 period. But even Smethurst agrees that many farmers were still poor and unable to withstand a run of bad years. See Francks 1987: 479.

[48]Hadley 2003. It is likely, as with income, that relative equality promotes political stability, whatever the regime. Korea and Taiwan, which also undertook land reform, remained undemocratic for an additional three decades, quite possibly because income equality removed at least one common reason for political dissatisfaction.

[49]The logic was Hobson's (1902), later adopted by Lenin (1916), that imperialism necessarily followed from the advanced stages of capitalism in which oppressed labor could no longer consume, forcing companies to move abroad in search of new markets.

[50]Tiedemann 1971. Jeffry Frieden (1994) points out that investors in raw materials are more likely to favor territorial acquisition than are traders who can access markets without owning the territory.

[51]Grew 1944: 339.

territorial imperialism was undertaken by a narrow group of imperialists for geopolitical strategic reasons rather than at the behest of Japanese financiers and businessmen.

Education and Access to Information

A third set of Occupation reforms centered on building a pluralistic political culture, to unburden the Japanese of outmoded worldviews that could be incompatible with democracy. Political culture is an idea with a venerable pedigree, dating back at least to Aristotle and finding modern expression in Max Weber's ideas about "democratic personality" and in Almond and Verba's "civic culture."[52] Good institutions can foster a democratic culture by creating mutually reinforcing expectations of cooperative and productive decision-making processes. But institutions alone may be insufficient, not only if income inequality creates expectations of instability, as we've discussed, but also when a collectivist culture provides an opening for demagoguery.

The official U.S. opinion about Japanese civic culture, influenced by former ambassador Grew and others who had watched political expression flourish during the 1920s, was that the Japanese people were fundamentally capable of peaceful and democratic self-rule if only they were rid of militarist control. In the U.S. view, the problem was that the Japanese public had been gagged and blindfolded, but were neither brainwashed nor comatose, so the solution was a matter of nurturing intellectual and political pluralism.[53] The decision to leave the imperial institution intact, albeit in a much attenuated form, was also undoubtedly influenced by the desire to use the emperor's popularity to rally support for the new democratic institutions.

CONCLUSIONS

In this chapter, Japan's institutional experiments have shed light on some enduring questions in political science. What are the conditions under

---

[52] Aristotle 1998; Weber 1946; Almond and Verba 1965.

[53] Dower 1999: 411. Of course, U.S. officials were not able to resist the temptation to make use of their extraordinary control of information through the education system and media. They did not stop at dismantling the censorship exercised by the militarist government, but also undertook extensive censorship of the media and school curricula to eliminate criticism of the United States or other Allied nations, and criticism of the Occupation and its policies, including the U.S.-written constitution.

which democracy is more likely to emerge and thrive? Does late industrialization foster the development of strong state institutions that undermine a pluralistic civic culture most conducive to stable democracy? Does late development also promote territorial aggrandizement by creating large economic conglomerates that bend governmental power in service of their quest for new markets and raw materials?

One might think that the brief flourishing of democracy in Japan in the 1920s was doomed to fail because late development had created powerful state institutions that worked hand in glove with grotesquely concentrated business conglomerates.[54] This picture overlooks the fact that by the 1920s, all but a very few of the original Meiji oligarchs had died, and power had become dispersed over many different groups in society and sectors of the economy. There was talk of amending the Meiji Constitution to reduce the powers of the Privy Council in order to strengthen party rule.

It is true that, when in a few short years the military assassinated the prime minister and installed a military government, the public did not deeply mourn the passing of democracy. The political parties had become unpopular because of their grubbing for the zaibatsu money with which they bought votes. Part of the blame lay with the Meiji Constitution, which had established an institutional structure designed to impede the development of democratic forces by subordinating parties to extraparliamentary forces that controlled the emperor. It is harder to assign blame for the unintended consequences of electoral rules, passed by the parties themselves, that created incentives for politicians to contest elections with bribes instead of policy platforms. Without well-functioning institutions to foster a culture of trust in the democratic process, public support for parties was weak when the military decided to strike.

It also seems plausible, on the face of it, that Japan's economic concentration contributed to military expansion. But Japanese industry followed, rather than led, the charge into war. The zaibatsu most actively engaged in trade with China initially opposed the war for fear of losing their markets. When war appeared inevitable, they accommodated themselves rather

---

[54]The Canadian historian and diplomat E. H. Norman (1940) is most associated with this argument in the English language, but it is a view held more generally among Japanese Marxist historians. Norman, investigated by the U.S. Senate for his Communist sympathies, committed suicide in April 1957 when he was the Canadian ambassador to Egypt. Declassified documents from Norman's personnel file are available on the digital archive of the University of Victoria at http://web.uvic.ca/ehnorman/.

quickly to military rule and began investing in munitions industries. The military further concentrated industry in order to ensure that all available resources went to the war effort, and businessmen saw that their best way to survive was to do the military's bidding.

The Japanese historical record from the end of the Tokugawa period through the Occupation suggests the utter indeterminacy of approaches that rest on underlying economic structure such as income levels, the distribution of income across society, or the timing of industrialization. Paying close attention to the strategic behavior of elite actors is crucial to understanding choices over economic and military policy, as is an appreciation of the rules that governed political competition among those actors. The next chapter explores how postwar constitutional arrangements and electoral rules shaped political competition and party structure in Japan for decades to come.

Finally, a theme of this book is that domestic political and economic arrangements can be affected profoundly by external forces. Since the mid-nineteenth century, the overthrow of the Japanese political and economic status quo by the intrusion of outside forces has repeated itself. With each disruption, domestic actors scramble to arrive at new allocations of political and economic resources, only to have the outside world intrude again. Political actors share a powerful drive to protect their positions, and to share resources only as widely as necessary toward that end. Political coalitions produce policies that create economic winners and losers and lock in benefits for the winners. But those arrangements survive only as long as the government can dictate its own rules. Markets thrive on innovation and eventually find ways to outstrip political attempts to regulate them. Sooner or later, the narrowly drawn political bargains collapse, either because outsiders crash the game and enforce new rules, or because outside options induce some players inside the winning coalition to strike a new deal.

In the late nineteenth century, the intrusion of the Western powers, symbolized by Perry's black ships, was the spark that ignited the Meiji Restoration. The upheaval cleared 250 years of underbrush that had collected during the country's politically enforced closure, and precipitated dramatic changes in the political, social, and economic order. In the decades that followed, Japan struggled to create a new political and social equilibrium, the failure of which led to a military coup and ended with the largest intrusion of all, war followed by foreign occupation. The end of the Occupation, in turn, left Japan with yet another set of political arrangements. A large political party supported by a coalition of big firms and small farmers underwrote a system of "convoy capitalism" characterized by closed and cartelized markets, heavy subsidies, and expensive, personalistic elections. The next chapters tell the story of this clubby postwar deal and how it, too, eventually collapsed when the government was unable to fend off the latest "black ships": the globalization of economic and financial markets.

CHAPTER 4

The Old Japanese Politics, 1955–1993

INTRODUCTION

The first thing that comes to mind when one thinks of postwar Japan is surely its economic "miracle" that stretched from 1960 through 1990, and the decade and a half of economic stagnation that followed. But a close second might be the political dominance of the Liberal Democratic Party, which spanned roughly the same period. From 1955, when the party formed, through 1993, when it split and lost its parliamentary majority, the story of Japanese politics was, more or less, the story of the LDP. Just how did the party stay on top for so long, and why did it finally give way to coalitions and even some alternation in government? There are many superb studies of politics during the era of LDP dominance, and we cannot do more than summarize the highlights in this short chapter. What we hope to add is a frame to inform our discussions of LDP-era political economy in chapter 5, and of the postreform Japanese politics and political economy in chapters 6 and 7, respectively.

The basic puzzle of LDP dominance is that the party managed to win repeated majorities (of seats, if not always of votes) despite an electoral system that required *intraparty competition within each electoral district*, setting up internecine blood feuds that threatened continuously to tear the party (or any would-be large party) into several pieces. The factions that bedeviled LDP politics from the day the party formed are testament to the powerful centrifugal forces of the Single Nontransferable Vote (SNTV) electoral system. The Opposition progressively fragmented as well. What started out in 1955 as a "one-and-a-half party system,"[1] with a large LDP majority and a half-as-large Japan Socialist Party (JSP), splintered into a system with at least five stable parties, but with all of the newcomers in the Opposition camp. Somehow, the LDP was able to avoid disintegrating,[2] but the Opposition was not.

[1] Scalapino and Masumi 1962.

[2] The New Liberal Club represented the one split on the government side, formed by LDP defectors in 1976, only to fold back into the LDP less than a decade later.

The LDP solved the electoral puzzle through a combination of electioneering tactics and policies that represented a sort of "best response" for a long time, but ultimately these tactics ran their course. What disturbed this cozy equilibrium was, more than anything, globalization. The LDP's policy mix could not survive the economic forces that pushed the government to open the economy to foreign competition and investment, and that offered the party's strongest clients—big business, especially—better opportunities than those the LDP could offer. The party used money—pork-barrel spending and patronage—to spackle over the cracks in its coalitional edifice, but this only resulted in a steady stream of increasingly spectacular campaign finance scandals and in the end could not keep the house from collapsing.

Until the world intervened, however, the LDP maintained what might be called a coalition of steel and rice.[3] The LDP's survival depended on massive donations of political finance from modern, competitive sectors of the economy, which it then fed to individual candidates' political machines to mobilize the votes of the uncompetitive, traditional sectors, especially farmers. The same transfer of resources occurred at the policy level, with the government taking in tax revenues from profitable sectors (as well as savings from shackled consumers) to fund enormous subsidy programs for farmers and inefficient small businesses that could not have survived otherwise. Money came from big business and votes from farmers. One of the groups left out of the bargain was consumers, who faced high prices and limited choice in the marketplace, but who were growing ever wealthier in any case as the rising tide of rapid growth really did raise most ships. Another outsider group was unionized workers, who showed their dissatisfaction by supporting, in vain, the LDP's rivals.

SNTV AND THE CHALLENGE OF INTRAPARTY COMPETITION

The reason that the LDP needed so much campaign finance is tied to the rules of the Lower House electoral system used through 1993, known as the Single Nontransferable Vote (SNTV). SNTV was first introduced in 1925 as a product of bargaining among three medium-sized parties.[4] After a single election using a large-district PR (proportional representa-

---

[3]By the end of the period we discuss here, "steel" had been supplanted by automobiles and consumer electronics. For excellent book-length treatments of the LDP's increasingly unwieldy coalition of special interests, see Calder 1988 and Pempel 1998.

[4]Soma 1986.

tion) electoral rule in 1946, the Occupation authorities returned to SNTV in 1947, and similar results (a moderate number of medium-sized parties) prevailed. But it was not until the LDP formed that a majority-seeking party had tried to contend with the full implications of its centrifugal pressures.

Under SNTV, each voter could cast just one vote, for an individual candidate, but in a district that would send multiple winners to the national legislature. Nearly all districts elected between three and five MPs, with an average of four. Many electoral systems around the world use multimember districts, but in most of those, voters vote not for individuals, but for parties, and each party is awarded a share of the seats up for grabs in that district that matches its share of the vote. If a party were to win, say, 60 percent of the vote in a five-seat district, it would earn three seats, and the top three people on the party list would be elected.[5] Under SNTV, any party seeking to win two or more seats in a district would have to nominate as many or more candidates, but then, crucially, the party's supporters could not simply vote for the party but would be forced to choose *among* those copartisan candidates. This made same-district copartisans the bitterest of rivals engaged in cutthroat competition for the same types of voters.

As importantly, it raised the question of how copartisans could differentiate themselves in the eyes of voters.[6] Party leadership did not want its candidates to squabble publicly over policy—with one candidate taking, say, a hawkish stand on policy, and another a more moderate stand—because to do so would confuse voters as to what the party stood for, and might shrink the pool of voters in which the candidates were fishing. Copartisan candidates had to find ways to distinguish themselves without really disagreeing with one another. The "solution" to this dilemma was personalism. Candidates focused to some degree on "home turf" neighborhoods, and campaigned on promises (and, for incumbents, track records) of pork and patronage. They would compete to provide favors to constituents, to direct pork-barrel spending from the national budget, and to provide all manner of constituency service. They would attend

[5]The system just described is called closed-list proportional representation. There is an "open-list" variety as well, in which voters may (but do not have to) indicate a favorite candidate or candidates within a party list, in the attempt to revise the party's initial ranking of candidates. Open-list PR is closer in its effects to those we describe for SNTV (see, e.g., Carey and Shugart 1995).

[6]This discussion of product-differentiation strategies draws on McCubbins and Rosenbluth 1995; Cox and Thies 1998; and Hrebenar 1986, among many other works on LDP campaign tactics.

scores of weddings, funerals, and birthday parties, always armed with generous gifts. Watanabe Michio, a seasoned LDP politician, once quipped that he always had a black tie in one pocket for weddings and a white tie in the other for funerals.

> In Japan, when we attend funerals or go to the hospital to console patients, it is traditional to bring a big wreath and a cash gift. Nobody gives such a small amount as 1,000 yen or 2,000 yen [$10–$20]. Everybody gives 10,000 or 20,000 yen, and flowers cost another ¥20,000.... People die every day, you know. Diet members... say that if they do not attend these, they will lose in the next election.[7]

Politicians also organized junkets to hot springs or sports tournaments for their supporters. In short, each constructed (or inherited) and then worked hard to maintain a personal political machine (*koenkai*). Votes were not actually "bought" in the literal sense—the secret ballot made that impossible. Rather, each candidate cultivated and nurtured a personal support network and then used copious amounts of money, as well as the advertising and speechifying opportunities of the (short) formal electoral campaign, to mobilize supporters at election time. A voter faced with a choice among two or more LDP candidates typically went to the polls at the urging of one of those candidates, who had already established himself as that voter's political patron.

The party helped to sustain this system of parallel political machines, district by district, by overseeing a division of labor among same-district candidates. Sometimes, if two or more candidates in a district hailed from different hometowns, a natural home-turf-centered division of voters would emerge.[8] But in many districts, geographical differentiation was insufficient, so the party would enforce a functional division, by means of nonoverlapping policy specialization. All candidates could toe the party line in terms of policy platform, but each individual candidate would get to stake a particular claim to expertise and influence over some subset of policy areas, with each candidate claiming credit for a different subset. The party enforced this by assigning same-district copartisans to different committees. With the important exception of candidates from farming districts and membership on the agriculture committee, it was rare for two LDP MPs from a single district to find themselves on the same committee. The reason we say that the party had to "enforce" this division of credit-claiming opportunities is that no individual MP had an incentive

[7]Watanabe Michio, quoted in Hirose 1989: 14.
[8]Tatebayashi 2004; Hirano 2006.

to leave his rival's turf unmolested. Left to their own devices, every candidate would try to claim credit (or avoid blame) for everything that the LDP did. It required the intervention of party leaders, who wished to maximize the total number of party seats, to ensure that each of its members had a policy patch to call his own. This functional specialization, then, informed the targeting of the MP's personal-vote seeking. Each MP would naturally seek support from those constituency groups whose interests were most closely tied to the policy areas for which he could most credibly claim influence.

That this Byzantine sort of intraparty organization was so closely linked to the imperatives of intraparty competition under SNTV is underscored by what happened when SNTV was abandoned in the 1994 reforms. Almost immediately, the LDP lifted the restriction on membership in its internal policy committee structure, telling all MPs that they could participate in any committee they liked. And MPs jumped at the chance to "expand their territory" even to the point where the party, which had maintained detailed committee rosters for thirty years, stopped keeping track of who participated on what committees altogether.[9] With SNTV gone, there was no longer any need to help MPs carve out and defend areas of specialization.

THE FIRST POSTWAR PARTY SYSTEM

The LDP (along with its nemesis, the JSP) formed in 1955, after several years of raucous, fragmented politics that saw frequent changes in government, heated ideological battles, street demonstrations, and violent strikes. After two decades dominated first by total war and then by an extended occupation, Japanese democracy was vibrant, exciting, and even a little bit dangerous. Two conservative parties, the Liberals and the Democrats, two Socialist parties (called the Left Socialists and Right Socialists no less), a small Communist Party, and such other tiny parties as would appear and disappear made for fascinating electoral politics and frequently shifting coalition politics.[10]

One might argue that the beginning of the end of these "interesting times" occurred in 1955 with the formation of the LDP and the JSP, to be followed by nearly four decades of boring, predictable routine. The LDP

[9]Krauss and Pekkanen 2004. Importantly, executive positions on these committees were still rationed—and allocated with factional balancing in mind—but general membership became a sort of free-for-all.

[10]Kohno 1997.

controlled both houses of the National Diet[11] continuously until 1989, its seat share varying election to election, and its tenure punctuated by sporadic scandals, but rarely with any real concern that it would lose power, not to an Opposition that seemed more and more incompetent and out of touch all the time. Much as the advent of the Tokugawa dynasty in 1600 ended centuries of civil war, closed Japan off to the world, and ushered in more than 250 years of quiet, complacent isolation, the ascension of the LDP appeared to end the excitement of Japanese democracy in favor of quiet, complacent domestic political hegemony.

If the party mergers of 1955 foreshadowed a passage into political predictability, it was the Security Treaty Crisis of 1960 that sealed the deal. The U.S.-Japan Mutual Security Treaty was promulgated as a condition of the end of the postwar Occupation in 1952, and throughout the 1950s security issues made for frequent and contentious debate. Right-wingers complained that the treaty was an offense to Japanese sovereignty, reminiscent of the "unequal treaties" that Japan had been forced to sign when the Tokugawa dynasty was humiliated, by American military might, into ending its splendid isolation. Those on the left condemned the treaty because it tied Japan too closely to an America now obsessed by the Cold War, having already fought a real war next door in Korea. These opponents argued that Japan's defeat in the Pacific War ought to have taught it to be pacifist, to avoid foreign entanglements altogether.

As the LDP government of Prime Minister Kishi Nobusuke made clear its intention to renew the treaty, protests swelled in the streets,[12] and violence spilled into the Diet itself, with opposition party members attempting to physically prevent the Speaker from calling for the vote.[13] Eventually, the vote was called, and the LDP prevailed, but Kishi resigned immediately afterward, to take responsibility for the unrest that had accompanied the decision. Kishi's successor, Ikeda Hayato, made a speech soon thereafter,

---

[11]The Lower House (or House of Representatives) is the more powerful chamber, with exclusive authority over the choice of prime minister (Article 67 of the constitution), budgets (Art. 60), and treaties (Art. 61). But for all other legislation, the Upper House (House of Councillors) must also assent, unless the Lower House can override an Upper House veto with a two-thirds majority, but this happens very rarely. The distribution of powers actually makes the Japanese Upper House one of the most powerful among bicameral parliaments, somewhere between the Italian Senate and the German Bundesrat, and considerably more important than its counterparts in the United Kingdom, France, and Canada. See Druckman and Thies 2002; Tsebelis and Money 1997; Patterson and Mughan 1999. Of course, the fact that the LDP controlled both houses for thirty-four years rendered the relative power of the two chambers a moot point during that period.

[12]In the student riots outside the Diet building, a female University of Tokyo student, Kamba Michiko, was trampled to death in a stampede by armed police.

[13]Scalapino and Masumi 1962.

putting the Security Treaty debate firmly in the past, and promising that his and future governments would dedicate themselves to economic growth. Famously, he pledged that average income would double by the end of the decade. As some might put it, "the rest is history." Ikeda's pledge was more than fulfilled, and by the time the Security Treaty again came up for renewal, in 1970, most Japanese were indifferent. The 1970 protests staged by the opposition parties and remaining student activists were but a shadow of the 1960 chaos.[14]

The Opposition Parties

The LDP did lose some support after 1960, and the combined vote share of its candidates dipped below 50 percent within a few years. But because the anti-LDP vote was dispersed among a fragmenting set of opposition parties, and owing to the increasing pro-LDP malapportionment that resulted from large migrations from rural to urban areas without concomitant redistricting, the party was able continuously to convert its vote share into parliamentary majorities and control over government.

THE SOCIALISTS

The leader of the Opposition from 1955 through 1993 was the Japan Socialist Party.[15] The JSP was, on the one hand, a fairly typical labor party. Its platform called for redistribution from capital to labor, and for workers' rights. Accordingly, it found most of its vote support, as well as campaign finance, candidates, and activists, in the labor movement, especially the more militant public-sector unions under the umbrella organization *Sohyo*.

On the other hand, the JSP had a second identity, as the so-called Japan Peace Party. The JSP was the staunchest defender of Article 9 of the postwar constitution, which renounced Japan's right to wage war, and outlawed "land, sea, and air forces, as well as other war potential." The JSP feared that the LDP wished to repeal Article 9, and fought every effort, including the Occupation-era creation of the Self Defense Forces (SDF), to stretch Article 9 into meaninglessness. The JSP called instead for "unarmed neutrality," an end to the U.S.-Japan Mutual Security Treaty, and a ban on the Rising Sun flag and the wartime national anthem.

---

[14]See Marotti 2009 for a discussion of the protest politics of 1968, centering on the U.S.-Japan security relationship.

[15]The JSP later changed its name to the Social Democratic Party of Japan, but we will use the original name, to avoid confusion.

Over the 1960s, 1970s, and 1980s, while the LDP maintained its single-party majorities in both Diet chambers, the JSP saw its support decline, and it fell victim to new parties that offered voters alternative ways to oppose the LDP. Despite the secular decline in blue-collar labor in a rapidly modernizing economy, the JSP was unable to moderate its strongly leftist platform. This was mostly because it was so utterly dependent on the unions' organization, but it was also due to the blackmail potential of the JCP. Sitting hard on the JSP's left flank, the JCP essentially anchored the JSP, and kept it from moving in a more social-democratic direction, lest it lose its more radical supporters to the Communists.[16]

It was difficult as well for the JSP to find new issues with which to challenge for power. In the 1960s, one major by-product of Japan's rapid development was terrible air and water pollution. Green activists managed to defeat LDP incumbents in local elections on environmental platforms, and the JSP tried to jump on the bandwagon, hoping that it could leaven its calls for redistribution by condemning the externalities of an overheated economy.[17] But this promising issue turned out to be a poor wedge issue for the Socialists, precisely because expensive environmental regulation would raise costs for firms, and its labor supporters would feel the pain as well.

And while the JSP was perhaps unable to moderate its social/economic platform, it was just unwilling to update its foreign policy platform. Its pacifist, neutralist positions made the JSP popular early on, but as time passed without any resurgence of Japanese militarism, and without Japanese entanglement in American wars, the JSP's platform seemed more and more quaint, and contributed to the party's image as unfit to govern.

After decades of slow rot, the JSP's greatest electoral triumph came in 1989 when its popular leader Doi Takako led it to an Upper House victory over the LDP and cost the latter its majority (see appendix 3). But this also proved to be the party's last gasp. The JSP was not able to duplicate its victory in the 1990s Lower House election (see appendix 2), and when the LDP split in 1993 and its defectors set up new parties of the center-right, voters jumped at the chance to abandon the fading JSP in favor of the new parties. Since the electoral reform, the once-proud leader of the Opposition has all but disappeared from the stage.

THE OTHER OPPOSITION PARTIES

The first split in the Opposition occurred in 1960 (see fig. 4.1), when the right wing of the Socialist camp split off to form the Democratic Socialist

[16]Kohno 1997.
[17]McKean 1981; Reed 1981.

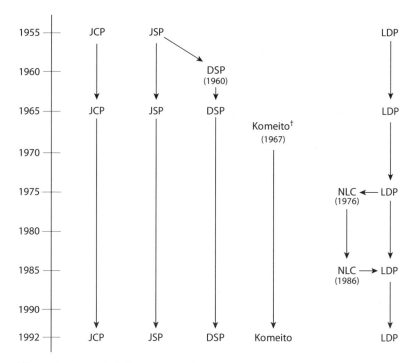

Figure 4.1. Japan's Political Party System, 1955–1992
†The Komeito supported candidates in the Upper House as early as 1956 but did not endorse Lower House candidates until 1967. Numerous small parties appeared and disappeared over time, especially in the Upper House, but these are omitted for purposes of clarity.

Reproduced by permission of the publisher from Frances Rosenbluth and Michael F. Thies, "Politics in Japan," in *Comparative Politics Today: A World View*, ed. Gabriel A. Almond, G. Bingham Powell, Jr., Russell Dalton, and Kaare Strom (New York: Addison Wesley Longman).

Party (DSP). The primary support base for the DSP was the moderate enterprise unions, under the umbrella of the *Domei* Federation, having replaced postwar radical unions after the failure of the February 1947 general strike. Public sector unions remained staunch supporters of the Japan Socialist Party. The other way that the DSP distinguished itself from the JSP was over foreign policy. The DSP was hawkish, sometimes more so than the LDP, and supported the U.S.-Japan Mutual Security Treaty, and the existence of the Self Defense Forces (SDF), both despised by the JSP. Despite this more moderate economic and foreign policy platform, or perhaps because of it, the DSP found itself squeezed ideologically between the LDP and the JSP, and never managed to obtain as much as 10 percent of the national vote before it disbanded after the 1994 electoral reform.

The Japan Communist Party (JCP) also benefited from the 1960 events, growing from near extinction to a consistent 5 to 8 percent of the Diet seat share. The party is the longest-lived in Japan, having been founded in 1922, though it was banned from politics by the military governments of the 1930s. It was legalized by the Occupation authorities after the war, but was not helped by the Reverse Course that followed the start of the Cold War and the Communist takeover in China. The JCP has been willing to participate in parliamentary politics, but with a platform that condemns the whole bourgeois enterprise. The JCP nurtured ties with its Chinese and Soviet counterparts until formally parting ways in the mid-1960s, and called for abrogation of the treaty with the United States, peace with the USSR and China, dissolution of the SDF, an end to the centuries-old imperial system, and an overthrow of the new postwar constitution.

The JCP is the most disciplined party in Japan, with a strong hierarchical organization down to the neighborhood level, which produces consistently high turnout and activism by its small number of loyalists. Throughout the pre-1994 period (and a little beyond) it insisted on nominating a candidate in every electoral district across the country, no matter how remote those candidates' chance for success. The JCP has survived, even flourished, on the strength of sales of its daily newspaper, *Akahata* (Red Flag), and other ideological tracts. The party has long been popular among many white-collar intellectuals, including a large number of attorneys and teachers. Interestingly, however, the JCP is more than a band of ideologues. It also cultivated the image of a "lovable" party. It regularly nominates and elects more female candidates than any other party. It participates constructively in local politics and is generally perceived to be the only party that is completely unsullied by the corruption that plagues Japanese politics.[18]

In 1964, the Clean Government Party (usually called by its Japanese name, *Komeito*) arrived on the scene, a political arm of the lay Buddhist organization *Soka Gakkai*.[19] Komeito's platform called for "world peace, humanitarian socialism... Buddhist democracy, and the eradication of

[18]Berton 1992, in Hrebenar 1992: 116–147.

[19]Fifteen candidates endorsed by Soka Gakkai won seats in the 1962 Upper House election, and Komeito was created two years later. Soka Gakkai is an organization associated with Nichiren Soshu, a sect of Buddhism that is unusual in Japan for its evangelistic fervor. To most Japanese, who are religious eclectics, the proselytizing is off-putting and has limited the appeal of the Komeito as a result.

corrupt politics."[20] The party is virulently anti-Communist and, perhaps not coincidentally, most resembles the JCP in its rigid hierarchy and neighborhood-level "cell" organizations.

Komeito formally broke with Soka Gakkai in 1970, after considerable criticism of its overt mixture of religion and politics, but it still draws nearly all of its financial and electoral support from Soka Gakkai adherents. Komeito finds most of its constituency in lower-middle-class, urban households, especially among women. Its supporters are extremely loyal and active, which means that the party does particularly well when general turnout is low (its voters show up no matter what), and relatively poorly when general turnout is high.

Over time, Komeito has settled into the center of the ideological spectrum, with mostly moderate, pragmatic positions on everything from the economy to foreign policy. Beginning in the mid-1970s, when the LDP's majorities looked fragile, Komeito, together with the DSP, began musing publicly about coalition governments and offered itself as a potential partner. Although the LDP regained its Lower House dominance, it did in fact turn to Komeito for support in the Upper House, after it lost its majority there in 1989. The best-known example of Komeito's Upper House leverage came in 1992. The LDP government of Kaifu Toshiki sought Diet approval to send troops to participate in UN-sponsored peacekeeping operations. Because no Japanese troops had set foot abroad since 1945, and in light of the "peace clause" in the postwar constitution, this was a matter of great controversy.[21] Komeito and the DSP agreed to support the PKO bill, but only after an extended public negotiation over the nature of their duties, their weaponry, and their rules of engagement. Western observers might have been bemused by Komeito's insistence that the troops carry no guns (or, in the end, only sidearms), but the larger political point was that Komeito was pivotal for the bill's passage, and that it used this leverage to bargain, rather than obstruct. This reasonable approach to policy compromise foreshadowed the formal LDP-Komeito coalitions that governed between 1998 and 2009 (see chapter 6).

Whatever vote share the LDP lost during the 1960s and 1970s went mostly to these new parties, as the JSP gave up even more ground. By the mid-1970s, the LDP's majority was razor thin. In the 1976 and 1979

[20]Hrebenar 1992: 157.

[21]The LDP was desperate to participate in peacekeeping operations, in large part to counter the perception that it had been allowed to "free ride" on the efforts of the UN-backed coalition that fought the Gulf War to push Iraq out of Kuwait. Japan had contributed $13 billion (more than any country other than Saudi Arabia) but was the only member of the coalition to send no troops.

Lower House elections, its victorious endorsed candidates did not gain a majority of seats, but each time, the party was able to invite enough conservative independent winners into the fold (sort of a postelection endorsement) that the LDP never had to share power, let alone relinquish it. The 1980 and 1986 elections[22] were landslide LDP victories, while the 1983 and 1990 elections saw more modest LDP wins. Only in 1993, owing to a preelection party split, did the LDP finally fail to garner a majority of Lower House seats and tumble into opposition for the first time since its birth.

So, as we said, the story of Japanese politics between 1955 and 1993 was more or less the story of LDP politics. But we would disagree with anyone who might argue that predictable LDP majorities made for boring politics. Undoubtedly, it pushed a lot of the most interesting aspects of politics behind the scenes. As long as one party could control both legislative chambers and the executive (not to mention most local governments), it could ensure that its proposals nearly always passed into law without much in the way of public fireworks. Instead, most of the action took place behind closed doors, within the LDP itself, and between the party and the various private interests that it endeavored to satisfy and balance through its policies. So if Japanese politics and policy making seemed somewhat somnolent to the average voter after 1960, that was because it was opaque, not because it was either undemocratic or overly harmonious.

Factional Politics and Money Politics

As discussed, the LDP was able to "solve" the centrifugal incentives[23] in the SNTV electoral system well enough to stay in one piece even as the Opposition fractured. But the electoral rules still took their toll on the party, by sustaining a system of parallel, hierarchically organized factions. Nearly every party member was obliged to join a faction even before his first election to office, and to remain in that faction throughout his career. Factions performed many functions for their members: securing the official party endorsement, collecting and distributing campaign finance, and facilitating appointments to Diet or internal party committees, and eventually, the cabinet. In exchange, faction members gave their votes in proxy

---

[22]In both 1980 and 1986, elections for the Lower House were held on the same day as the regularly scheduled Upper House polls. Whether or not the "double elections" helped the LDP is difficult to know.

[23]Cox 1990.

to their factional leaders when the time came to choose the next party president (who, by virtue of the party's legislative majority, would become prime minister). Each faction would, en masse, back either its own leader, or the candidate designated by its leader, for the top job.

Most large, heterogeneous parties in most democracies around the world suffer factions of one sort or another, as loyalists gather behind potential party leaders, or as like-minded subgroups within parties form around policy positions. But those sorts of factional fractures tend to be more temporary and fluid than the LDP's version. LDP factions were rigid—with any changes in affiliation coming only as the result of a factional split, or a failed transition when a factional leader left the scene. And the factional organization followed an electoral logic. Because the LDP was obliged to field multiple candidates in each SNTV electoral district, and because, as discussed, those copartisan rivals would compete on the basis of patronage, credit claiming, and the expensive maintenance of personal support machines, they relied on their factional bosses for support. Accordingly, it is not surprising that no faction liked to support more than one candidate within a single electoral district—spending double the resources to compete with itself—so each LDP candidate within a given district was backed by a different faction.[24] When endorsement opportunities came open due to retirement, or because an Opposition-controlled seat looked vulnerable, factional leaders would bargain over which as-yet-unrepresented faction in that district would be allowed to name the new party endorsee.

Among incumbent LDP MPs, then, one's access to committee posts, junior ministerships, or even cabinet portfolios was mediated by one's faction. Through the 1970s, the factions that had supported the current party president's bid for that position (known as the "mainstream" factions) were rewarded with a more than proportional share (and the most prestigious) of the various government and party posts, while those factions that had backed the wrong horse (the "antimainstream") received a little less than their fair share.[25] Whether a faction was in the mainstream or the antimainstream would vary over time, and no faction was cut out

---

[24]Reed and Bolland (1999) have argued that this explains why the number of factions eventually settled down to five. Because the party could endorse as many as four candidates in a given district, an extension of Duverger's Law implies that there should be 4 + 1 = 5 factions fighting for those slots in a cutthroat game of "musical chairs" (Reed 1994). Often, LDP incumbents would lose to challengers backed by other factions, and just as often, they would return to office, knocking out another copartisan in the process. See also Cox 1997 and Reed 1990.

[25]Sato and Matsuzaki 1986; McCubbins and Thies 1997.

of the division of spoils entirely, but the point is that posts were allocated based on factional affiliation. After the "Civil War" in 1978–1979 that nearly split the party along mainstream/antimainstream lines and cost it its majority, the LDP decided to lower the stakes of the leadership contest, allocating posts as proportionately as possible, based on faction size.[26] Throughout the 1980s, this faction-based universalism became the norm.

Oddly, given how central factions were to the LDP's internal politics, most observers did not detect any ideological logic to their organization. The main explanation for this again points to the SNTV electoral system. Because each district with multiple LDP incumbents must necessarily evince multiple factional links, there was no real geographical distinctiveness (with any corresponding difference in socioeconomic, sectoral, or other regional bases of support) to factions. Each looked like a microcosm of the entire party, with urban and rural members, eastern and western members, and so on.[27] Because faction members tended to back their leaders' initiatives on most things, it was not completely irrelevant for policy which factions were in the mainstream at any given time and which were in the antimainstream. Any differences among factional leaders could be reflected in policy outputs as the factional composition of the mainstream and antimainstream shifted,[28] but it seems clear that those differences were small, and probably more a matter of priorities than of any large ideological disagreements.

One might characterize the battle within each electoral district as a factional proxy war. Each faction wanted to grow, to win greater influence within the party, and the only way to do that was to help incumbent MPs to keep their seats, and help prospective newcomers to win seats, in the face of competition from other factions' candidates. Each LDP candidate (or factionally backed, but unendorsed conservative independent) needed access to large pots of money to build and sustain his personal campaign machine, and that money came, by and large, through his factional pipeline. An individual MP rose within the factional hierarchy by demonstrating his ability to become a net contributor to his faction's coffers, raising even greater amounts than he personally needed to spend.

At the same time that the LDP was finding ways to manage intraparty

[26]Sato and Matsuzaki 1986; Ramseyer and Rosenbluth 1993.

[27]Any conservative politician who wished to join the LDP would have to secure factional backing but could choose only among factions that did not already have a candidate in his district. So, often, choice of faction was constrained by a "process of elimination," such that a best fit in terms of policy preferences or priorities was not always possible (Ramseyer and Rosenbluth 1993).

[28]McCubbins and Thies 1997.

competition while keeping the party from disintegrating, it also had to keep an eye on the other parties in the system. And here, electioneering rules came into play. The LDP, by virtue of its perpetual majorities, could unilaterally decide the rules for campaigning. So it is no coincidence that it chose rules that would help it to solve its own vote-division problem while simultaneously making life difficult for the Opposition. Formal campaign periods were short (and shortened further over time), television and radio advertising were prohibited,[29] and low limits were placed on posters and handbills. Door-to-door canvassing was also outlawed, as were polling, mass meetings, unscheduled speeches, multiple campaign vehicles, and parades.

Clearly, such a regime was frustrating for would-be challengers. In such a short time (only a couple of weeks), and with most of the obvious campaign activities outlawed, it was very difficult for a challenger to increase his name recognition among voters, to say nothing of getting his policy message across. Because the LDP had the most incumbents, it benefited the most from this restraint of trade.[30] But there was more to the LDP's advantage than the incumbent-protection effects of the stifled campaign. Note that the LDP alone, because it needed to find a way to induce optimal vote division among several candidates, would not have benefited much from the ability to broadcast policy appeals. Those might warm voters up to the party as a whole but would not sort out the intraparty competition problem. What is more, because the LDP was the governing party, there was not much new to tell voters about its platform. By contrast, candidates from opposition parties, unencumbered by copartisan competition, would have profited immensely from the ability to issue mass appeals with alternative policy ideas, via TV or radio ads. Thus the electioneering activities that were outlawed would have helped challengers more than incumbents, and small parties with single candidates more than big parties with multiple candidates. These rules helped the LDP to keep the Opposition divided and enfeebled, so that it could concentrate on vote division and mobilization.[31]

[29]Each candidate was granted two five-minute slots on television during the campaign. But these were far from the expensive, high-production-value advertisements familiar to U.S. voters. Instead, they proceeded as virtual cattle calls, in which a stream of candidates would line up and take a turn in front of a stationary microphone, reciting a series of vanilla policy promises before exiting stage right and giving the next person a turn. These parades of platitudes were so pointless that very few voters bothered to watch. We thank a reviewer for reminding us to describe these somewhat surreal exercises.

[30]Hrebenar 1986.

[31]Cox and Thies 1998.

As discussed, mobilization under SNTV required money. There were restrictions on spending and fund-raising, of course, but these were the most difficult to enforce. It would be hard to hide a parade or a TV commercial—but exceeding official limits on contributions, or spending more than the legal limit on political activities, especially outside the official campaign period, was not very difficult to pull off. LDP politicians would periodically be caught breaking these rules, and would be forced to pay a fine, or even to quit politics for a short time. But the LDP's insatiable need for political money to grease the wheels of intraparty competition, coupled with its control over the governmental apparatus that would have to enforce the restrictions on such money, meant that such punishments were the exception rather than the rule.

LDP politicians raised this money largely from business groups. Some groups, such as *Keidanren* (the Federation of Economic Organizations) would contribute to the party proper. But many others would choose to support specific faction leaders or even individual candidates. Tanaka Kakuei, for example, was notorious for his deep ties to the construction industry, and he reaped the lion's share of their largesse in return for massive public works projects to "remake the Japanese archipelago" before, during, and after his brief term as prime minister (1972–1974). Thus firms or industry organizations would in essence "purchase" regulatory favoritism with their donations, government policies that would protect them from foreign competitors and enable them to cartelize markets to keep newcomers out and profits high. In the national tier of the Upper House, interest groups would even insist on the endorsement of particular candidates, to represent their interests directly in government.

As we discuss more thoroughly in the next chapter, however, the LDP over time found itself with more and more mouths to feed, and often the policy demands of these various groups were mutually incompatible. Farmers and owners of inefficient small businesses wanted expensive subsidies and protection from imports, while big-business interests wanted cheap raw materials and finance and unfettered access to foreign markets. Keeping this coalition together became more and more expensive, in terms of fiscal deficits, inflationary bubbles, and inveterate corruption.

Moreover, rapid migration after the war from rural to urban areas made the task ever more difficult. Redistricting did not keep up with population shifts, so farmers managed to retain disproportionate political influence, but the swelling urban populations were much trickier for LDP politicians to organize and mobilize. Urban voters had new and different policy demands, some of which (e.g., pollution, welfare) were more incompatible with those of the LDP's business clients than were the simple subsidy demands of farmers. But they also were more atomized and peripatetic than traditional rural households—they lived far from where they worked and worked far from their neighbors; they were younger and less tied down to one community—and so they were much more difficult for LDP politicians to capture with koenkai-based patronage machines.

Through the 1980s especially, it became harder for the LDP to buy everyone off, and the interests of steel started to diverge from those of rice.[32] Once foreign governments brought pressure to bear on the Japanese policy process, demanding access to Japanese markets, and threatening sanctions against Japanese export industries, the tensions within the LDP's support base increased. Why, asked profitable export firms such as Matsushita and Toyota, should we be punished by foreign governments just because the LDP insists on coddling farmers? Still, as long as the economy was chugging along, and the average Japanese was getting richer, the teetering house of cards stood, and farsighted reformers were met with the short-term mantra "If it ain't broke, don't fix it."

Then, at the close of the 1980s, the stock market and land-price bubbles burst, the economy stopped growing and even began to decay, and more politicians began to think more seriously about the political antecedents to economic restructuring. Still, the LDP bounced back from an embarrassing Upper House defeat in 1989 to win a Lower House election in February 1990 (albeit with a reduced majority—see appendixes 2 and 3), so an internal effort to reform the electoral system ran aground on the shoals of complacency and risk-aversion. As it turned out, the 1990 win was to be the LDP's last under SNTV, as the frustrated reformers would engineer a party split that would lead to the collapse of the first party system and the elimination of SNTV once and for all.

Conclusions

If one's definition of democracy requires actual alternation in government, then Japan between 1955 and 1993 (or at least 1989) might look a little suspicious. Most observers would concede that Japan ought to be considered a democracy anyway,[33] albeit a democracy flawed by corruption.

---

[32]Calder 1988; Pempel 1998.

[33]For one thing, while the LDP held on to power continuously, individual LDP members were always "running scared"; reelection rates for incumbents were much lower than in the United States, for example.

On this view, the LDP's long, uninterrupted reign can be put down to a combination of popular policies (and favorable outcomes) and the sheer ineffectiveness of the opposition parties. The key to democracy is accountability, wherein voters can assess the performance of those in power, and either reward them with a renewed electoral mandate or else punish them by replacing them with their opponents. It is the *possibility* of alternation that is important. Indeed, in an ideal world, incumbents would always do a good job and would continuously be returned to office. There is no doubt that the LDP had a lot of policy success of which it could be proud, and good luck for which it could be thankful. Two generations and more of peace, prosperity, rule of law, domestic tranquility, and relatively low socioeconomic inequality make for an enviable track record. That many of these results depended on an unsustainable mix of policies in a fast-changing international marketplace did not worry voters, or therefore politicians, very much until the bills came due in the 1990s, so the LDP rode the wave of success for a very long time.

Still, by the mid-1960s, despite pro-LDP malapportionment, more Japanese voters voted for opposition party candidates than for LDP endorsees, so general approval of LDP performance is not a sufficient explanation for LDP longevity.[34] Some of the answer, as we have discussed, pivots on the LDP's ability to overcome SNTV by virtue of its control over government spending—creating a virtuous cycle[35] for the party that happened to get a majority first. But the rest of the explanation comes down to the inability of the opposition parties to convert a combined majority of the votes into a majority of the seats. The *intraparty* vote-division problem that bedeviled the LDP manifested as an *interparty* problem for the opposition parties. Too often, they divided the anti-LDP vote too thinly, because they were unable to coordinate on an optimal number of candidates. They could not agree on a set of issues that would unify their anti-LDP message, and if ever they managed to find such an issue (antipollution demands in the 1960s, for example), the LDP was savvy enough to jump on the bandwagon and carry out sufficient policy change to diffuse its electoral effect. For the most part, the only winning issue for the opposition parties was corruption, and their fortunes would wax and wane as the LDP's campaign-finance and related scandals erupted and faded away.

The 1990s, however, brought a great deal of change. As we will discuss in chapters 6–8, the collapse of the economic bubble and the changes in

---

[34]Scheiner 2006.

[35]Scheiner 2006. Of course, a virtuous cycle for the LDP was a vicious one for opposition parties.

Japan's geopolitics that came with the end of the Cold War gave Japanese voters a lot more to be worried about, and the equation (however over-simplified) of "LDP" with "peace and prosperity" took a hit. Soon, the electoral rules would be changed, reducing the LDP's incumbency advantage, and at the same time increasing the likelihood that the Opposition could get its act together and finally wrest power away. Before we turn to these developments, however, we shall examine the political economy of the LDP era. Just what was the policy mix of that time, why was it politically optimal for such a sustained period, and why did it eventually collapse?

CHAPTER 5

Japan's Postwar Political Economy

Introduction

The Japanese economy grew at a stunning rate in the postwar years, achieving a tenfold expansion of nominal GDP between 1965 and 1990. Japan went from a country laid waste in World War II to one that appeared poised to rule the world economy. Tokyo was awash in money. Eight of the world's top ten banks, measured by loan assets, were Japanese, and Japanese companies were on an extended buying spree around the world, not only to set up production plants overseas, but also for luxury destinations such as five-star golf courses and Rockefeller Center in New York City. Tokyo cafés had trouble keeping up with the demand for coffee adorned with gold shavings, and there was talk of filling half of Tokyo Bay with landfill to add office and living space at the cost of over ¥2 trillion. No wonder American managers yearned to discover the secrets of Japanese efficiency and management genius.[1]

The collapse of Japan's economy was equally spectacular, after the asset bubble burst in 1990. The Nikkei stock market index dropped from its record high of 39,000 in December 1989 to less than 15,000 in the fall of 1990 (see fig. 5.1). Property prices plummeted by 80 percent in the space of a few months. Not only did the markets in stocks and property crash, but Japan's economy languished in a recessionary trough for more than a decade (see fig. 5.2). Bankruptcies and suicides rose in tandem.[2] Japanese banks that had dominated world rankings in assets were found to be sitting on enormous mountains of nonperforming loans, and construction of skyscrapers in cities and of massive concert halls in rural towns stalled in midproject for lack of funds.

---

[1]Self-deprecating humor in America in those years included a joke about President George H. W. Bush awaking from a coma, nervous about what might have happened to the U.S. economy while Vice President Dan Quayle presided on his behalf. "What is our growth rate?" "Five percent, sir." Surprised, Bush asked about interest rates and unemployment. "They're both around five percent as well," answered Quayle. "How did you do that?" the president asked, genuinely astonished. "We asked the Japanese to take over our economy," came the answer.

[2]Amyx 2004: 2.

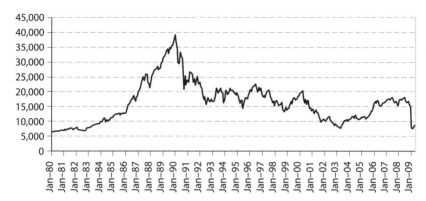

Figure 5.1. From the Stock Market Bubble in 1990 to the Global Financial Crisis: Nikkei Index at Close of Each Month's Trading, January 1980–April 2008

Source: Nikkei Inc., Nikkei Digital Media, Inc. http://www3.nikkei.co.jp/nkave/data/month4.cfm. See also Endo 1999, 318, for a visual comparison of stock prices and land prices.

How did Japan tumble so quickly from an economic powerhouse to a basket case? In this chapter, we argue that an economic growth strategy based on industry protection contained the seeds of later failure from the very beginning. Japan's rapid economic development in the postwar years and its later decline were both products of a postwar political deal to protect big investors in war industries after World War II. Industry grew quickly in a pro-business climate, to be sure, but protectionist policies accommodated increasingly large amounts of deadwood into the Japanese

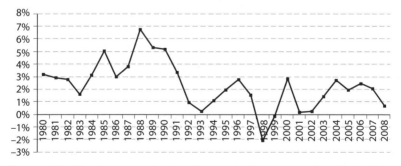

Figure 5.2. The Lost Decade-Plus: Economic Stagnation after the Bubble Burst. Annual Japanese GDP Growth (Constant Yen—Base Year = 2000)

Source: International Monetary Fund, *World Economic Outlook Database, October 2008*. http://www.imf.org/external/pubs/ft/weo/2008/02/weodata/index.aspx.

economy, especially in the nontraded sectors that were most sheltered from competition.

Japan's industrial policy was supported by well-known economic institutions—the main bank, cross-shareholding, and lifetime employment, to name just three. The minimalist nature of the Japanese welfare state, and the unequal opportunities for women in the workforce, are also well documented. A political logic undergirded the entire system of "convoy capitalism,"[3] propping up firms and whole industries that would have failed in a less-regulated economy, and foisting on Japanese taxpayers high prices and taxes, limited choice in the marketplace, and rigid career paths.

For the staying power of the postwar system, we blame Japan's rules of electoral competition that pitted LDP politicians against each other in multimember districts. As we described in the previous chapter, LDP politicians were unable to campaign on the basis of a party platform, however public spirited they may have been, and therefore had to "sell" protective regulation in exchange for campaign contributions. Any notion of the "public good" was swamped by the flood of patronage doled out to specific private interests. Moreover, the multimember-district system lent itself to creating new protected groups, and before long big business in Japan had to share policy favors with farmers and small business proprietors in sectors of the economy not engaging in international trade and who were therefore under less market pressure to innovate. Along the way, so many different producer groups were cut in on the bargain that, as it turned out, Japanese economic development proved to be relatively egalitarian.

Over time, the LDP had to spend ever more to keep all of its diverse group of supporters in tow. It was only when the economy finally collapsed under the weight of massive resource misallocation that the hidden costs of convoy capitalism became clear. Reformers within the LDP demanded an end to money politics, splitting the party and destroying its parliamentary majority. Within a year, the politicians agreed to change the electoral system to one that would foster party-based competition. We describe the process and the political effects of that reform in chapter 6, and the economic policy effects in chapter 7. In the remainder of this chapter, we lay out the logic of Japanese convoy capitalism, and explain how global economic integration in the 1980s and early 1990s pulled the rug out from under the LDP's money politics.

---

[3] The metaphor of the "convoy system" evokes the image of a naval flotilla that moves only as fast as the slowest ship. It has long been used to describe postwar Japanese financial regulation, and we follow Schoppa 2006 in extending the metaphor to refer to Japan's postwar political economy as a whole.

THE WAY OF HEAVY INDUSTRY

Toward the end of the U.S.-led Occupation of Japan, American officials increasingly ceded control of the economy to the Japanese government. The United States was no longer worried about resurgent militarism in Japan and instead hoped that Japan would contribute to the American-led defense against encroaching communism in Asia. Prime Minister Yoshida Shigeru (in office 1946, 1948–1954) worked hard to deflect American pressure on Japan to spend more on defense, for although the United States had imposed on Japan a "peace constitution" that forbade Japan to rearm, the U.S. government had changed its mind and was pressing for a flexible reading of Article 9 that would permit rearmament.[4]

The Yoshida government was less alarmed than was the United States by the prospect of Communist expansion, and would have normalized relations with Mao's China if the United States had permitted; but the Japanese also knew that a strong alliance with the United States would be cheaper than full-scale rearmament. Thus was born the Yoshida Doctrine, to "concede to the United States as much as necessary but as little as possible" to keep the alliance strong. In this way, Japan was able to reserve more government spending for economic recovery.[5]

The Japanese government still had many choices to make concerning how to marshal its resources for recovery and growth. Given the shortage of capital and an abundance of labor, Japan's comparative advantage in world trade should have been in light manufacturing. The textile industry had been the engine of Japan's economic growth before the military coup in 1932, and a number of economists, including Bank of Japan governor Ichimada Hisato, argued that Japan's government would be best served by the decentralized, small-scale capitalism of the prewar period.[6] In theory, Japan's investment in heavy industries during the war constituted a misallocation of resources and should have been considered unrecoverable sunk costs. But in politics, as Gary Becker famously noted, there is no such thing as sunk costs.[7] Political backing can alter

---

[4]The U.S. government was frustrated with Yoshida's staunch opposition to bigger Japanese defense budgets and began to push the candidacy of the more hawkish Hatoyama Ichiro behind the scenes. See, for example, the now-declassified top secret Department of the Army document 0029 of August 17, 1955, on the merger between the Democratic and Liberal Parties.

[5]By Hugh Patrick's estimate, Japan's economy would have been 30 percent smaller by 1976 if it had allocated 4–5 percent of its GNP to defense rather than the 1 percent it spent (Patrick and Rosovsky 1976).

[6]Inoue 2002.

[7]Becker 1983.

economic calculations, because government policies such as subsidies and regulatory favoritism can make an otherwise inefficient business proposition into a profitable investment.

Thus big business in Japan came through the war with portfolios skewed toward heavy industry, since cooperation with the military government had been the firms' path to survival.[8] Companies with large investments in steel, cement, shipbuilding, and machinery lobbied for a development strategy favoring heavy industry, and received favorable regulations from politicians of the ruling Liberal Party in exchange for campaign contributions. Once the Liberal and Democratic Parties merged to form the LDP in 1955, they developed an even greater appetite for campaign contributions.[9] With two sets of incumbents seeking seats under a common party label, LDP politicians pumped large sums of money into personal support networks to be electorally competitive against each other in multi-member districts, putting a premium on campaign finance.

Japanese businesses were willing to bankroll the LDP in exchange for a favorable business climate. This did not mean wanton public expenditures for any business desiring a handout, because that would have caused ruinous inflation. In exchange for campaign contributions, the LDP gave businesses protective regulation and low-interest loans from the postal savings system, but kept outright budget subsidies within modest limits so as to maintain fiscal and monetary responsibility. Although Ichimada lost the argument about Japan's trade policy, he served in the first LDP cabinet as the minister of finance and worked hard to keep the government budget in balance.[10]

Industrial Policy—the Coalition of Steel and Rice

The Japanese government's heavy industrial development policy (*keisha seisan hoshiki*), administered principally by the Ministry of International Trade and Industry and reinforced by other agencies and quasi-public banks, favored heavy industry in a variety of ways.[11] The MITI Heavy

---

[8]Tiedemann 1971.

[9]Behind the push for the merger were business groups seeking more generous government financing and protective regulation. They got rid of Ichimada as the Bank of Japan governor, because he was holding to a tight monetary policy. *Asahi shimbun*, March 16, 1954, p. 4, and August 16, 1954, p. 1. At the same time, businessmen worried aloud that the Liberal Party's spending would cause inflation. *Asahi shimbun*, September 7, 1954, p. 3. Supporting favored groups in a fiscally responsible way became the LDP's central creed.

[10]*Asahi shimbun*, October–December 1955, various issues; Inoue 2002.

[11]Johnson 1982.

Industries Bureau limited entry and often regulated pricing to help stabilize profits. Favored industries received some government budget subsidies and tax breaks, as well as tariff protection and favored access to foreign exchange. Heavy industrial firms also enjoyed privileged access to cheap loans from the Japan Development Bank.[12] The Japan Development Bank was the largest of several quasi-governmental financial institutions funded by the Fiscal Investment and Loan Program (FILP) which pooled millions of savings accounts from post offices around the country. The FILP is sometimes referred to as the "second budget" because the enormous sums of money it disbursed in the form of low-interest-rate loans through a range of financial institutions were comparable to the sums in the government's general account budget.[13]

Japan's industrial policy was a boon to heavy industrial firms, at least in the short run. But without import competition, many businesses that grew rapidly in this hothouse environment failed to keep innovating and eventually proved incapable of competing globally. It is true that Japan's GDP grew at an annual average rate of over 10 percent in the decades between the 1950s and the 1970s, a feat that stunned the rest of the world. But the firms and sectors that received the most JDB loans, subsidies, tariff protection, and tax relief actually grew at a slower rate and showed lower productivity growth than did the rest of the Japanese economy.[14] Steel and cement manufacturing, shipbuilding, and mining, for example, lagged behind the less favored electronics and auto sectors.

The incentives that Japan's electoral rules gave politicians to develop loyal personal support provided an opening for new interest groups besides big business to find representation in the LDP. The Occupation Era reforms had redistributed land to millions of tenant farmers at bargain prices, and in the late 1950s the LDP brought farmers into the fold in response to successful bids by the Socialist and Communist parties for the new "small farmer" vote.[15] The result was a "steel and rice" coalition backing the LDP, whereby heavy industry provided money for campaigns and farmers turned out the vote in large numbers.[16] As with Bismarck's "iron and rye" coalition in nineteenth-century Germany, both members of the coalition were willing to make a costly trade for the bigger prize of protection. Japan's heavy industry would have preferred protection for

[12]Uriu 1996; Noble 1989; Beason and Patterson 2004.
[13]Calder 1988.
[14]Beason and Weinstein 1996: 289.
[15]Calder 1988.
[16]This point echoes Calder 1988 and Pempel 1998.

themselves but open markets in agricultural products to lower food prices and therefore wages. Farmers would have preferred open markets in industrial goods to lower the costs of food production while keeping their own markets closed to foreign competition. Instead, the LDP brokered a deal to give each group its highest priority, of market protection, at some cost to each group—and especially high costs to consumers—of higher prices.[17]

In the late 1950s and early 1960s, small businesses also joined the LDP support coalition, forming the third leg of the stool that propped the LDP's long-term tenure in office. Mom-and-pop retailers, as well as small manufacturers and subcontractors of the manufacturing giants, were present all around the country and were organized into many LDP Diet members' support networks. In exchange for their votes, the LDP gave small stores regulatory protection from retail giants,[18] and leniency on tax reporting.[19]

Policy advantages enjoyed by farmers and small business proprietors were, it seems clear, political favors rather than plans to put resources to their best use. The supposed security advantages of self-sufficiency in agriculture made for politically convenient rhetoric, but stockpiling foreign rice would have been a far cheaper way to achieve that goal.[20] Although Japanese agriculture and retail are known for their low productivity of labor, allowing the market to winnow out the less productive enterprises would have been counterproductive for the LDP, which liked them precisely because of their large numbers that could turn out at elections and vote in predictable ways.

Japanese Corporate Governance: Main Banks and Keiretsu

Kent Calder once called Japan's political economy a Banker's Kingdom because of the centrality of banks to the investment decisions of Japanese

---

[17]Calder 1988. Not only did the government block imports of foreign rice, but it ensured that farmers received artificially high prices for rice through a buying scheme paid for by the general government budget. During the 1970s, Japanese rice farmers received up to seven times the world price, though consumers were able to buy at only three or four times the world price, thanks to government subsidy.

[18]Schoppa 1997; Upham 1993.

[19]Kishiro 1985. The street wisdom about who paid what in taxes is known as 9-6-4 (*kuroyon*): wage workers paid taxes on 90 percent of their income; small businesses paid taxes on 60 percent of their income because they systematically underreported; and farmers paid on 40 percent of their income because their books, too, were not carefully monitored, and because all land under cultivation was taxed at a far lower rate than other land.

[20]Hoshi, Kashyap, and Scharfstein 1990.

corporations and, indeed, to the direction of the entire economy.[21] Banks are one piece of an interlocking set of economic institutions that characterized the postwar Japanese system of corporate governance: banks loans and stable shareholding arrangements released management from short-term thinking, and lifetime labor contracts motivated workers to invest in productivity-enhancing skills and routines.[22]

The Occupation authorities had broken up the zaibatsu holding companies with the U.S. antitrust model in mind, and for a time stock market shares were widely held by individuals. But when the Occupation ended, many companies regrouped into families of firms referred to as *kigyo shudan* or *keiretsu*.[23] Keiretsu firms bought each other's shares to maintain internal control over shareholding, and beginning in the 1960s when the terms of Japan's accession to the articles of the IMF included acceptance of inward foreign direct investment, keiretsu firms bought even more shares to defend against the possibility of hostile foreign takeovers.

From the standpoint of the Anglo-American model of corporate governance, shielding incumbent managers from market discipline is a bad idea.[24] While shareholders, as the firm's owners, want to maximize profits, managers, as salaried agents of shareholders, may prefer some mix of goals that includes their job security and leisure. In a stock-market-based system of corporate finance, share prices provide a constant measure of how well managers are marshaling the firms' assets, and a low share price can trigger takeovers or otherwise result in the replacement of management.[25] To solve the potential problem of managerial slack, according to the Japanese model of corporate governance, banks monitor firm performance and play a managerial role if necessary. If they get it right, the system is nearly perfect: cross-shareholding allows corporate managers to take the long-term view, while oversight by main banks ensures that managers do not use the freedom from short-run performance metrics to enjoy job security at the expense of the firm.

[21]Calder 1993.

[22]Aoki 1988, 2007.

[23]Japanese refer to groups of firms with interlocking shareholding patterns as *kigyo shudan*, or "corporate groups." In American scholarship on Japan, the term *keiretsu* has been popularized, perhaps first by Japan watcher James Abegglen, to refer to the same phenomenon. In Japan, *keiretsu* is a generic term that means linkage and is more often used in connection with the vertical relationships between parent companies and subsidiaries (Hoshi and Kashyap 2001).

[24]Berle and Means 1932; La Porta et al. 1997.

[25]In the Anglo-American model, performance-based executive compensation is a way to align the interests of managers with those of owners, and an outside board of directors is an additional monitoring mechanism.

But there is more to this argument. Not only do banks keep managers on their toes, but long-term bank loans also make it possible for firms to offer employees long-term labor contracts, and this is crucial if workers are key players in the Japanese model of the firm. Job security motivates workers to invest in firm-specific skills, making possible the Japanese manufacturing techniques of team production and quality control that rely extensively on inputs from skilled labor, and that are central to productivity in Japanese manufacturing.[26] According to this model, Japanese workers are not merely replaceable cogs in a generic production process. Instead, because of their superior loyalty and stock of knowledge, they are suppliers of indispensable ideas and techniques that make Japanese products of reliably high quality.

Lifetime labor contracts first emerged on a large scale after World War I when Japanese manufacturing firms found a ready market in a Europe still prostrate from wartime destruction. An export boom in Japanese textiles created a scarcity of skilled workers for whom companies competed with attractive contracts. This was a new phenomenon in Japanese labor markets that had been characterized by high levels of mobility among artisans.[27] When the Japanese economy gained momentum after World War II, labor scarcity again drove companies to compete with one another for scarce labor with offers of lifetime employment.

There is much truth to this characterization of the generic Japanese corporate model, which Masahiko Aoki has labeled the "J-firm." The Japanese have shown that there are multiple efficient ways to produce things, only one of which is the U.S. way of using low-skill labor to fill in the cracks around capital-intensive production processes. Highly skilled and motivated workers have been protected from layoffs in economic downturns through a variety of measures. But this rosy picture of Japanese stakeholder capitalism is only one part of the story. Banks were sometimes poor monitors, and the companies that relied on long-term bank loans did not in fact become the engines of Japanese economic growth.[28] The banks, moreover, were recipients of political favors in their own right.[29]

[26]Aoki 1988; Soskice 1990; Jackson 2001; Vogel 2006.

[27]Thelen and Kume 2001; Streeck 2001.

[28]It should also be noted, however, that banks probably increased the quantity, if not the quality, of capital going into industry in the 1950s and 1960s, and main banks gave borrowers the security to keep investing borrowed money even in tough times.

[29]Our view of Japanese corporate governance takes seriously its political roots, and is consistent with Gourevitch 2003 and Gourevitch and Shinn 2005, who argue that strong labor unions and the PR electoral institutions that helped to translate union strength into

Banking Regulation

In prewar Japan, stock and bond markets accounted for much of firms' external financing.[30] This changed during the war, however, when the military government forced bank mergers on a massive scale, squelched the stock and bond markets, and channeled private savings into bank deposits for loans directed to munitions industries.[31] After World War II, attempts by SCAP to reduce the market power of the largest banks were cut short by the Reverse Course, and by 1947, the Occupation authorities began to prioritize the health of the banking system over economic deconcentration.[32] SCAP abolished holding companies and drafted an antimonopoly law that prohibited banks from owning more than 5 percent of any company's shares, but otherwise banks could retain close ties to "family firms" as before.

Along with steel and construction, banks were among the three biggest contributors to the LDP's electoral coffers in the 1960s through the 1980s. In exchange, banks enjoyed various regulatory favors including a low ceiling for interest rates paid on savings accounts, which prevented banks from competing away the spread between their cost of money and the rates at which they could lend to growing businesses. The Ministry of Finance (MOF) implicitly guaranteed the solvency of banks, not by requiring banks to hold capital in reserve against the possibility of bad loans, but by regulating the competition among banks and across different types

political clout underpin "stakeholder capitalism" in the coordinated market economies of Europe. By contrast, weak unions and majoritarian electoral rules in liberal market economies such as the United States and the United Kingdom give shareholders far more scope for ensuring regulation that favors shareholders over other "stakeholders" in the corporation. In Japan, workers were politically weak, but their scarcity motivated employers to compete for them with long-term contracts. See also Pagano and Volpin 2005 for the way regulation and corporate governance are shaped by electoral rules.

[30]Prewar banks sought capital requirements and other entry barriers to consolidate the banking sector but were thwarted by the prewar Diet, where small banks retained considerable clout. In 1892, Shibusawa Eiichi, of the Tokyo Bankers' Association and founder of the Daiichi Bank, proposed minimum capital requirements, but without success. Sakairi 1988: 191; Ramseyer and Rosenbluth 1995: 104.

[31]Alexander Gerschenkron (1966) argued that late developers tend to establish bank-centered finance as a way to play *economic* catch-up, but the reason for concentration of finance into banking rather than in a decentralized stock market in both Germany (under Bismarck) and Japan (under the military government in the 1930s) was to build a war machine.

[32]Hadley 1949; Tristan Beplat, an economic officer in charge of banking, remembers that the Japanese bankers soon learned to come to him over regulatory issues rather than to the Occupation's antitrust office. Tristan Beplat, personal communication, 1987.

of financial institutions in a way that maintained even the weakest as a going concern.[33]

In trying to maintain the stability of the banking system by suppressing competition among financial institutions, the MOF incurred considerable risk that bank failure would sully its reputation (and after the bubble burst in 1990, the MOF's worst nightmares came true). The MOF had attempted repeatedly to shift more responsibility for financial system stability onto banks themselves through prudential rules of various kinds, but in each instance the ministry was thwarted by LDP politicians with close ties to the banks.[34] As we have argued, LDP politicians were more preoccupied with providing particularistic policy favors to big campaign contributors than with formulating public policy with the average citizen in mind.[35] Banks were favored players in the postwar economy because they were able to parlay their market concentration, via the political influence of massive campaign contributions, into profit-padding regulation.

The Politics of Trade Policy

Japan's most productive firms, in automobiles and electronics, typically had lower than average dependence on main banks. When the MITI in the 1960s pressured the smaller automobile companies to merge with either Toyota or Nissan, they were able instead to solicit capital investments from foreign firms: Mitsubishi from Chrysler and Isuzu from General Motors in 1971, Mazda from Ford in 1979, and Suzuki from General Motors in 1981. By the mid-1980s, when firms such as Toyota or Canon or Panasonic began to look good to banks, those firms no longer needed loans. They had become profitable enough to finance their investments through retained earnings, and had established corporate credit ratings that gave them access to the cheapest sources of capital in the world. International product competition and internal competition for the top corporate jobs, rather than monitoring from banks, kept the management of these firms on their toes.

---

[33]The MOF regulated competition among banks and between banks and nonbank financial companies in a way that ensured the viability of weaker institutions. For example, big banks for many years were not allowed to offer ATM services beyond the hours that smaller banks (which could not afford ATMs) kept their doors open. Simultaneously, the MOF enforced walls separating commercial banking, investment banking, life insurance, nonlife insurance, agricultural cooperative banks, postal savings, and so on.

[34]The final version of the Banking Act of 1982, for example, gutted the MOF's proposals for stiffer capital adequacy requirements. See Rosenbluth 1989.

[35]Rosenbluth and Schaap 2003.

It would be an exaggeration, however, to say that these exporting firms grew hardy in the thin air of laissez-faire, for they, too, were recipients of a variety of government measures to promote domestic businesses. Until the mid-1970s, the Japanese government protected domestic manufacturers from international competition behind a high wall of import tariffs. Japan (like Germany) also benefited from having its currency fixed at a low level against the dollar.[36] Although a weak currency was appropriate when Japan was recovering from the ravages of the war, by the 1960s the weak yen was seen as artificially depressing the prices of Japanese goods on world markets, thus rendering them artificially competitive. By 1967, Japan (and Germany) had begun running chronic trade surpluses against the United States, prompting calls for exchange rate revision.[37] When Japan refused in the late 1960s and early 1970s to revalue the yen to make Japanese goods more expensive on international markets, the Nixon administration took the dramatic step of bringing down the entire fixed rate system by allowing the U.S. dollar to depreciate against gold in 1971.[38] The Japanese yen floated upward and did cut into export profits, but not enough to turn the tide.

Throughout the 1970s and 1980s, chronic Japanese trade surpluses against the United States aroused ferocious pressure from the U.S. Congress. The Japanese responded with a string of concessions, including the elimination of import tariffs on manufactured products by 1978, voluntary export restraints on steel, automobile, and textile exports to the United States, and promises to buy more U.S. products. But farmers and retailers continued to hide behind protectionist barriers. Moreover, although many of the visible barriers to trade in manufactured goods were out of the way by the 1980s, American trade officials complained that the real problems were invisible "structural impediments," including the

[36]Fixed exchange rates were a pillar of the postwar international monetary system hammered out principally by the British economist John Maynard Keynes and American Treasury official Harry Dexter White at Bretton Woods, New Hampshire, in 1944. Their hope was to prevent a repeat of the spiraling worldwide depression triggered by competitive rounds of currency devaluation before the war. The other Allied nations, including the Soviet Union, were represented at the Bretton Woods conference as well, but the American and British views dominated the planning for the postwar international financial institutions including the World Bank and the International Monetary Fund.

[37]Kindleberger 1972.

[38]Closing the gold window on August 15 was the second of two "Nixon Shocks" that summer. On July 15, the trip to Beijiing by U.S. National Security Advisor Henry Kissinger to begin rapprochement with China had caught the Japanese off guard, because they had been forced in 1952 by the American government to recognize as the official government of China Chiang Kai-shek's government on Taiwan. Nixon took both actions without consulting the Japanese in advance.

keiretsu and main bank arrangements just described,[39] while Japanese trade officials countered that Japanese companies were just better at manufacturing. There was truth to both sides: companies like Toyota were outcompeting American companies wherever they met, whereas other industries, including agriculture, food processing, construction, and transportation, were backwaters that could not survive without props. The LDP had supported its tenure in office for decades by selling these props—budget, tax, and regulatory favors—in exchange for votes and money, at least until the whole edifice was toppled by its own excesses.

The Politics of the Japanese Welfare State

Japan's welfare state does not fit easily into typologies that have been built around European and American examples.[40] Like the liberal market economies of the United States and the United Kingdom, Japan is a chary welfare state as measured by direct government spending on welfare as a percentage of GDP. On the other hand, much of Japan's labor market is characterized by long-term labor contracts, as in the coordinated market economies of Europe. Japan has universal health insurance, but because pensions are employment based and relatively modest, many Japanese citizens sock away a large chunk of their wages into savings accounts to make up the difference.[41] This jumbled picture does make sense, however, once one understands the nature of Japanese political coalitions.

We have argued that the distributional patterns in Japan's postwar economy cannot be understood without an appreciation of electoral politics and the demands of the LDP's favored constituents. The same can be said about social insurance policies. Here, as elsewhere in Japanese policy making, we find a pattern of favoritism to corporate contributors. Indeed, we argue that the notable egalitarianism that accompanied Japan's rapid postwar economic growth was substantially a by-product of business-coddling, anticompetitive regulations that kept weak firms and industries operating (and their employees working) at the expense of high corporate taxes and restrictions on the market behavior of the more competitive firms. Convoy capitalism was not designed in order to produce a rela-

[39]Schoppa 1997.

[40]Esping-Andersen 1990.

[41]Dekle 2005. Since the bubble burst, however, Japanese household savings have declined precipitously, from 11.4 percent in 1997 to 7.9 percent in 2000 to only 2.2 percent in 2007 (Noble 2009).

tively equal distribution of wealth and welfare, but whatever its attendant inefficiencies, that was one of its effects.[42]

Employment Protections

Long-term labor contracts in Japan emerged in conditions of labor scarcity but not labor political empowerment, first after World War I and then in their current form after World War II.[43] Unlike the continental European model, in which the interests of organized labor were championed by strong social democratic parties that participated in, or even dominated, governments, the LDP's coalition excluded labor.[44] Japan has no counterpart to the legislative protections of labor that European labor parties have succeeded in incorporating into the industrial bargaining landscape.[45]

Japanese employers were gratified by the government's suppression of industry-wide unions and the resulting establishment of quiescent firm-level unions during the Occupation. Unions organized at the level of the firm are more willing to restrain *wage demands* because their livelihood is tethered to the firm's competitiveness vis-à-vis other firms. *Lifetime employment* is another matter, because that reflects the interests of employers themselves. Long-term labor contracts were designed and implemented by firms for whom skilled labor was central to their production method. Firms wanted to avoid training workers only to have them leave for greener pastures, and therefore back-loaded wages in a system of seniority advancement. Since workers were underpaid in their early years and overpaid in their later years, they had incentives to stay.

Firms' willingness to avoid layoffs even during economic downturns had the effect of maintaining social stability and softening the bite of recession, even if it was motivated by their interest in maintaining their reputations as good employers for the better years ahead. In contrast to

[42]A much more thorough treatment can be found in Estévez-Abe 2008. She characterizes many of these welfare-affecting economic regulations as the "functional equivalents" of more explicit public-goods-oriented welfare programs. The differences lie in the means by which certain outcomes are produced, and especially the extent to which benefits are targeted to favored groups.

[43]Moriguchi and Ono 2006.

[44]Pempel and Tsunekawa 1979.

[45]Swenson 2002 points out that strong labor unions could be, in some circumstances, useful to businesses in managing production cartels. Negotiations over wages could also be used to anchor production quotas. But businesses in Japan did not need the help of labor to form cartels, since the government was protective of business interests.

European arrangements, however, where the terms of wage bargaining typically cover all employed workers, Japan's lifetime employment applies only to the 25 percent or so of the workforce who are cultivated as core, skilled workers. For the rest of the labor force, employment is less secure and less well remunerated.

The biggest group to be left out of corporate largesse is women, for whom Japan's long-term labor contracts have been a disaster. As labor economists noted decades ago, employers who expect to invest in employees over the course of a career will avoid hiring or promoting women as long as women are more likely to quit or take time off for child rearing and other family work.[46] Women should look like particularly bad investments when lifetime employment is common, and Japanese women have, in fact, fared poorly in Japan's labor markets. Any weakening of lifetime employment, then, should be a relative boon for women, because it would level the playing field somewhat by making men less secure about their own employment (that is, more like women in that regard).

Pensions

The distribution of retirement benefits in Japan, keyed to earned wages, bears more similarity to that of the liberal market economies of the United States and the United Kingdom than to those in the coordinated market economies of continental Europe. As with employment protections, pension benefits in Japan overwhelmingly hinge on employment status. The public pension is universal and pays out a flat rate that is not enough to live on in Japan generally, let alone in Tokyo, one of the most expensive cities in the world. Workers rely instead on Employee's Pension Insurance, which is linked to salary and length of employment. Retirees received a monthly pension of about 50 percent of their average monthly wage, though as we will see in chapter 7, Japan's aging population, combined with its shrinking workforce, has made the traditional payout rate unsustainable, leading to a downsizing of pensions in 2000.[47] The point we wish to make here is that pensions, like employment protections, rest on workers' market power rather than on their feeble political clout.[48]

---

[46]Mincer 1968; Polachek 1978; Estévez-Abe, Iversen, and Soskice 2001.

[47]Clark and Mitchell 2002. Chopel, Kuno, and Steinmo (2005: 22, 30) note that the United States and Japan are similar not only in their generally low levels of social spending, but in the large shares of those small amounts devoted to the elderly. For Japan, with its low fertility rate, this poses a far bigger fiscal problem. In 1973, 25 percent of the Japanese government's welfare spending went to the elderly; by 2001 it was 68.7 percent.

[48]Estévez-Abe 2006.

Health Insurance

Health insurance, which is provided universally at a far lower price than the private health insurance scheme in the United States, is one of Japan's success stories. But even this ostensibly social welfarist outcome bears the unmistakable mark of Japanese politics. National health insurance is an umbrella for substantially unequal plans that are based on employment status and wages.

SCAP initially put forward a more progressive, redistributive plan that would have brought together Japan's patchwork system of public health insurance into a comprehensive social insurance system on the British model, but this ran into insurmountable opposition in both the United States and Japan.[49] The Occupation itself had lost its New Deal flavor by 1947, and the so-called Dodge Plan of 1949 aimed at balancing Japan's government budget by cutting social welfare spending. Japanese businesses insisted on separate programs for industrial workers where they could control insurance premiums and ceilings, given the political power of doctors to balk at managed rates.[50]

By 1962 when the government passed health insurance legislation, the Japan Medical Association (JMA) had persuaded the LDP to leave substantial control of treatment and fees to doctors, a feat that is often attributed to the colorful Takemi Taro, who was JMA president from 1957 to 1980. We will never know how much he was bluffing, but Takemi threatened to mobilize doctors to bring down fifty LDP members in the following Lower House elections if the LDP did not agree to physician latitude in treatment methods and payment.[51] The result is health-care coverage that is universal but not unified because doctors retain considerable freedom in treating their patients, while firms control premiums, copayments, and benefits of their employees.[52]

In summary, Japan's welfare system, in health as in other categories, is

[49]SCAP Public Health and Welfare 1946; Sheingate and Yamagishi 2006.

[50]When health-care costs began to climb at a faster rate in the 1970s, the business community insisted that the LDP put a tighter lid on them.

[51]Takemi Taro won the gratitude of the medical profession when he demanded of the LDP that the health insurance law of 1962 guarantee physicians' professional freedom and give the JMA a say on any changes in fee schedules. See Steslicke 1973; Campbell and Ikegami 1998; Khoon 2006.

[52]Campbell and Ikegami 1998: 107; Sheingate and Yamagishi 2006: 158. Premiums range from 7.3 to 9.5 percent of the wage base. According to empirical analysis by Komamura and Yamada (2004), firms passed along the costs of employers' contributions toward health care to employees but not the costs of long-term-care insurance, reflecting relative demand for each.

more extensive than a measure of direct government spending would indicate[53] because many of the benefits provided by governments in other countries are, in Japan, tied to employment. This requires, in turn, that employment, at least for a substantial percentage of male heads of households, be stable.[54] And stability of employment, in turn, requires either a powerful union movement that bargains for job security, or else a corporate governance system that shelters firms from the discipline of the market for ownership and can therefore afford to carry their employees through hard times. In Japan, labor was weak, but cross-shareholding arrangements and main bank relationships were the keys to employment protections and hence welfare protections.

We noted above that the system of lifetime employment led to discrimination against women in the workforce—it was a greater risk (or higher cost) to commit to a female employee who might leave the firm to have children.[55] Absent any state provision of child-care or elderly-care services, women were expected to provide those services for their families at home.[56] This arrangement again depended on stability of employment (and sufficient salary) for their husbands. Families could afford to have one spouse stay home and take care of children and grandparents only if the other spouse earned enough money, and was protected sufficiently from the risk of a layoff, to make a one-career household feasible. As Leonard Schoppa has elaborated, women could choose between careers (albeit not as well remunerated or upwardly mobile as those open to men) and motherhood, but the Japanese social welfare system depended on their not being able to have both. Over time, however, Japanese women increasingly have chosen careers, and have opted to postpone or even eschew marriage and motherhood altogether. This has sent the Japanese fertility rate plummeting and contributed significantly to the rapid aging of Japanese society. "Traditionalists" might bemoan the fact, and feminists applaud it, but there is no disputing that the choice of more and more women to "exit" the role of unpaid welfare provider in favor of

[53]Estévez-Abe 2008.

[54]Schoppa 2006.

[55]Of course, we do not mean to imply that there were not also other causes of gender discrimination. But lest we assume that the ultimate source of gender discrimination is some notion of Asian patriarchy, it is worth noting that women are more likely to be employed in Taiwan, where the small-firm economy is characterized by fluid labor markets, compared to Japan and Korea (Brinton 2001).

[56]Indeed, as has often been noted, housewives were most likely to be responsible for the care not of their own parents, but of their in-laws.

paid employment has contributed to the "unraveling" of the Japanese welfare system, and perhaps to convoy capitalism writ large.[57]

GLOBALIZATION AND THE COLLAPSE OF THE POSTWAR ECONOMY

Japan's economy overheated in the 1980s for reasons having to do with its reaction to pressures of economic globalization. But the reasons for the government's response, which was to turn on the spigots of money supply, reach back into the early postwar years, and to the structure of Japan's political system itself. The LDP was simultaneously trying to satisfy exporters and import-competing sectors, a task that looked increasingly like a stunt rider standing astride two horses that have begun moving in different directions.

The world economy began exerting pressure on Japan even before the strain was perceptible. In the early postwar years, although Japanese exports were bolstered by an artificially low exchange rate and a variety of tariff and nontariff barriers, successful exporting nevertheless required investing enormous assets in learning about foreign markets and improving productivity. By the late 1970s, owing to pressure from the United States, Japanese firms lost much of their tariff protection and exchange-rate protection. This forced exporters to improve productivity, while firms in the nontraded sectors of the economy, such as local service providers, invested instead in political lobbying for collusive deals to limit competition.

With advances in transportation and communication technology worldwide, the category of goods and services that were considered to be naturally "nontraded" shrank over the years. Time was when farmers, retailers, and bankers enjoyed such a home-country advantage that they had relatively little to fear. But as time passed, overseas farmers found ways to ship even delicate produce, such as strawberries, profitably to Japan; foreign retailers could offer lower prices than could mom-and-pop grocery stores, thanks to computer-assisted inventory management; and foreign financial-service providers with global investment strategies could offer higher yields than could domestic providers. The natural barriers of distance and cultural knowledge lost much of their power.

For decades, embattled producers of goods and services sought to pro-

[57]Schoppa 2006; Campbell 2002.

90 • Chapter 5

tect their "nontraded" status. LDP politicians unfailingly came to their aid, because the party's divide-and-conquer electoral strategy protected them from mass consumer movements, and, for that matter, from political competition by parties that might take up the cause of consumers and taxpayers who were feeling ripped off. The LDP government responded to globalization's early losers with legislation including the Large Scale Store Law of 1975, which gave small firms the ability to block the entry of large stores in their neighborhoods, and backed Japanese farmers against foreign growers of oranges, beef, and rice. Although the LDP leadership sometimes made timely concessions for the sake of the U.S.-Japan alliance, the LDP politicians who represented the farmers earned the sobriquet of "Vietcong," because of their dedication to the cause of agricultural protection "until death."[58]

Early signs of disaffection of Japanese manufacturing exporters toward backwater sectors appeared during the mid-1970s, when the post–oil shock recession put a severe strain on the government's budget. Firms competing in export markets were leery of government budget deficits, lest taxes rise or inflation raise their input costs, cutting into margins on foreign sales. The Administrative Reform movement of the early 1980s, backed by the captains of Japanese industry, singled out agriculture, Japan National Railways, Nippon Telephone and Telegraph, and the national health system for special attention, because of the size of the government budget subsidy allocated to each. Not yet ready to inflict a full measure of pain on farmers,[59] the LDP government met the demands for budget discipline in agriculture by raising the consumer price of rice rather than cutting the price going to rice producers.

By the 1980s, foreign ire aimed at Japanese protectionism threatened to impose on Japanese exporters costs even greater than the tax burden of outright subsidies. In response to Japan's enormous and growing trade surplus, the country's trading partners insisted that Japan either revalue the yen (to make Japanese products less competitive overseas) or throw open Japan's domestic markets to foreign manufactured goods.[60] The

---

[58]"Vietcong" in Japanese, *betokon*, also sounds amusingly similar to *beikon*, shorthand for the *Beikakondankai*, or Rice Price Deliberation Council, which set the producer price of rice each year. This was a supremely political decision, because it required setting the amount of the subsidy going to agriculture from the General Account Budget.

[59]But see Thies 1998.

[60]Why Japan's trade surplus was so large is another question. Part of the answer, no doubt, is simply that Japanese automakers outperformed their American counterparts, but the weak yen also contributed, as did various tariff and nontariff barriers against foreign imports.

Japanese government opted for exchange-rate adjustment in hopes of blaming the pain of economic adjustment on market forces.

Following the Plaza Accord of 1985 and the Louvre Agreement of 1986 in which Japan agreed to allow substantial appreciation of the yen, the Japanese government reduced real interest rates to zero as a domestic painkiller.[61] The LDP wanted to ease the adjustment to market forces for Japanese exporters and import-competing firms, but in the process produced one of the biggest asset bubbles of the twentieth century. Banks and corporations went on an enormous spending spree with nearly free money, bidding up the price of real estate and other assets until the land under the Imperial Palace in Tokyo (about three square miles) was valued as highly as the entire real estate of California.[62]

For successful Japanese manufacturers who could compete without government favors, foreign anger against Japanese protectionism soon struck home. The U.S. Congress equipped the 1988 Omnibus Trade and Competitiveness Act with a zinger clause, known as Super 301, which authorized the administration to retaliate against countries considered to be engaging in unfair trading practices. Although the Reagan administration and congressional Republicans resisted a full embrace of economic protectionism, bipartisan support for a more activist American trade policy gelled around the national security angle. The Exon (D-NE)-Florio (D-NJ) amendment to the 1988 Trade Bill granted the president authority to block an acquisition by a foreign firm in the event of "credible evidence" that a "foreign interest exercising control might take action that threatens to impair the national security." Fujitsu, a Japanese electronics company that had signaled an interest in purchasing Fairchild Semiconductor Corporation, backed off rather than stumble into a thicket of hostile congressional scrutiny.[63]

Japan's bubble economy of the late 1980s eliminated government budget constraints, temporarily relieving one of the pressures on the LDP's shaky electoral coalition between exporters and the nontraded sectors. But the bubble finally burst in 1990 when the Bank of Japan began raising interest rates. The collapse of the stock and real estate markets came

---

[61]The Bank of Japan set the nominal discount rate at 2.5 percent, which left the real rate at zero, controlling for inflation. The BOJ raised the rate to 3.25 in mid-1989, and to 4.25 by the end of the year, still only marginally above the rate of inflation.

[62]Wood 1992.

[63]Crystal 2003. Ironically, Fairchild at the time was owned by Schlumberger, a French oil field services company that was courting Fujitsu as a buyer.

as a genuine shock to the many people who had thought that Japan would come to dominate the world economy.

After the market crashed, the voting public in Japan expressed unprecedented disenchantment toward the ruling Liberal Democratic Party, and politicians began running for cover in every direction. Now that firms and jobs were in mortal danger on account of the asset collapse, the Japanese government that had once looked like the proud managers of a first-rate economy looked like a bunch of incompetent (and corrupt) bumblers. There was no papering over the opposed interests of traders and antitraders in an economy for which export revenues are so important to growth and livelihood.

In years past, the LDP had held the productive and unproductive groups together by reminding each that they needed the other. While export businesses oiled the LDP's electoral machines with campaign contributions, the farmers and shopkeepers were equally indispensable because of their mobilizational capacity to turn out the vote. This symbiosis between money and votes eroded, almost imperceptibly at first, when steady and ultimately vast migration from rural into urban areas turned Japan into a nation of "floating" voters untethered from the communities of their rural ancestors. While farmers and shopkeepers remained motivated as ever to protect their livelihoods, they had become vastly outnumbered by company employees and other urban dwellers for whom high grocery bills were an irritant and the prospect of foreign protectionist retaliation a real threat to their careers.

Conclusions

Japan's economic miracle was operating on borrowed time. Government protection from competition made for some spectacular early achievements, and some Japanese companies went on to become household names around the world because of their successful production strategies and desirable products. Many other companies, particularly those in the nontraded sectors, mistook a lack of competition for success and settled into comfortable lassitude.[64]

Japan's postwar political economy was built on a complex but delicate web of political coalitions and economic policies. The LDP relied on

[64]These are the companies that would become the source of massive nonperforming loans in the postbubble world when banks once again had to evaluate loans on a more realistic basis.

votes from farmers and small business owners in exchange for protectionist regulations, government subsidies, and tax breaks. The party also depended on enormous campaign contributions from big business, and had to maintain a favorable investment environment (secure bank loans, low interest rates, an undervalued currency) and diplomatic efforts to keep foreign markets open for Japanese products. As long as the government could hold foreign finished products at bay, could force Japanese firms to raise their capital domestically, and could subsidize inputs, the "steel and rice" coalition was viable. But once the regulatory net began to tear, the unraveling came quickly.

One source of strain on regulatory protection was foreign pressure. Japan's trading partners, particularly the United States, demanded the opening of Japanese markets to imports and threatened retaliation against Japanese exporters. Big Japanese manufacturers, the firms that had driven the economy's spectacular growth, took these threats seriously and pressured the LDP to jettison the most heavily protected sectors, which were in any case an enormous drain on the national budget.

Other leaks appeared when, as Schoppa tells us, Japanese firms that sought flexible, lower-cost labor markets abroad, and women, who exited the home in favor of paid employment, undermined the Japanese system of welfare provision.[65] And of course the excesses that led to the formation of the bubble economy in the late 1980s were the result of incomplete regulation even of the domestic economy. Individual lenders and borrowers took advantage of loopholes and the bad incentives of "free money" to amass a mountain of ultimately unrecoverable loans.

The concentration of wartime industries goes far toward accounting for business's privileged position in Japan's postwar economy, but leaves unexplained how rigidities survived for decades and to an extent not seen in many other countries. Japan's postwar electoral rules, by forcing politicians from the Liberal Democratic Party to spend most of their money and effort differentiating themselves from one another in multimember districts, were an important reason for Japan's convoy capitalism. One implication of this argument is that overlaying different institutions onto the same material conditions would have generated pressure in different directions. Majoritarian institutions of the Anglo-American variety would have pushed politics toward broader coalitions, reducing the premiums

---

[65] A similar source of partial "exit" had begun in the late 1970s when the strongest Japanese firms began to raise capital on the Euromarkets rather than depend on loans from domestic banks (Rosenbluth 1989).

captured by organized groups with extreme preferences, and appealing more to the interests of unorganized voters. Proportional representation would have given labor a persistent and politically potent voice of the kind we see in continental Europe.[66] We realize this is a strong claim, that material conditions are filtered by electoral competition in powerful and predictable ways. The next two chapters take advantage of the electoral rule change of 1994 to see how well our logic holds.

[66]Rogowski and Kayser 2002; Schaap 2002; Bawn and Thies 2003.

CHAPTER 6

Japan's New Politics

INTRODUCTION—THE KOIZUMI PUZZLE

Koizumi Junichiro would have been an interesting politician to watch in any democracy. But in Japan, he was a mold-breaker. As prime minister from 2001 to 2006, he achieved celebrity status at home and abroad for all the ways that he defied the stereotype of a staid Japanese politician. He had a preference for rolled-up sleeves in lieu of suit and tie, sported a mane of wavy hair, was an unabashed fan of all things "Elvis," and was the first divorcé to achieve the premiership. His adoring fan base greeted his public appearances screaming his name or his self-chosen nickname, "Lionheart."

Koizumi stood out from his peers and predecessors in more than just superficial ways. He was an avowed internationalist, a believer in a strong Japan that would have an impact on world events befitting its economic might, and, most important, a bold reformer who disavowed many of the preservationist principles of the conservative party he led. He ignored factions in his cabinet appointments and sought systematically to undermine the electoral support networks (*koenkai*) of LDP politicians who opposed his reformist agenda. He sought and won Diet agreement to send Japanese troops to help in the rebuilding of Iraq, and became the first Japanese leader to travel to North Korea. He attacked two pillars of traditional LDP governance by denouncing the quasi-corrupt practice of *amakudari*[1] and by cutting back on pork-barrel public works spending. "Reform, with no sacred cows" was one of his slogans, along with the even more provocative "Change Japan by changing the LDP."

Recall from chapter 2 the Japanese proverb that "the nail that sticks up gets hammered down" *(deru kugi wa utareru)*. By Japanese politics standards, there has never been a politician at the national level who has drawn attention to himself as ostentatiously as has Koizumi Junichiro.

---

[1]Literally translated as "descent from heaven," *amakudari* is a practice whereby retiring central-government bureaucrats take cushy jobs in the very firms that they had spent a career regulating. Some retiring bureaucrats would run for political office, almost always for the LDP.

But far from being "hammered down," he rose to the top and stayed there. It is natural to wonder how such a man rose to power, and how he served for five years (tied for the second-longest tenure in the postwar period). Koizumi stepped down at the time of his own choosing, at the height of his popularity. As prime minister, he was better loved outside his own party, but he led his party to several consecutive electoral triumphs. He did not get everything he wanted in policy terms, nor did he lack detractors, as we shall show. Nonetheless, Koizumi is a puzzle that merits explanation.

Koizumi may appear to be a one-off anomaly against a backdrop of dull gray suits, particularly given the nondescript prime ministers that succeeded him in office. But Koizumi's ascendancy signified bigger changes afoot in Japanese politics. However important his iconoclasm and personal charisma were in their own right, a politician like Koizumi could never have become prime minister under the "Old Politics" described in chapter 4. But he fit the logic of the "New Politics" exceptionally well.

Changing the Rules of the Game: The Electoral Reform of 1994

The transition between the old and new versions of Japanese politics was a long time coming, and in some ways it remains incomplete. But in looking for a watershed moment, one's attention turns first to June 18, 1993. That day, after thirty-eight uninterrupted years in power, the LDP suffered a major party split and its government lost a vote of no confidence. In the ensuing election, it failed to recoup its legislative majority and saw its defectors form new parties that combined with most of the traditional opposition groups (all but the Communists) to construct the first non-LDP government in two generations.

This turn of events, while certainly dramatic, was important not because it pushed the LDP temporarily into opposition, but because it spurred an institutional change that had much broader and longer-term implications. The replacement of the SNTV electoral rule with a mixed-member majoritarian (MMM) system has had ramifications for everything from the party system to campaigns to government formation to policy, and constitutes the basis of what we term Japan's New Politics.

Japan's New Politics is characterized by parties that are more programmatic and centralized than the personalistic and fragmented LDP during its era of dominance. Although a pure two-party system is still unlikely, alternation in government between parties or coalitions centered on competing policy visions is now more likely than at any time since before the LDP's debut in 1955. Electoral competition focuses now on explicit party manifestos, on the personalities and perceived abilities of party leaders, and on campaigns that are national in scope, in sharp contrast to the district-level personalism and internecine "blood feuds" that dominated elections prior to the electoral reform. Campaigns are less expensive and more policy oriented. Policy has taken a turn away from the expensive coddling of inefficient farmers and small businesses to appeal more to the ordinary consumers whom the new electoral laws encourage parties to court.

The political upheaval of 1993 did not come as a complete shock. It arose from the pathologies of the old system, in both politics and economics. While even seasoned observers could not predict the precise timing of the rupture, the exact shape of the post-1993 rules, or the resultant "new logic" of politics, it was not at all surprising that the old equilibrium proved unsustainable. Pressure had been building within the party since at least the mid-1980s as wave after wave of corruption scandal combined with the finance, production, and employment losses of a postbubble economy (not to mention the international disgrace of "checkbook diplomacy" surrounding the Gulf War) to threaten LDP hegemony. For years, a plurality of voters had tolerated the LDP's campaign finance peccadilloes because the party had overseen an economic "miracle" of rapid and fairly equitable growth, while simultaneously charting a secure and steady course in international relations. Corruption and other improprieties had tarnished the party's image, and it had long since ceased to be the favorite of a *majority* of voters. But the LDP lingered in power because the opposition parties could not convince enough voters that the system was broken, did not manage to offer any plausible vision for how they might fix things, and could not coordinate sufficiently to defeat vulnerable LDP incumbents.

The dirty secret behind Japan's rapid economic growth was the unsustainable means by which it was produced, not to mention the terrible inefficiencies that were tolerated, even nourished, by government policies. The "Japanese model" of export-led development became an example for other late-developing economies, especially in Asia, and it loomed as an apparent threat to earlier developers such as the United States and Western Europe. But it was a model that, to succeed, required a tightly regulated domestic market. When the forces of globalization outstripped the government's ability to regulate its way to political and economic stability, the house of cards collapsed.[2]

The bursting of the stock and land-price bubbles at the beginning of

---

[2]Pempel (1998) makes a similar argument, as does Rosenbluth (1989).

the 1990s underscored the need for drastic policy changes. Nevertheless, politicians beholden to antireformist interest groups were reluctant to make any but the most minor, piecemeal adjustments. The snowballing bad loan problems in the financial sector were met with forbearance, and the post-bubble slowdown in production was parried with pointless public works spending. Predictably, these responses only exacerbated the problems.

Reformers inside and outside the ruling party had complained for years of the inefficiencies of government policy, especially the mounting subsidies needed to keep farmers, small banks, uneconomical layers of retailers, and "zombie" companies in business. Likewise, the media bemoaned the high cost of electoral politics. Finally, with a far-reaching and drawn-out stocks-for-favors scandal in 1988–1989, and the LDP's unprecedented defeat in the 1989 Upper House election (see appendix 3), a growing number of LDP politicians decided that the time had come to restructure. In 1990–1991, an internal party committee chaired by Hata Tsutomu produced several versions of an electoral reform proposal that recommended the elimination of SNTV in favor of a mixed system of single-member districts and proportional representation, but this effort was torpedoed by a block of veteran MPs who insisted that the bad times would pass, and that the party should not abandon a system that it had mastered for so long. Electoral reform was shelved (yet again) in September 1991. Kaifu Toshiki declined to seek a second term as party leader and PM, and was replaced by Miyazawa Kiichi, an electoral-reform opponent. By August 1992, however, electoral reform was back on the agenda, thrust there when the "Sagawa Kyubin" scandal reminded reporters and voters that nothing had changed.[3] Calls for political reform multiplied.

Miyazawa read from the script the LDP had followed for thirty-five years, proposing a new system of five hundred single-member districts, with plurality rule, well aware that it would fail.[4] This time, the reformers upped the ante. The opposition parties counterproposed a German-style mixed system of single-member districts and proportional represen-

[3]The most notorious aspect of the Sagawa Kyubin scandal was the police discovery of hundreds of pounds of gold bars, millions of dollars' worth of stock certificates, and piles of cash in the home and office of former deputy prime minister and LDP vice president Kanemaru Shin in 1992. To add insult to injury (from the perspective of aggrieved voters), his punishment for this offense was merely a nominal fine.

[4]Reed and Thies 2001a. Electoral reform had been on and off the agenda going back as far as the 1950s. Each time, the impetus was a scandal, and each time the LDP proposed a pure plurality system (although other systems were discussed). The newspapers would run simulations that purported to show that pure plurality would lead to overwhelming LDP majorities, and the opposition parties would back down.

tation, and a group of reformers within the LDP, led by Hata and Ozawa Ichiro, threatened to leave the party in protest at Miyazawa's insincere posturing. When Miyazawa pushed his bill to a vote on June 17, 1993, it was defeated. The next day, forty-six LDP members supported a no-confidence vote against the Miyazawa government and resigned from the party. A general election was held one month later, on July 18, and although the LDP remained the largest party in the Lower House, it found itself in opposition for the first time ever, while a seven-party coalition led by the LDP defectors assumed control of government. The new government was headed by the leader of the Japan New Party (a former LDP prefectural governor), Hosokawa Moriichi, who announced that his first priority would be political reform, including the replacement of SNTV.

This was easier said than done. With the LDP finally in opposition, the other parties had a chance to change the rules to something that would work to their own advantage—but they were too heterogeneous a group to agree on what that might be. The Socialists were the largest party in the coalition, but they saw the writing on the wall. The Cold War that had defined many of their policy positions[5] was over, and the party's dependence on public-sector labor unions for votes, candidates, and finance was an albatross in the increasingly postindustrial Japanese economy. Accordingly, the Socialists called for as proportional an electoral system as possible, knowing that more majoritarian rules would most benefit big parties, and that they were not likely to be big for much longer. The parties made up of LDP defectors, as well as such centrist groups as the DSP and Komeito, saw the calculation differently. They hoped to combine to form a large party that could challenge the LDP for control of government on a consistent basis, so they coveted the big-party bonuses typical of more majoritarian rules.

The unwieldy coalition compromised on a mixed system under which roughly half of the Lower House would be elected under plurality rules from single-member districts, and half would be elected from party lists, under proportional representation. The plan passed the Lower House but died in the Upper House when a large group of Socialists opposed it, insisting on a stronger PR component. Hosokawa, who had staked his government's existence on political reform, faced a choice between conceding to the Socialist demands, which would undermine any future attempt

---

[5]As discussed in chapter 4, these included opposition to the U.S.-Japan Mutual Security Treaty, the existence of the Self Defense Forces, and such symbols as the national anthem and even the Rising Sun flag. See chapter 8 for a more thorough discussion of the politics of foreign policy.

to unite the anti-LDP forces into a single party, and going hat in hand to the LDP itself for support. He chose the latter path. The LDP's price was a shift in a more majoritarian direction, increasing the number of plurality seats and decreasing the number of PR seats, among other changes. Indeed, the eventual compromise looked almost exactly the same as the system that the LDP's internal committee had proposed back in 1990–1991.[6] Whereas party dinosaurs had killed the idea then, now they had been chastened sufficiently—by the party split and a few months out of power—to go along. The bill passed into law in January 1994.[7]

Scholars and practitioners have long recognized that the details of democratic institutions affect the behavior of political actors by defining the rules of the political game. Rules do not determine outcomes—the players still have to make choices—but they make some outcomes more likely than others, by defining what it means to "win," and by creating incentives for and imposing constraints on the players. A change in the rules, therefore, ought to induce changes in player strategies, in political outcomes, and, eventually, in policy choices. Accordingly, as soon as the new electoral law was passed in 1994, and even before it was used for the first time in 1996, observers rushed to predict the consequences of the new system.[8] The most immediate effects were expected to show up in the political party system, including such attributes as the number and relative sizes of parties, the internal organization of parties, the campaign strategies of parties and candidates, and, perhaps, in the logic of coalition formation within the parliament. Policy changes were harder to predict, but certainly they would come down the road, once politicians figured out the optimal *organizational* responses to the new rules of the game.

In this chapter, we assess Japanese politics in the sixteen years since the electoral reform. To cut to the chase, we see important and far-reaching changes in the logic of Japanese politics. This is not to say that no vestiges of the old politics remain—whatever our theories about political equilibrium might predict, because human beings are involved, change is much more likely to be evolutionary than revolutionary.

Nonetheless, we feel confident arguing that the old political logic has been overthrown, and while we do not believe that the transition is complete, enough time has passed that we can sketch out the new landscape.

---

[6]Christensen 1994.

[7]See appendix 1 for a comparison of the old and new electoral systems. The 1994 system reform was passed along with another law requiring the gradual tightening of campaign finance rules.

[8]See, e.g., Cowhey and McCubbins 1995.

The party system has consolidated, moving closer and closer to bipartism. Naturally, the two big parties are not internally homogeneous, but they are considerably more centralized than the LDP was during its heyday. Intraparty factions persist, but they are pale shadows of their notorious predecessors in terms of organizational strength, and they no longer seem to serve any purpose.[9] Campaigns are considerably more issue oriented than they were under SNTV, as politicians in single-seat districts are free of intraparty competition and in pursuit of the mythical median voter, and as the PR tier gives parties no choice but to run on their policy platforms.[10] All governments since 1993 (save one minority caretaker) have been coalitions, so policy making requires regular cross-party compromise. Also, because a single majority party cannot make decisions behind closed doors, policy debates have become more public and, for want of a better word, interesting. In the remainder of this chapter, we describe these components of Japan's New Politics.

THE PARTY SYSTEM

If political scientists agree about anything, it is that electoral rules affect party systems,[11] so changes in those rules ought to produce changes in the party system. But one might glance at the Japanese case and argue that, after a few years of chaos, it resembles nothing so much as its former self. The party system heading into 1993 contained five main parties: the longtime majority LDP, its chief opponent—only half as large—the Socialist Party, and the much smaller Komei, Democratic Socialist, and Communist parties. And now? The LDP remained the largest party for fifteen years after the 1993 reform, the Communists and Komeito (now called "New Komeito") are still there and roughly the same sizes as before, and there is a big party heading the anti-LDP opposition, although it is no longer the Socialist Party, which has shrunk to near irrelevance. The lead rival is now the Democratic Party, which was created by LDP defectors, former Socialists, and former Democratic Socialists. The DPJ is ideologically more moderate (and, lately, more successful) than the Socialists ever were, but one might look at the current partisan lineup and wonder what all the commotion was about.

In fact, as we show in figure 6.1, quite a lot has happened in the years

[9]Giannetti and Thies 2008.
[10]Köllner 2007.
[11]Duverger 1954; Rae 1971; Lijphart 1994; Cox 1997.

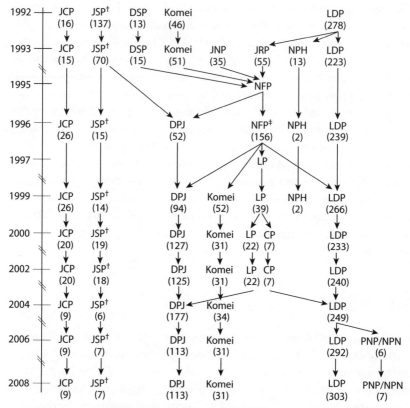

Figure 6.1. Japan's Political Party System, 1992–2009

The numbers in parentheses are the number of Lower House seats that each party held at several points in time. There were also nine independents, and one seat was vacant as of January 13, 2009.

†The JSP changed its name to Social Democratic Party in the early 1990s, but we retain the old name for purposes of clarity. Parties are arranged ideologically left to right (relative placement of DPJ and Komeito is tricky, with the DPJ more to the left owing to its inclusion of many JSP refugees and the Komeito's long-standing coalition with the LDP).

‡When the NFP disbanded in 1997, it spawned several small, short-lived parties. All besides the LP eventually joined one of the existing parties shown in the figure.

Reproduced by permission of the publisher from Frances Rosenbluth and Michael F. Thies, "Politics in Japan," in *Comparative Politics Today: A World View*, ed. Gabriel A. Almond, G. Bingham Powell, Jr., Russell Dalton, and Kaare Strom (New York: Addison Wesley Longman).

since the electoral reform. The 1993 election that preceded the reform, and which led to the LDP's brief sojourn in opposition, saw the creation of two new parties (the Japan Renewal Party and *Sakigake*) created by LDP defectors, and the emergence of a wholly new party, called, appropriately enough, the Japan New Party (*Nihon Shinto*).[12] After forming a coalition government that included every party except the LDP and the JCP, the first postreform attempt to create a single, large counterforce to the LDP resulted in the birth of the New Frontier Party (*Shinshinto*). The JRP and JNP joined in this merged entity with the longtime opposition stalwarts, the Democratic Socialists, and Komeito.

The new party immediately became the second largest in the Diet, and the early predictions of a two-party system, encouraged by the single-member-district component of the new electoral rule, seemed well on their way to fruition. However, after a quite successful 1995 Upper House showing (even outdoing the LDP in the Upper House PR tier), the NFP began to splinter in the lead-up to the October 1996 Lower House election. A month before the voting, NFP and Socialist defectors formed yet another new group, the Democratic Party of Japan. The NFP and DPJ split the anti-LDP vote in many of the 300 single-member districts, which helped the LDP to capture as many as 239 of 500 seats overall. Having failed to unite the anti-LDP vote, and suffering from its own internal heterogeneity, the NFP collapsed later that same year, spawning a slew of tiny new parties, as well as the resurrection of the Komeito. Within a few months, most of the remaining NFP refugees joined up with the DPJ, but enough returned to the LDP that the latter regained its single-party-majority status.[13]

Thus by mid-1997 the postreform party system had already accordioned twice. The Komeito participated in the first effort, but not the second, choosing instead to remain independent, and in 1999 it joined the LDP in coalition. The JSP was the main victim of the partisan flux, having alienated its left flank by partnering for more than two years with the LDP, and then seeing most of its members jump to the DPJ.[14] The rest

---

[12]The JNP had run candidates in the 1992 Upper House election, but 1993 marked its Lower House debut.

[13]Another small "refugee party," the Liberals, survived long enough to form a coalition with the LDP in 1998 and then split, giving way to its offshoot, the Conservatives. In 2003, the rump Liberals formally merged with the DPJ, while the Conservatives were absorbed by the LDP. The leader of the Liberals, who had also led the initial defection from the LDP in 1993, was Ozawa Ichiro, later the head of the DPJ itself.

[14]A tiny Socialist Party still exists, but it includes only a few die-hard members.

of the parties that either burst into existence in 1993 or appeared when the NFP collapsed in December 1997 all disappeared just as quickly, into one or the other of the two large parties. The only opposition entity not affected at all by the waves of fission and fusion was the JCP, whose antisystem ideology rendered it effectively inert.[15]

Importantly, both the NFP and the DPJ were explicit attempts by politicians to form a single, large alternative to the LDP. As political scientists predicted at the time of the electoral reform, the logic of plurality elections has created a strong incentive for consolidation into two large parties. The small parties that have endured to this point, Komeito and the JCP, depend entirely on the PR tier to survive. Thus the most important change in the party system is the emergence of a viable alternative to the LDP. What had been a system with a dominant majority party and a fairly stagnant panoply of hopeless opposition parties has been transformed into a system with two large parties that battle it out in each and every single-member district (SMD),[16] and two small parties with loyal but limited support bases, hanging on thanks to the PR tier.[17] As we describe in the epilogue, the DPJ has finally unseated the LDP in government. We expect alternation in power to become a regular feature of Japanese politics.

Coalition Politics

Perhaps the most obvious contrast between prereform Japanese politics and the postreform variety has been the turn to coalition government. The defining feature of the previous period had been the LDP's uninterrupted thirty-eight-year run as sole governing party. The LDP lost control of the Upper House in 1989, and its Lower House dominance survived another four years. Since the party split in 1993, however, every Japanese government but one has been a coalition of at least two parties, and sometimes three or more.[18] Even when the LDP managed to scrape to-

[15]Over the last few years, the JCP has finally dropped some of its Cold War–era shibboleths and made itself available as a potential coalition partner, mirroring the examples of its European counterparts.

[16]As we will discuss below, there have been a few exceptions in which the LDP has refrained from fielding a candidate and instead thrown its support behind the candidate of its current coalition partner (the Conservatives in 2000, and Komeito since then). Effectively, these small party SMD candidates have "represented" the ruling bloc.

[17]Occasionally other small parties win a PR seat or two (see appendix 2).

[18]The exception was a minority government headed by Prime Minister Hashimoto Ryutaro that continued after the Socialists withdrew from coalition in November 1996.

gether a Lower House majority by repatriating some NFP survivors, it chose to form a coalition with Komeito, rather than go it alone. Interestingly, it did not waver from this decision even after its overwhelming triumph in the 2005 Lower House election (in which it garnered 296 of the 480 seats).[19]

Neither the LDP's split in 1993 nor its ensuing brief stint in opposition led to its demise. Even the institution of the new electoral system failed to threaten the LDP, but this is perhaps least surprising, because the LDP had prospered for thirty-eight years *despite* the centrifugal incentives of SNTV, not *because* of SNTV—and recall that the party had negotiated a more amenable version of mixed-member rules at the last minute. Still, after the LDP had governed alone for nearly four decades, it now forms coalition governments. For several years (roughly 1994–2003), it changed partners frequently, but since 2003, it has continued a monogamous—if not always harmonious—coalition with Komeito. Some have speculated that the Japanese party system might eventually resemble Germany's during most of the postwar period, with Komeito playing the centrist, kingmaking role of Germany's Free Democratic Party, alternating between one big party and the other to form coalition governments. It is not coincidental that Germany's mixed-member electoral system is very similar to (and was for many the inspiration for) the new Japanese system, and in both cases, the small, centrist party survives only because of the PR tier, never earning any SMD seats on its own.

One important difference between the German version of MM and the Japanese version, however, is worth considering, because it could matter for the future prospects of both big parties, and of alternation in government. The German version of MM (also used in New Zealand, Scotland, and, briefly, in Venezuela), is generally called MMP, for "mixed-member proportional." This is in contrast to the Japanese (also Russian, Mexican, and Ukrainian) variety, called MMM ("mixed-member majoritarian"). Under MMM, single-member district seats and PR seats are counted independently. There is a fixed number of seats assigned to each tier, and each party "earns" its proportional share of the PR seats, *plus* as many SMD seats as its candidates win. Under MMP, however, the PR vote alone determines the total number of seats that a party earns, and any SMD seats that its candidates win count against that total.[20]

---

[19] This was largely because the party still needed a partner in the Upper House (Druckman and Thies 2002).

[20] A quick example will highlight the importance of the difference. Suppose a (rather large) party were to win 160 of 300 SMDs, and 40 percent of the vote in a 200-seat PR tier.

The key difference, then, is that *under MMM, every district counts.* To some extent, parties in an MMP system do not really care how many districts they win, because the PR vote determines their overall representation. One implication of this is that MMM is better for large or geographically concentrated parties, because they have the best chance of having their candidates place first in the single-seat districts. Another implication is that, under MMM, parties that might end up forming coalition governments together would do well to maximize their joint seat share by cooperating instead of competing with one another in the SMDs. They should strike mutual stand-down agreements, deciding which is stronger in a particular district, and then having the weaker partner stay out of the race and try to convince its supporters to vote for that "coalition candidate." This binds the parties together in a relationship of electoral codependence.

The LDP has used this tactic to good advantage since the advent of the new electoral system. In 2000, its then-partner, the Conservative Party, won seven SMD seats in large part owing to the absence of an LDP candidate in any of those districts. Since the LDP solidified its coalition with Komeito, the process has deepened. Komeito is an urban party, strongest in the places where the LDP is weakest. In a few districts, the LDP has stepped aside and asked its voters to support Komeito candidates. In more, however, the LDP has used Komeito's formidable vote-mobilization machinery to get its own candidates elected to urban seats, in exchange asking its voters to cast their PR-tier vote for the Komeito list. In this way, Komeito has won more PR seats than it would have on its own, and the LDP has won many more urban seats than it could have without the support of Komeito voters. Because the two parties depend on each other, not just to muster legislative majorities to pass bills, but to win the very seats that add up to those majorities, they cannot take each other for granted. If Komeito were to switch its allegiance to the DPJ, not only

---

Under MMM, its total take would be 160 + (.40*200) = 240 seats. Under MMP, however, it would earn 40 percent of the total number of seats, so only .40*500 = 200 seats overall. The purpose of the districts under MMP is merely to determine how many of those 200 winners come from the districts (160 of them in this example) and how many are topped up from the party lists in the PR tier (40 in this example). Now modify the example by supposing that the party still wins 40 percent of the PR vote, but only 140 SMDs. Its seat total under MMP would not change—it would remain 200 seats, but now the top-up from the list would be 60 instead of 40, to compensate for the smaller number of district winners. Under MMM, however, the party's take would be reduced by exactly the reduction in SMD wins—so it would see its total fall from 240 to 220 seats.

would the LDP be left without a coalition partner and perhaps short of the number of votes needed to pass laws—it might also shrink because it would lose the urban seats that Komeito voters deliver to it. Were Komeito to make the same electoral pact with the DPJ instead, the DPJ would grow, perhaps enough to take over the government in coalition with Komeito, with a much-diminished LDP in opposition.

This logic goes a long way to explain why the LDP did not part ways with Komeito after the former's huge electoral triumph in 2005. Having won 296 of 480 seats, the LDP no longer needed Komeito's 31 Lower House MPs to pass legislation. But its having won that many seats in the first place was due in large part to Komeito's electoral assistance. The LDP, at present, is too dependent on Komeito voters to contemplate going it alone.

So why does coalition government matter? The LDP has to compromise. During the 1955–1989 period, the LDP could use its majority control of both Diet chambers to convert its platform into policy. The LDP frequently made small concessions to opposition parties in exchange for a more harmonious legislative process, but it never had to make important substantive changes, and if push came to shove, it would ram bills through without any Opposition support. Once the LDP lost its Upper House majority in 1989, it found that it had to compromise to get things done.[21]

But even during the 1989–1993 period, the LDP did not share control over the cabinet, nor did it risk its own position to a no-confidence vote, nor did it even have to compromise on the annual budget, all because it retained its Lower House majority. Since the electoral reform, however, the LDP has only occasionally mustered a Lower House majority, and, as just discussed, it has depended on the electoral cooperation of its legislative partners to pull that off. Accordingly, it has shared cabinet posts with its partners in all postreform governments, and even allowed its first postreform coalition partner, the Socialists, to assume the prime ministership for eighteen months.[22]

---

[21]We discussed in chapter 4 the concessions the LDP made to Komeito to secure Diet support for Japanese participation in UN-sponsored peacekeeping operations after the Gulf War. See Ehrhardt 2009 for a discussion of the convergence of LDP and government policy decisions under Koizumi and long-standing Komeito positions, which the author argues is no coincidence.

[22]After the 2007 Upper House election, not only did the LDP have a coalition partner (Komeito), but the two partners' combined strength in the Upper House was no longer sufficient for a bicameral majority. For the first time, the Upper House was controlled by the opposition. Not surprisingly, in the first six months of this arrangement, not a single piece of legislation was passed.

The Internal Organization of the LDP

Just because a party label survives for a long time, and even if it evinces a good deal of continuity in its membership, it does not follow that it is the "same" party as before. It might adjust its ideological position, becoming more moderate or more extreme. It might change the way it organizes itself internally, from leadership selection to candidate endorsement. It might campaign in different ways, chasing different groups of voters or using different sorts of messages and tactics. It might undergo a split or merger that makes the resultant party more or less homogeneous and unified. In Japan, since the early 1990s, the evidence shows that while remnants of prereform politics survive, quite a lot has changed, along all of the dimensions just enumerated, and more.

The Fate of Factions

During the LDP's period of dominance, an oft-repeated mantra had it that "the Liberal Democratic Party is neither liberal, nor democratic, nor a party." Others echoed at least the last of these sentiments, calling the LDP more a "coalition of factions" than a true party.[23] Some saw factions as peculiarly Japanese, a political version of the general predilection within Japanese culture to favor hierarchical groups, and groups within groups.[24] But others noted that intraparty factions were not unique to Japanese politics (with the Italian Christian Democrats the usual comparison), and argued that they were sustained by the intraparty competition faced by large parties under SNTV.

The 1994 electoral reform set up a nice test of these competing hypotheses. The elimination of multiseat districts means that no party should run more than a single candidate in one place at one time. A voter no longer has to choose among copartisans but can vote for the sole representative of her favorite party. In the PR tier, voters simply choose *among* party lists and have no opportunity to choose favorites *within* those lists. If the lifeblood of factions was intraparty competition (as we argued in chapter 4), then factions as we knew them should not have survived the electoral reform. And it appears that they did not.[25] As quickly as the first election under the new system, in 1996, record numbers of LDP candi-

---

[23]Leiserson 1968.

[24]Nakane 1970; Ishida 1971.

[25]See Cox, Rosenbluth, and Thies 1999, and Giannetti and Thies 2008 for more complete discussions.

dates, especially newcomers, chose not to join any faction at all, a choice that would have almost guaranteed defeat under SNTV. Under the old rules, even (conservative) candidates who failed to secure the official LDP endorsement would obtain the backing of a faction, with the financial resources and organizational support that that entailed. But under the new rules, there was no need to choose a subgroup patron, so most newcomers eschewed factional affiliation.

Other than campaign support, the main roles of factions during the period of LDP dominance were leadership selection (namely, the choice of party president and hence prime minister) and post allocation (the divvying up of cabinet positions, and other committee and party organizational positions). Factions lost control over leadership selection almost immediately after the electoral reform, as three successive contests demonstrate. First, in 1995, LDP President Kono Yohei was seeking reelection. He met with the various faction leaders within the party, offering plum cabinet and party leadership posts in exchange for faction leaders' promises to throw their members' party presidential votes his way. This was the usual method of backroom deal making, but this time it failed. Kono's rival, Hashimoto Ryutaro, realized that Kono had locked up enough factional endorsements to win, as long as all backbenchers followed their (respective) faction leader's marching orders. So he tried another tactic: he appealed to younger members from *all* party factions to ignore their factional bosses' wishes and support him instead—presenting himself as the man most likely to help the party as a whole. When Kono realized that the promises he'd received from those faction leaders would not be fulfilled, he dropped out.

In the very next party presidential race, in 1998, eventual winner Obuchi Keizo had to compete against a competitor, Kajiyama Seiroku, from his very own faction. This had never happened before the reform, since party leadership contests were a main reason that factions existed. As importantly, in both 1995 and 1998, the members who thumbed their noses at their faction leaders were not punished for doing so. Even Kajiyama, who challenged his own boss, maintained his position within the faction.

Finally, when Obuchi was incapacitated by a stroke in April 2000, party elders hurriedly installed Mori Yoshiro, in what turned out to be an immensely unpopular backroom deal. They argued that there was no time for a proper election, but voters were furious. The party set about establishing new rules for leadership selection to avoid a repeat of this sort of backlash, and held a new election in April 2001. Under the new rules, prefectural party branches held direct elections (among party members) to name their choice for party leader, and each prefecture's choice was then allocated three votes, to be counted along with the votes of sitting LDP Diet members. The Diet members retained enough votes to trump those from the local branches if necessary, and since the popular favorite, Koizumi Junichiro, was far from a favorite among his colleagues, there was some chance that the party would decide to reverse the expressed will of the party rank and file. As it turned out, however, the support for Koizumi in the prefectural votes (which was known by the time the MPs took their turn) was so overwhelming (he won forty-three of forty-seven prefectures) that the MPs realized that they would have to go along—that choosing as party leader someone with widespread support among party rank and file was the smarter course. Not only had factions lost control of the leadership selection process, but the party elite as a group had realized the wisdom of courting public opinion.

Thus the factional stranglehold on both individual electoral campaigns and party leadership selection weakened immediately after the electoral reform, and has never reemerged. Faction-based post allocation, however, persisted a while longer. Indeed, most of the party newcomers who steered clear of factional affiliation while trying to get elected in 1996 ended up joining factions once elected.[26] Presumably, continuing members, who had waited in the factional queues for their chance at top posts, were loath to give up their places in line. Soon enough, however—since old-style factions no longer had roles to play in elections or leadership battles, and insofar as the numbers of and sizes of factions had been tied up with the old multimember-district system (see again chapter 4)—their discipline began to break down, and party presidents felt less constrained to treat them as units across which patronage appointments should be shared. This came to a head with Koizumi, who announced publicly that he would ignore factional affiliations in allocating cabinet and party posts, instead assigning these to the individuals he deemed most appropriate for the jobs in question. Whether or not he actually did match jobs to talents is a matter of opinion, but there is no doubt that his appointments departed from factional balancing, as he had promised they would.[27]

It is important to note that today's LDP still contains groups that are called factions. But these are not the factions of the 1960s–1980s. For one thing, there seem to be a much larger number of (necessarily) smaller

---

[26]Cox, Rosenbluth, and Thies 1999.

[27]Krauss and Pekkanen (2004) point out that factional balancing still seems to matter for subcabinet appointments such as the allocation of leadership positions on internal party committees.

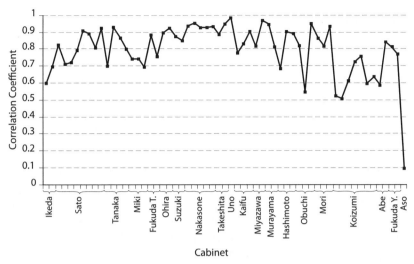

Figure 6.2. Factional Strengths[†] and Cabinet Shares,[‡] 1963–2009
Source: *Kokkai benran*, various years.

[†]"Factional Strengths" counts faction members from both Diet chambers.

[‡]"Cabinet Shares" refers to ministerial posts, including the prime minister, only. Subcabinet posts (vice ministerships) are not included in this calculation.

Ignoring the extreme outlier of the Aso cabinet, the mean correlation coefficients are 0.789 for the Ikeda-to-Fukuda Takeo period (1963–1978) before the "LDP Civil War" forced a more proportional sharing of posts, 0.904 for the Ohira-Miyazawa period (1978–1993), and 0.760 for the (postreform) Murayama-Fukuda Yasuo period (1994–2008). Difference of means tests show that the differences between the first and second periods and between the second and third periods, respectively, are both statistically significant at the 0.05 level. Including the Aso cabinet of course lowers the mean correlation for the postreform period and increases the difference from the prereform period. Similar tests that include parliamentary vice ministers along with ministers show statistically significant differences between the late prereform period and the postreform period, but not between the early and late prereform periods.

groups than the steady state of five main factions that persisted during the earlier period. Second, membership is more flexible and often harder to pin down. Third, the factions look more like groups within large parties the world over—as somewhat ad hoc support groups for individual party grandees, and not as semipermanent organizations.[28]

---

[28]It is also possible that factions might begin to differentiate themselves along policy lines in the future. Under SNTV, most observers failed to find any appreciable ideological variation

Party Centralization

One consequence of a party organized around and dependent upon factions is weak central leadership. LDP presidents were merely "first among equals" within the party, at best the leader of just one of several factions, and not endowed with very much discretion.[29] As just discussed, post allocation and endorsements were shared among factions, and they were rotated very regularly. Cabinet ministers would often hold their posts for only a year before making way for the next MP in the queue to get a turn. Even party presidents were held to two-year terms, and after Sato Eisaku held the job from 1964 to 1972, they were limited to only two terms and four years total.[30] Factions also controlled the accumulation and allocation of political money, so the ability to raise campaign finance and dole it out to others was the path to becoming a faction leader.[31]

The LDP president was sharply constrained in his role as prime minister as well. The PM's office was extremely weak in comparison with its counterparts in other parliamentary democracies. It was understaffed and in direct control of almost no areas of policy. Of course, the fact that the PM was on a short leash within his own party, to be replaced by the next person in line (nearly always from a rival faction) as soon as his popularity ratings dipped low enough, did him no favors in his official role.

Since the electoral reform, the LDP has begun to centralize in earnest. The reforms themselves created public financing for electoral campaigns, and mandated that all private contributions could be made only to parties, and not to individuals. Of course, now that each party endorses only

---

across factions (Ramseyer and Rosenbluth 1993; but see McCubbins and Thies 1997 for a slightly different view). Then, because no two LDP candidates within a district hailed from the same faction, every faction had members all across the country. This meant that each faction looked, in terms of regional, and hence occupational, representation, like each other faction. Now, without that constraint, politicians are free to form factions that have distinct policy priorities. There is as yet no systematic evidence that this is happening (Giannetti and Thies 2008), but further work is needed.

[29]Hayao 1993. After especially juicy or far-reaching scandals, when every true power broker (*jitsuryokusha*) within the party either was implicated or just did not want the job at the time, the party would sometimes anoint a "Mr. Clean," a relative weakling lacking a substantial power base of his own, to hold the post until voter anger died down and the real top dogs could return from the shadows. Miki Takeo (1974–1976), Uno Sosuke (1989), and Kaifu Toshiki (1989–1991) are perhaps the best-known examples of such hapless front men.

[30]Nakasone Yasuhiro was voted an extra year to reward him for the party's landslide victory in 1986. The term has since been changed to three years, which explains why Koizumi was in office for five years.

[31]Iwai 1990; Sasaki et al. 1999.

one candidate per district, the distinction between candidate and local party office has blurred,[32] but the extent to which factional leaders (actual or prospective) can amass their own campaign war chests, and then distribute largesse to allies, has declined dramatically.

Recall from chapter 4 that under the old rules, because the LDP had to nominate at least two candidates per electoral district, and since factions bankrolled the candidates, copartisan rivals within a district never came from the same faction. In fact, there were often more factions represented in a single district than there were official endorsees—because candidates with factional backing could and did run as conservative independents, only to join the party after the election if they managed to win. What all of this meant is that the LDP's approach to endorsement was really more a balancing act among self-interested factions than it was a well-considered optimization solution by party strategists. All incumbents were endorsed, and when targets of opportunity arose (due to retirements, or because the party thought it could win seats currently held by opposition parties), the factions competed to be allowed to bestow the official party endorsement on "their" candidates. Often, these additional endorsees were former MPs who had lost an election or two, and were eyeing comebacks.

Since the advent of the new electoral system, each party nominates only one candidate per district, so it benefits everyone if the endorsement goes to the candidate most likely to win (which nowadays means "finish in first place," not just in the top four or five). The LDP has responded by centralizing its decision making, and establishing new and stricter rules to increase the "electability" of its field of candidates.[33] Those who have lost SMD races twice are not given a third chance: SMD losers may not appear on the party's PR list the next time around. The party also instituted an age limit on PR-list candidates, to increase turnover and reduce the advantages of seniority.

Moreover, with voters now freed of the need to choose between same-party competitors, they can rely on the general reputations and platforms of parties to guide their decisions. Every party now does well to project a unified message, and to choose leaders who (they hope) best represent and articulate that message for the party as a whole. Within the LDP, the first inkling that the party leader would become, more than ever, the "face" of the party came in Hashimoto Ryutaro's successful challenge of Kono Yohei for the party presidency in 1995, described above. Hashimoto based his appeal to those who eventually bucked their faction leaders'

[32]Sasaki et al. 1999.
[33]Asano 2006.

orders on his greater popularity among regular voters and on promises to lead the party back to the top.

If Hashimoto was the first leadership aspirant to reject the backroom factional deal-making route in favor of an appeal to his personal popularity, Koizumi perfected the new approach. As discussed, Koizumi ascended to the party presidency and premiership over the objections of most of his fellow LDP MPs, precisely because his iconoclastic image (personally and politically) was so admired by the general public. Amazingly, in the normally monotone world of LDP politics, Koizumi was able to leverage his personal appeal again and again to win victories over his rivals within the party. He contested elections as party leader by, in effect, running against his own party, specifically the antireform elements who resisted him, vowing to "change Japan by changing the LDP." Of course, Koizumi's opponents within the party could have toppled him, but they realized that doing so would be self-defeating. Many hated what Koizumi stood for and resented his rock-star image, but they also realized that the party as a whole was benefiting at the ballot box with Koizumi in charge. When, in 2005, a group of fed-up MPs dared to rebel against Koizumi's postal savings reform bills (see next section), he ejected them from the party, called an election, endorsed attractive challengers to the rebels,[34] and led the party to its greatest electoral triumph ever by convincing voters that the election was a referendum on Koizumi himself.

Most recently, the same lesson has been repeated, only with the reverse outcome. Koizumi stepped down near the peak of his popularity, giving way to the considerably less charismatic Abe Shinzo. In fact, Abe was probably more assertive and image-conscious than most prime ministers over the postwar period, but compared with Koizumi, he was unskilled and uninspiring. At the same time, the opposition DPJ picked as their new leader none other than Ozawa Ichiro. Ozawa is something of a political celebrity himself, having led the LDP split back in 1993, engineered the formation of the NFP in the mid-1990s, created the Liberal Party a few years later, and served as the leading voice for political reform throughout that time. When Abe's LDP squared off against Ozawa's DPJ in the 2007 Upper House Election, it was a debacle for the former. Certainly, the electoral reversal had more causes than the changes in party leadership, but it is clear that voters saw Abe as a poor successor to Koizumi,[35] and a weak counterpart to Ozawa. Abe was obliged to

---

[34]Many of these challengers were female celebrities of one sort or another, and were quickly dubbed by the tabloids the "lipstick ninjas."

[35]Indeed, Abe was seen by some as having betrayed Koizumi's legacy, because one of his first acts as party leader was to repatriate many of the "postal rebels."

resign as LDP leader and prime minister, and the LDP tabbed old-hand Fukuda Yasuo as a sort of caretaker. Fukuda resigned a year later in favor of the more charismatic Aso Taro, who it hoped would be a more attractive "face" to lead them into the 2009 Lower House Election (see the epilogue to this book).

The enhanced importance of the vote-getting ability of party leaders goes hand in hand with the increased centralization of power both within parties and in the office of the prime minister. If a party wishes to lean more heavily on its leader's personal popularity,[36] and to ask that leader to articulate its platform and to project "leadership," then it should invest that leader with greater decision-making and administrative authority once he is in office. If a voter is to choose a party in part because of the qualities of its leader, then she must have some confidence that the leader will be able to deliver on his promises, and not be hopelessly hamstrung by factional infighting and empty suits.

We have already discussed the weakening of factions within the LDP, largely as a consequence of the elimination of intraparty competition under the new electoral rules. But the party has taken positive steps as well to strengthen the hand of its leadership, both within the party itself, and in those leaders' governmental roles. Koizumi owes a debt to the man he defeated for the top job, because the centralization of power actually began in 1998 when Prime Minister Hashimoto oversaw an important reorganization of the national bureaucracy that consolidated some ministries and agencies, and greatly increased the authority and resources of the prime minister's office. Hashimoto's successor Obuchi continued this downsizing and centralization the next year, cutting the number of bureaucrats by as much as 25 percent,[37] and revising the Cabinet Law to empower the prime minister both to oversee the line ministries and to take the lead in times of crisis. Several new advisory councils, responsible directly to the prime minister, were created as well. In general, the goal was to take back agenda-setting authority from individual ministries, who had long enjoyed a sort of gatekeeper role, and to vest it in the prime minister and the cabinet office.

Some have described these changes as revolutionary.[38] On this view, Japanese politicians finally wrested power from the unelected bureaucrats who had usurped it,[39] claimed their constitutional birthright as the

[36]McElwain 2009.

[37]Nakano 2002: 243–255.

[38]Nakano 2002: 18.

[39]This argument is best summed up by Chalmers Johnson's famous aphorism that "the politicians reign and the bureaucrats rule" (Johnson 1982: 154).

democratically elected representatives of the sovereign people,[40] and, in a sense, completed Japan's long transition to democracy. We see the shift differently. During the decades of LDP dominance, the party controlled both Diet chambers, not to mention most local governments, and could delegate extensively to bureaucrats because it could control that delegation quite easily.[41] Because the LDP maintained legislative majorities by dispensing pork and patronage rather than competing with other parties over public policy, the LDP had little incentive to empower a single leader. The stronger imperative was to decentralize policy formulation and credit claiming to the ministries and the internal party committees that mirrored them.

But now, with coalition governments the new order of the day, and with alternation in power a real possibility, politicians feel less sanguine about such extensive delegation. Moreover, because voters focus more on party platforms under the new electoral rule, the premium on strong leadership and centralized policy formulation is much higher than before.[42] Parties now need leaders who can actually lead (rather than merely manage), and they invest those leaders with formal authority to set the legislative agenda, and with the resources, through the office and within the party, to see that agenda at least presented to the legislature for deliberation and decision. The centralizing reforms of the Hashimoto, Obuchi, and Koizumi administrations therefore represent a logical adaptation by politicians to the new rules of the game. They recognized that the old ways of governing were no longer optimal given the new electoral incentives for individuals and parties, and given the shifts to coalition government and party-based competition that characterize the New Japanese Politics.

THE NEW ELECTORAL MAP

So far, we have explained the incentives of the new electoral system, and we have explained their effects on the electoral and organizational behavior of politicians and parties. While it is clear that the single-member-

---

[40]Article 41 of the Japanese Constitution stipulates that the National Diet "shall be the highest organ of state power, and shall be the sole law-making organ of the State."

[41]Ramseyer and Rosenbluth 1993. As in the United Kingdom, where single-party government is also the norm, the ruling party could delegate freely, secure in its ability to overrule any bureaucratic initiatives that it did not prefer without any need to secure the agreement of a coalition partner or an Upper House in opposition hands.

[42]Estévez-Abe, Hikotani, and Nagahisa 2008.

district component of the new electoral system has produced two large parties, and that the PR tier has allowed the survival of a few small parties with no SMD pretensions, what is not clear is the ideological basis of the new system. What will they stand for, and how will they differ from one another?

Maybe not much. The median voter theorem[43] suggests that the two parties should converge on the portion of the ideological spectrum that contains the most voters, the better to win over as many voters as possible with a single policy message.[44] But this raises the question: what is the main dimension of politics? In most places, and most times, absent ethnic or other ascriptive cleavages that can divide a society politically, the main dimension tends to be economic, with advocates of bigger government and more fiscal redistribution on the "left," and their opponents on the "right." This was indeed an important organizing principle during the 1955–1993 period, with Communists and Socialists appealing to union workers and other "have nots" with promises of redistribution, and the LDP more interested in protecting the interests of the businesses that drove economic expansion. But as we discussed in chapter 5, over time this distinction became less and less clear. As the LDP's catchall strategy led it to champion enormous subsidies for small businesses and farmers, the economic dimension seemed to shrink and compress.

Moreover, the economic dimension was overlaid, and sometimes overshadowed, by the foreign policy dimension, with the parties of the Left opposing strong ties to the United States, the SDF, and anything with a whiff of nationalism, and the LDP (joined by the DSP) on the other side of those issues. However, with the end of the Cold War, this issue dimension atrophied for a time. More recently, with the international opprobrium heaped upon Japan for its "checkbook diplomacy" surrounding the Gulf War, and with the unpopularity of Japan's more recent participation in Afghanistan and Iraq, the rise of China, and the recent tensions involving North Korea, foreign policy has become considerably more complex. As we will discuss in chapter 8, the LDP has pursued a more active foreign policy role for Japan, but it is noteworthy that support for this tack includes many opposition party members, while disagreement also crosses party lines.

---

[43]Black 1958; Downs 1957.

[44]Of course, convergence is unlikely to be complete, as parties must concern themselves with such things as abstention and the "blackmail potential" of more extreme parties (for example, a center-left party that moves too far toward the center could be outflanked by a "true" leftist party that picks off the voters most alienated by the moderation.

One of the most important changes during the era of LDP dominance was the rapid urbanization of the Japanese population. Only one in four Japanese lived in an urban area in 1945 but now two in three do. By one estimate, the 300 single-member constituencies in the new system can be pretty neatly divided into 100 rural districts, 100 urban districts, and 100 mixed districts. In postreform elections through 2003, the LDP has dominated the rural third, and is dominated by the DPJ in the urban seats, with the middle, mixed, third being competitive.[45] So one might expect that an urban-rural cleavage would form the basis of the new Japanese party system, with the pro-rural LDP in favor of continued protectionism and governmental largesse for farmers, and the urban DPJ (and Komeito, for that matter) calling for fiscal retrenchment and liberalization.

For a time, that looked about right. The defection that split the LDP in 1993 left the party even more rural than it had been, as mostly younger, urban members bolted to form new parties. Big business organizations immediately announced that they would donate campaign finance to those new parties, in the hope that they could induce a policy mix that was less solicitous of expensive and inefficient farmers. But this was a losing proposition for the LDP. The party would have to find a way to appeal to urban voters, to at least make those districts competitive as well, or it would be doomed by rural attrition.

Enter Koizumi Junichiro, and his platform of "reform, with no sacred cows." His calls to dismantle many of the subsidy programs and profit-padding regulations that had been the LDP's stock-in-trade for forty years resonated well with urban voters. His signature reform, recall, was to break up and privatize the post office, its massive savings system, and, really, the backbone of most rural LDP support networks.[46] He also pushed to decentralize tax authority to local governments, and to end the stream of subsidies whereby more than half of most rural government budgets were paid for by block transfers from the national treasury. Rural members of the party, of course, opposed these plans, and delayed and scuttled many of them. As mentioned above, when the defeat of the postal privatization plan in 2005 culminated in expulsions and a landslide win for Koizumi and the LDP, the bulk of the party's seat gain was in urban districts. Urban voters were fed up with high food prices, low interest rates on their savings, and wasteful public works that led to unsustainable budget deficits, especially in an economy that had stagnated for more than a decade. They took a chance that Koizumi really could break the

[45]Scheiner 2006.
[46]Maclachlan 2004.

LDP free from its rural roots and remake it as a consumer-friendly, economically liberal force.

Koizumi stepped down a year later and turned the reins over to Abe Shinzo. Abe, however, squandered Koizumi's gains. He invited most of the postal rebels to rejoin the party, which infuriated urban voters who had hoped that their expulsion would not only do away with some anti-reform elements but would cow any holdouts into submission. Abe also devoted much of his time and political capital to foreign policy, following the path laid out by Koizumi and others toward enabling Japan to become a "normal country," no longer traumatized or hamstrung by memories of World War II. While his moves in this area were not hugely popular, they seemed to many voters to be beside the point, as the economy still struggled to emerge from the postbubble recession and restructuring, and a pension-record snafu called the LDP's competence into question.

The upshot of this was the LDP's worst-ever defeat, in the 2007 Upper House election. In party-based elections, where platforms and perceptions of competence trump the qualities of individual candidates, swings from election to election can be quite large if voters decide that the government of the day is performing poorly. If an election is seen by voters as a referendum on the prime minister and cabinet, then a small change in preference can switch a voter from yes to no, and single-member districts will amplify a small, relatively uniform change in vote share into a huge seat swing.[47]

An especially intriguing subplot of the 2007 House of Councillors election was that the DPJ, led by the ever-opportunistic Ozawa Ichiro, took advantage of the anger of rural voters who would bear the brunt of Koizumi's reforms, and "out-LDP'd" the LDP, promising a restoration of rural subsidies. The success of this tactic was most evident in the DPJ's success in the rural single-seat districts, where its candidates routed LDP incumbents. There are two reasons that this is such an intriguing result. First, it is rare indeed for a party to leapfrog its rival in ideological terms, to respond to the rival's push toward the center by "hopping over" to the abandoned policy ground, and, in effect, swapping platforms. It is unlikely that the DPJ can become the antiliberal, proregulation party without splitting asunder (or that it would want to). Even when the DPJ had opposed Koizumi's postal reform bills in 2005, its public justification was that they did not go far enough. For the party to beat the LDP in 2007 by

[47]The swing from LDP triumph in 2005 to DPJ triumph in 2007 (albeit across two different chambers) resembled the huge party swings that sometimes occur in the United Kingdom and Canada, among other places.

promising a restoration of rural handouts was a brilliant tactical move in the short run but seems unsustainable.

The second reason that this was an interesting turn of events, however, is that it reminded us that party-based, plurality-rule elections[48] do not necessarily produce liberal, proconsumer outcomes.[49] The flip side of appealing to the *interests* of the median voter is populist pandering to the short-term *passions* of the median voter.[50] Since 2007, it is clear that the remaining LDP conservatives have been saying, "We told you so," and have dragged the party away from the reform agenda, rather than stay the course of economic liberalization and give up the farmers once and for all. In the wake of the global financial crisis that crested in September 2008, current prime minister Aso Taro has prioritized fiscal stimulus over reform. Interestingly, this has proved a political disaster, and Aso's initially high approval ratings have plummeted since he took office. As we shall explain in chapter 7, we think that further liberalizing reforms can only be postponed, not avoided altogether. Whether the LDP survives and rededicates itself to reforms, or whether it finally loses control of government to the DPJ, the only sustainable course, both economically and politically, is further liberalization.

CONCLUSIONS

We have argued that the electoral reform of 1994 changed Japanese politics profoundly. The most important mechanical effect was the elimination of intraparty competition. Second-order effects include the weakening of factions and the centralization of authority within parties and in the prime minister's office. The third-order effect, which we explore next, is on policy. Parties now face strong incentives to appeal to the interests of the median voter, and that has already led to extensive dismantling of the policy mix that sustained the economy and the LDP for so long.

---

[48]In Japan's Upper House, the electoral rule for the district tier is actually SNTV, but most districts in fact elect only a single representative in a given election (half the house is up for election each time), so it "plays" like an SMD-plurality system in all but a few urban districts. Even in the two-seat districts, it is rare for a party to go after both seats, so all of the intraparty competition problems described in chapter 4 are absent. See Cox, Rosenbluth, and Thies 2000.

[49]This is a counterexample to the general proliberal bias of plurality-rule elections demonstrated by Schaap 2002, and Rogowski and Kayser 2002.

[50]When his party was voted out of office in 1945, Churchill mused, "In my country the people can do as they like, although it often happens that they don't like what they have done" (Gilbert 2000: 864).

We hasten to add, however, that the electoral reform was no panacea. It neither eliminated all of the pathologies of the old system nor lacked problems of its own. The word "reform" generally connotes "for the better," and in some ways the jettisoning of SNTV and its attendant intraparty competition will serve Japanese politics well. But our goal has been to focus on the more neutral notion of "change." Because the rules were changed, some incentives changed and some outcomes changed as well. But the version of mixed-member system (MMM) that Japan uses is not as complete a break from the previous system as it might have been (as, say, the German/New Zealand MMP version would have been). The strong majoritarian component that focuses parties on the median voter should lead to more public-goods-oriented policy, but it is, correspondingly, less representative of the diversity of opinion in Japanese politics and gives strong bonuses to large parties. The PR tier allows small parties to survive, and perhaps even to be pivotal in coalition formation, but their influence is marginal, not central.

Similarly, while the end of intraparty competition reduces dramatically the incentive for candidates to pursue personal votes, and hence their need for huge campaign war chests, the mixed-member system is not free of personal-vote seeking. Partly because it is difficult for old dogs to learn new tricks (and plenty of old dogs remain), and partly because the need to win a plurality means that every last vote counts, politicians still have a reason to trade on their personalities, their connections, and their constituency service.[51] The Japanese version of MMM actually emphasizes the importance of every last vote because a candidate may run simultaneously in a district and on a party list, and some parties have taken to ranking their lists according to how close these "dual candidates" come to winning their districts.[52] A close loss increases a candidate's chance of being saved by the list, so she is motivated to do everything possible to maximize her vote share even in a losing effort. If that means seeking personal votes to add to the base partisan support she receives, so be it. While personal-vote seeking is more difficult than it used to be—there are tighter restrictions on campaign finance; institutional opportunities for credit claiming through such things as committee memberships are fewer; and voters are now able to rely solely on party labels in the absence of intraparty competition—it is not impossible, so some vestiges of pre-reform politics persist.

[51]Cain, Ferejohn, and Fiorina 1987. For evidence that some "old tricks" are still employed in Japan, see Krauss and Pekkanen 2004.
[52]Reed and Thies 2001b; McKean and Scheiner 2000.

Still, all things considered, Japanese politics has a new logic, and this has important downstream effects on Japanese policy. Untangling the political origins of policy change from the effects of changed circumstances is tricky. For scholars interested in causal explanation, it is theoretically inconvenient that the LDP split and Japanese political reform came so quickly on the heels of the bursting of the economic bubble and the end of the Cold War. Even without electoral reform, Japanese policy was likely to change in some ways. The argument that we pursue in the next two chapters, however, is that an understanding of the ways that political incentives changed is necessary to explain the precise ways in which policy has changed. Of course, we argue that the coincidence of economic and political breakdown in 1990s Japan was not an accident—the two phenomena were intimately related. So, too, are the emergent policy and politics equilibria in the postreform period. We do not claim that the particular electoral system chosen in 1994 was chosen for the express purpose of facilitating needed economic policy reforms, but we do argue that the rules chosen have mattered for the nature and extent of those policy changes, many of which are still ongoing.

CHAPTER 7

Japan's New Political Economy

INTRODUCTION

Japan's electoral reform of 1994 brings in its wake two major shifts in policy orientation. The changed rules motivate politicians to aim policies toward the interests and preferences of the median voter, creating a more responsive political system than Japan's first postwar regime. At the same time, the new system introduces a neoliberal policy bias that has increased income inequality across society and insecurity for large numbers of voters. Although the global financial crisis of 2008–2009 pushed governments around the world, including Japan's, toward temporary fiscal expansion, the center of gravity in Japanese politics has moved from pork-barrel politics to fiscal conservatism in deference to the average taxpayer.[1] How should we think about these simultaneous trends? Have the Japanese failed in their attempts to engineer a better set of political institutions?

The choice of electoral rules involves making trade-offs between competing ideals. The old SNTV system supported Japan's strong middle-class solidarity by protecting the livelihood of many groups in society, including farmers, small businesses, and employees of large firms. It was also, after all, the system in place during the years of Japan's spectacular economic growth.[2] However, as we discussed in chapters 4 and 5, those protections came at the cost of massive misallocations of capital and inefficiencies, as well as budget deficits, limited consumer choice in the marketplace, and corruption.

Whatever the balance of merits and drawbacks of the first postwar system, returning to those rules is not in the cards. The challenges of competi-

---

[1] The LDP's supplemental budget in December 2008 included ¥2 trillion ($22 billion at the January 2009 exchange rate) in cash handouts directly to taxpayers, bypassing organized interests. *Yomiuri Shimbun*, January 6, 2009. Meanwhile, a backbencher rebellion in the LDP threatened to derail the part of the budget earmarked for road construction. *Asahi Shimbun*, January 6, 2009.

[2] See Yashiro and Morinaga 2007 for opposing views on Japan's growing wealth inequality. Yashiro takes the economist's view that more fluid labor markets will increase productivity and gains from trade, though he also favors stronger social insurance. Morinaga rues the loss of Japan's traditional employment guarantees that underpinned a decent life for many in the middle class.

tion in the global economy dwarf those of the past, and competitive Japanese firms are no longer willing to support an electoral system that hurts them more than it helps. Demographically, the balance has tipped away from rural voters, whose livelihood depended on agricultural protection, toward urban voters who care more about taxes and prices. The 1994 electoral rules underwrite a new coalition between competitive firms and urban taxpayers and consumers, all of whom prefer to keep the cost of government low, rather than to bankroll special favors.

The end of intraparty competition has reduced the need for enormous sums of money to build personal support networks freeing politicians to respond to issues of concern to average voters. Because of the preponderance of single-member districts in Japan's new electoral system, the party's electoral strategy targets the vast swath of voters in the political middle. In contrast to past decades, when the LDP effectively cobbled together electoral majorities out of numerous special interests, the strategy of targeting policy favors to narrow groups is now inferior to one based on broad appeals to average voters.

Of course, changing political incentives is not as simple as flipping a switch, because organized groups retain a political advantage over the unorganized regardless of electoral rules.[3] Groups with a high stake in a single issue are consistently willing to commit mobilizational resources in exchange for favors in a way that the median voter cannot. Worse yet, politicians often cannot be sure who the median voter actually is on any given issue, let alone when issues are voted on as a package deal at election time. Voters worry about rising taxes, but they also worry about economic insecurity, and the policy implications of these issues can cut in different directions. There may be no substitute for votes, but even informed and vigilant voters move their priorities across issue areas in unpredictable ways. The regulation of Japan's political economy has moved in a majoritarian direction, with an undermining effect on cartels, but special deals still survive in areas where voter interest is relatively low or voter priorities are unclear.

THE UNRAVELING OF INSTITUTIONAL COMPLEMENTARITIES

Japan's postwar market institutions of main banks, cross-shareholding, and long-term labor contracts were complementary and mutually reinforc-

---

[3]Stigler 1971; Becker 1983.

ing, as many scholars have pointed out.[4] Less noted was the regulatory underpinning of these market institutions that channeled competition in particular ways, some intended and some unintended. The government padded bank profits, ostensibly for the sake of banking system stability. But knowing that there are other ways to shore up banking system stability in which banks would shoulder heavier costs (e.g., with capital adequacy requirements or deposit insurance), grateful banks contributed money back to the LDP.[5] Protective regulation enabled banks to make long-term loans that shielded firms from business cycle downturns, allowed firms to engage in share swaps that protected firm management from hostile takeovers, and enabled firms to contract with workers for lifetime careers.

Our brief review of postwar economic history in chapter 5 documented the way economic organization mirrored the distribution of political power. Heavy industry prospered under a warm blanket of government protection without necessarily becoming globally competitive, while banks cashed in on a thriving loan business thanks to regulatory prohibitions against the payment of competitive interest rates to savers. Banks were free from the short-term discipline of stock market performance, but they competed on the margin of long-term loans to industrial firms. Firms, in turn, competed with each other for skilled labor, using that long-term bank funding to offer lifetime tenure to their choice employees. Skilled labor was in this way able to share in the rewards of Japan's economic growth, despite their lack of political strength. The political weakness of labor meant that core employees of big firms enjoyed secure wages and generous benefits in deals that did not cover the rest of the workforce, let alone the unemployed.

This chapter investigates what happened when the regulatory piece of the interlocking institutions was removed. Big segments of the edifice tumbled down, resulting in a configuration that reflects new government priorities. Electoral rules implemented in 1994 shook the hidden ballast undergirding the "Japanese variety of capitalism" by lessening political incentives to cultivate personal sources of campaign capital. With less need for money from business contributors, politicians were less beholden to their policy wishes.

Liberation from big business was, of course, only a matter of degree, for politicians always have an appetite for campaign contributions. But

[4]Milgrom and Roberts 1994; Manow 2001; Allen and Gale 2002.
[5]See Rajan and Zingales 2003 for a general argument about how incumbent financial institutions use political power to protect themselves from financial deregulation.

given that politicians now have to win votes from a broader swath of the public, rather than rely on targeted groups, they had to be more careful than before not to sell to industry policy favors that voters would not like. The "conversion rate" between money and electoral outcomes was worse under the new rules than it had been under the old.[6]

The policy consequences of the majoritarian turn are visible: with fewer and feebler regulatory shelters, capital has become more mobile in Japan's new political economy, which in turn has cut labor loose to a greater extent as well. Japan may or may not regain economic vigor as a result,[7] but the distributional consequences of mobile assets are similar in Japan to what has been seen elsewhere: dismantled logrolls will bring a greater dispersion of income and wealth.

The Big Bang

One of the first casualties of the new electoral regime was protective banking regulation. Under the old postwar banking regulatory scheme, the Ministry of Finance guaranteed bank solvency by limiting competition among financial institutions. The system worked well enough to protect savers from default, but at the cost of their getting below market interest rates on their savings. Ordinary bank-account holders packed no political punch under the old electoral rules, because unorganized individuals with small per capita stakes in policy outcomes would be of little use to politicians who needed to secure money from organized groups. Politicians had more use for campaign contributions from firms, including banks, that they could deploy to stitch together electoral support from personal loyalty cultivated by myriad small favors. Although the government was determined to avoid a financial system collapse that would threaten life savings and arouse the wrath of dormant interests, retail consumers of financial services were accorded the lowest regulatory priority.

The market collapse beginning in 1990 was of tsunami proportions against the Ministry of Finance's implicit guarantee against bank failure. So many banks were left with vastly devalued assets that the worst-case scenario of massive bank runs loomed large. The banking scene in Tokyo was being compared to the tulip mania in Rembrandt's time that temporarily ruined the Dutch economy.[8] The danger was that mass hysteria

---

[6] See Denzau and Munger 1986; Bawn and Thies 2003.

[7] There is much scholarly debate over whether relative fiscal stringency has helped Japan's economy (Vogel 2006). In the short run, tight budgets surely delayed recovery.

[8] Shiozaki 2002.

would envelope the investment world, and bankers would dump their collateral on a falling market while savers raced to reclaim whatever portion of their savings accounts they could salvage.

Under the old electoral rules, the government's response to economic downturns, as in 1964 and 1975, was to consolidate the convoy: merge weak banks into stronger ones, and provide tax relief and subsidies as necessary to shore up the remaining institutions.[9] The government did, in fact, infuse the banking system with taxpayer money in the 1990s crisis as well. But in 1995, the Japanese government allowed the regional Hyogo Bank to fail. Shocked, foreign lenders began extracting a "Japan premium" from Japanese banks in the interbank lending market.[10]

In November 1996, the LDP-Socialist coalition government under Prime Minister Hashimoto Ryutaro announced the "Big Bang" reforms that would liberalize the financial system, thereby putting more banks at risk of failure in a more competitive market. In an about-face from the old practice of maintaining financial stability through coddling and compartmentalization, Big Bang regulation permitted any type of financial institution to provide banking, brokering, investment, or insurance services in yen or any other currency with minimal regulation. The ban on holding companies was abolished, brokers' commissions were deregulated, entry into the currency exchange business was liberalized, and the Bank of Japan was given greater independence.[11] The "ships," so to speak, were cut loose from the convoy and urged to move at full throttle. The weakest would be put out of service rather than be allowed to compromise the whole system.

In 1997, the Hashimoto government allowed the bankruptcy of Hokkaido Takushoku, one of Japan's large "city banks." In 1998, the government established the Financial Services Authority, which separated the government's bank supervisory arm from the Ministry of Finance and augmented the oversight capacity with additional inspectors, stricter disclosure rules, and tighter accounting rules consistent with international standards.[12] Establishing the FSA was a high-profile attempt by the LDP to scapegoat the MOF for banking system failure, but few were fooled about the LDP's responsibility for having pampered the banking system into a state of weak capacity.

"Big Bang" may be too grand a term for what happened, because in

[9]Rosenbluth 1989: chapter 4.
[10]Peek and Rosengren 2001.
[11]Hoshi and Patrick 2000; Rosenbluth and Schaap 2003; Toya 2006.
[12]Miyajima and Yafeh 2003.

fact the FSA deregulated gradually (over the course of several years) to give Japanese banks a chance to adjust to stiff foreign competition.[13] Foreign financial institutions, particularly the globally competitive American banks that stood ready to expand market share, continued to be frustrated by the slow pace of reforms.[14] The London Big Bang of 1986, after all, was known for its "Wimbledon Effect": the City of London became a global center of finance by allowing foreign banks the freedom to compete and win.[15] The Wimbledon Effect was weaker in Japan, but some foreign-won matches aroused opposition from domestic players used to winning on playing fields that had been tilted in their favor.

One of the biggest players in Japanese markets after the Japanese Big Bang was Timothy Collins, chief executive officer of Ripplewood Holdings LLC, a New York–based private equity firm. In 2000 he organized a group of investors that beat out Japanese bidders to buy Long Term Credit Bank (LTCB), a failed institution that the Japanese government had nationalized in 1997 to prevent a meltdown in the banking system.[16] Ripplewood paid $1.2 billion for the bank and optimistically renamed it "Shinsei," Japanese for "new life." Collins and his group made about $2 billion a few years later by selling off 30 percent of their stake in the bank, but not before accepting taxpayer money in a government deal to buy some of LTCB's nonperforming loans.[17] Taxpayer frustration set the stage for good political theater, with the LDP and opposition parties sparring over who was to blame for the enormous sums of nonperforming loans being mopped up in part with public funds. Some politicians singled out foreign investors for the role of villain.[18]

[13]Endo 1999: 339–340.

[14]Japan Center for International Finance 2004.

[15]Pohl 2002: 14. The reference is to the All England Lawn Tennis and Croquet Club in Wimbledon, which is world famous and successful for its annual Open tennis tournament, despite the lack of British champions. The same is true, it is said, of the post–Big Bang financial sector in the City of London.

[16]Chuo Trust Bank and Mitsui Trust Bank, two Japanese banks that later merged, lost to Ripplewood on the bid for the Long Term Credit Bank.

[17]One of the more visible companies in the LTCB's portfolio was the ailing Sogo Department Store. Shinsei's refusal to roll over loans to Sogo put the store on the brink of bankruptcy. The LDP waffled over which would be worse: using taxpayer money to prop up the store, or allowing the company to fail, eliminating thousands of jobs. In the end, the LDP let the company go bankrupt. Meanwhile, Ripplewood took its profits from the sale of Shinsei shares to buy Japan Telecom in 2004 for $2.3 billion; it sold the company to Softbank Corp for $3.1 billion less than a year later. *Business Week*, July 12, 2004.

[18]Asao Keiichiro, a DPJ politician with an MBA from Stanford, published an article in a popular magazine entitled "Who Turned the Shinsei Bank into a Traitor?" (*Bungei Shunju*, September 2000). He wrote this in response to news that Shinsei investors had made $57

Most financial institutions have in fact remained in Japanese hands, and foreign banks sometimes complained that the new Financial Services Authority deliberately delayed licenses to wipe out the advantages of new financial products.[19] But Ripplewood still holds 30 percent of Shinsei Bank shares, and in contrast to the low-margin corporate lending business for which its predecessor LTCB was known, Shinsei has diversified into consumer finance, leasing, and hedge fund management.[20] Similarly, Citigroup's Salomon Smith Barney unit in Tokyo merged operations with Nikko Securities to form the Nikko Citigroup in 1999, joining other American investment banks, such as Morgan Stanley, in high-profile market making.

When the dust settled from the financial crisis of the 1990s, the Japanese government's new regulatory priorities came more clearly into view. In years past, convoy banking regulation had maintained banking system stability in the way that was most consistent with bank profits and big electoral campaign war chests. Big Bang legislation represented, instead, a move to regulation that was consistent with competition and better consumer services.

New Corporate Governance

Changes in financial regulation rippled through the rest of the Japanese economy.[21] Banks lost the regulatory cushion that enabled long-term lending on a large scale, and many firms sold large portions of their stable holdings of bank shares and other corporate shares in order to improve their access to alternative sources of financing. Short-term financial pressures in turn forced many companies to reduce the number of employees they could afford to keep in lifetime positions.[22]

It began with banks unloading shares of corporate clients. More competitive financial markets put banks under pressure to sell shares in companies below investment grade, while the need to secure funds to eliminate nonperforming loans motivated banks to sell shares of firms with

---

billion in profits in selling off a large chunk of shares after Asao argued that Ripplewood, being an investment fund, had fewer incentives than would an operating company to consider the long-term interests of the company and of the Japanese economy.

[19] Pohl 2002: 14.

[20] *Business Week*, June 13, 2005.

[21] An excellent source on financial deregulation in Japan is Hoshi and Kashyap 2001; for the relationship between financial regulation and corporate governance in general, see Aguilera and Jackson 2003.

[22] Foreign firms operating in Japan were the first to employ workers on short-term contracts, in exchange for higher salaries (Ono 2003).

high share prices. In 2001, banks sold shares at a rate of 40 percent, as measured by the number of corporate stocks sold by banks during a year divided by the number of corporate stocks held at the beginning of the year.[23]

Japanese firms sold bank shares as well, particularly shares of weak banks. The corporate sell-off of financial stocks was especially dramatic for profitable firms with easy access to capital markets.[24] It is now principally weak firms that buy and hold bank stocks as a price for retaining access to bank loans in the absence of better financing options.[25] The negative correlation between a main bank relationship and corporate profits is likely only to strengthen.

The depressed stock market also pushed many firms to unwind their stable mutual shareholding deals that corporate managers had put in place to protect each other from hostile takeovers. Holding each other's shares made sense both as antitakeover protection and as investment as long as the economy was lifting all share prices.[26] The stock market collapse may have made corporate management even more insecure than before and therefore bolstered one incentive for stable shareholding deals, but the weak market also made the price of this form of antitakeover insurance prohibitively expensive for many companies.[27]

As Japanese companies began liquidating large portions of their corporate holdings, the companies whose shares were being sold began repurchasing their own shares to keep their value from falling even further. In 1994 and again in 2001, the government enacted legislation that made it easier for companies to repurchase their shares that were being dumped on the market by previous corporate allies.[28] As a result of stock sales by allied firms and their own stock redemptions, cross-shareholding arrangements decreased from about 45 percent of all shares in the mid-1980s to 27 percent in 2002.[29]

Foreign investment in Japan is also easier now than before, hastened by revisions in the Commercial Code that simplify merger and takeover procedures.[30] Naturally, financial investment has responded to the re-

[23]Miyajima and Kuroki 2007:91.
[24]Miyajima and Kuroki 2007.
[25]Scher 2001: 19.
[26]Miwa and Ramseyer 2006.
[27]Milhaupt 2006. Some companies still engage in defensive cross-shareholding. A notorious example was New Japan Steel (*Shinnittetsu*), in 2007, where the incentives clearly came from insecurity rather than from a consideration of long-term productivity.
[28]Shishido 2006: 5; Kanda 2000: 9; Ogishima and Kobayashi 2002: 1.
[29]Miyajima and Kuroki 2007; Jackson and Miyajima 2007.
[30]Milhaupt 2003: 4.

laxed rules much more quickly than has direct investment. Japan's inward foreign direct investment doubled between 2000 and 2005, but it still amounted to only 2.4 percent of national output compared to 15 percent for the United States and between 30 and 40 percent for Germany, France, and Britain.[31] In contrast, by 2006 foreigners owned 28 percent of the shares of the one hundred companies in the Tokyo Stock Exchange first section, up from 5 percent in the mid-1980s,[32] and foreign ownership on Jasdaq, the small capitalization market, increased from close to zero to 23.5 percent in 2007.[33] This represents a major departure for Japan where formal and informal rules have played in favor of incumbent management against takeovers of any kind, domestic or foreign.[34]

Some observers partial to the old Japanese model lament that a move toward Anglo-American corporate practices will destroy the magic of what makes Japan tick. Foreign investors, and the Japanese firms that emulate them, are more likely to fire unproductive workers and abandon old supplier relationships.[35] Moreover, New York's financial meltdown in 2008 made it clear that radical deregulation had paved the way for excessive leveraging and systemwide instability. But if the fear is that Japanese corporate managers will no longer be free to take the long-term view, the concern is misplaced because it seems that many of them never did.[36] More realistic is the worry that Japan's economy will become less egalitarian. Even if the self-congratulatory view of Japanese socioeconomic equality during the "golden years" is an exaggerated one, the distribution of income will unquestionably grow more unequal.

JAPANESE LABOR MARKETS

Labor was never a part of the LDP's electoral coalition, even if some skilled workers did share in the fruits of economic growth because of their market power. In the new economy, more workers receive performance-based wages and have a reason to care about the overall productivity of the economy. These more free-floating workers, who have become the average

[31]"Gaijin at the Gates" 2007, 53.

[32]Tokyo Stock Exchange 2008.

[33]David Turner, "Jasdaq Foreign Ownership Soars," FT.com, June 25, 2007, http://www.ft.com.

[34]Katz 2005.

[35]For example, when Renault acquired a majority stake in Nissan, new CEO Carlos Ghosn cut personnel and ties with old suppliers in a way that Japanese managers have traditionally avoided at substantial cost.

[36]Weinstein and Yafeh 1998.

voter in Japan, have reason to oppose the special political deals that have for so long propped up the weak sectors of the economy.

Like falling dominoes, electoral rules affected labor markets by way of corporate finance: with banks no longer in a position to bankroll firms' labor contracts over multiyear periods, firms that had relied on banks were forced to cut their labor costs and move more and more workers to short-term contracts. On average, labor contracts have become more contingent on performance,[37] matching the new terms of performance-based loans. Groups of corporate "salarymen" will no longer walk in lockstep through their careers with seniority-based wages.

As we discussed in chapter 5, long-term financing of firms mirrored the shape of long-term labor contracts.[38] The chain of events we have re-counted shows that the connection goes back even a step further, because banks are capable of guaranteeing long-term access to funds only if they, the banks, are shielded from market competition. Under the new elec-toral rules, politicians no longer have the same incentives to reward banks for campaign money with protective regulation if that regulation makes politicians vulnerable in the polls to accusations of selling out to special interests. Politicians now compete with each other to be consumer friendly and taxpayer friendly, at least on issues on which the average voter has a big enough stake to care about outcomes.

How much electoral rules and new banking regulations have affected corporate hiring practices in Japan depends on the sector's reliance on bank financing. Lifetime employment has taken the biggest hit in two parts of the Japanese economy: at the weak end, for small and medium-sized manufacturers that lack access to international finance, and at the opposite end, for globally integrated service sector companies in banking, insurance, and commerce that compete for labor in the international mar-ket where labor contracts are based on short-term performance criteria.

It is worth noting that the most profitable Japanese manufacturing firms long ago dispensed with main banks but continue lifetime employ-ment, at least for their core workers.[39] But even for the firms that prefer to keep a long-term labor force, the unwinding of cross-shareholdings

[37]Abe and Hoshi 2007.

[38]Aoki 1988.

[39]The continuation of long-term labor contracts among Japan's premier manufacturers speaks either to the importance of fostering a workforce with firm-specific human skills that accumulate over a career, or of the difficulty of creating merit-based pay schemes in team-production settings. On the importance of investments in cospecific assets—for example, between employer and employee, or between a supplier and final producer—see Soskice 1999: 127. See also Alchian and Demsetz 1972.

and the increasing importance of the stock market in Japanese corporate finance have required them to whittle the lifetime employee cohort into a small, privileged group.[40] The percentage of lifetime employees in these firms has shrunk by at least half, down to 20 percent on average.[41]

Part-time and temporary workers have always served as the hidden cushion that enabled companies to retain the luckier core workers through thick and thin. When the economy was weak, part-timers were let go and, because they did not receive corporate pensions or other benefits, there were no up-front costs of firing them. In the new economy, these workers make up a growing share of the labor force even in the companies that continue to tout the lifetime model for an elite core of workers.[42]

As we discussed in chapter 5, lifetime employment practices tend to discriminate against women. Because lifetime employment requires the employer to make a calculated bet about the value of a worker's labor over the course of an entire career, employers avoided hiring and promoting women on account of the typical female pattern of quitting work in midcareer to care for children and family. Women were disproportionately in the expendable positions that firms used to augment personnel during business cycle upturns, only to be dismissed when business conditions worsened.

It follows that one consequence of the decline of lifetime employment is that women eventually will have a greater chance at employment on equal terms with men. In Japan's new economy, women will continue to face barriers to the (smaller number of) core lifetime jobs in the manufacturing sector, but more women will be hired in the segments of the economy that are moving toward flexible hiring and firing practices. It is not that women have gained job security,[43] but they have gained more equal access to the labor market as a whole at the same time as men have become more insecure. Men have lost some of the comparative advantage that comes from being able to commit to uninterrupted careers.

[40]Thelen and Kume (2006: 31) note that "Many companies are eager to preserve essential features of traditional practices even as they fine tune their reformed wage systems in order to maintain their institutional competitiveness."

[41]Miyajima and Kuroki 2007.

[42]The weak demand for full-time labor has hit young, first-time job seekers particularly hard. Neologisms appeared to describe the problem: "Freeters" are part-time and temporary workers, and "NEETs" are people not in education, employment, or training (the acronym was imported from Britain). As of 2005, over 2 million young people between the ages of 15 and 34 were unemployed, and 2 million more were Freeters. Patrick 2006: 7.

[43]Indeed, the immediate cutbacks driven by the prolonged postbubble recession have affected women more than men (Kambayashi and Kato 2009: 9–10). The most affected were women who were midcareer hires (as opposed to those who were hired as new college graduates).

Closing the Pork Pipeline

Pork-barrel politics has "been a key theme of postwar Japanese political economy."[44] Indeed, the LDP regime turned it into an art form. Just one notorious example is the *shinkansen* (bullet train) line that was built between Tokyo and Niigata, the remote, rural constituency of onetime prime minister (and lifelong "construction don") Tanaka Kakuei. Not only did this boondoggle benefit Tanaka's supporters most directly, but it was built to wind through several of the equally backwater districts of Tanaka's closest LDP allies. "Bridges to nowhere" abounded, as did beautifully paved highways all over the archipelago that are in little danger of excess wear and tear because they are so little used. Concrete flowed everywhere, from construction sites for concert halls in small villages to projects covering nearly all of the country's coastline.[45] Ethan Scheiner describes Japanese politics as basically clientelist and ascribes the LDP's stranglehold on power to its centralized control over the pipeline of particularism.[46] He argues that this pattern survived the electoral system change, and that really the Opposition's only chance to break through would have depended on its rallying public opinion against clientelism itself.

Ironically, the electoral backlash against the excesses of clientelism was led not by the Opposition but by the LDP, or, rather, by the anti-LDP leader of the LDP, Koizumi Junichiro. As we described in chapter 6, he led the LDP to electoral wins in 2003 (Lower House) and 2004 (Upper House) by "running against his own party," and that was just prologue to his resounding 2005 triumph. The LDP's 2005 landslide turned on the willingness of urban voters, who despised the wasteful particularism and the high food prices and enormous budget deficits that the strategy produced, to take a chance that Koizumi could actually deliver market liberalization, and a shift to public goods over particularism.

Interestingly, particularism was already waning before the 2005 election, and while Koizumi (who had been in charge since 2001) had a lot to do with that, the trend even precedes his administration. Public works spending dropped 40 percent between 1998 and 2008, and even more as

[44] Noble 2009: 9.
[45] Noble 2009.
[46] Scheiner 2006. Since access to the trough required contacts within the ruling party, it followed that the LDP was able to dominate local politics as well, and this, in a vicious cycle (from the perspective of the opposition parties), created a deep pool of talent from which the LDP could replenish its stock of candidates.

a share of GDP.[47] Reduced spending on agriculture was part of this, but a gutting of the Fiscal Investment and Loan Program (which we described in chapter 5) and the decoupling of postal savings accounts from the FILP mattered even more. The FILP was the main source for those pork pipelines, and Koizumi's reforms essentially drained the reservoir.

Under the new electoral rules, the LDP must weigh more carefully the benefits of favors to core voters against the costs of lost popularity in the general voting public.[48] Parties should move away from particularistic electoral strategies (no longer needed to deal with intraparty competition) and instead target the mythical median voter with programmatic, public-goods-oriented appeals. As discussed in chapter 6, there is evidence of this change on the ground, in campaigns themselves.[49] There is also evidence of it in the budget. "Spending on public goods... has increased virtually across the board. The share of the budget devoted to social spending, especially health care and pensions, has expanded rapidly."[50]

Farmers and small business proprietors were, by and large, economically unproductive but politically favored in Japan's postwar political economy. Their protected status came under attack beginning in the 1970s and 1980s when Japan's export success put the spotlight on the groups in Japan most obstructive of trade liberalization. Supporting these sectors also cost the government money at a time when exporting firms wanted the government to shrink the national budget in order to lower corporate taxes. Globally successful Japanese businesses pressured the government to cut subsidies to weak segments of the economy, but the LDP needed the reliable votes from these highly motivated and well-organized groups to forge a legislative majority. Farmers and small business proprietors continue to receive the special attention that all democracies reserve for well-organized groups, but their handouts are under attack.

Farmers

The agricultural lobby, because of its exalted position under the old electoral system, had the farthest to fall. Farmers enjoyed two enormous advantages: they were overrepresented in the Diet because urbanization had outpaced redistricting; and farmers were a nationally organized

[47]Noble 2009: 10.
[48]Bawn and Thies 2003.
[49]Köllner 2007.
[50]Noble 2009: 14–16.

group of voters mobilized around the single issue of agricultural protection. These are features of politics in many democracies, which explains postindustrial countries' peculiar attachment to agricultural sectors that employ a vanishingly small sector of the population and produce a tiny share of national output. But under Japan's old electoral rules, the ability of farmers to turn out the vote for particular LDP Diet members accentuated their clout.[51]

The 1994 redistricting, which dramatically reduced the overrepresentation of the rural vote, made both large political parties less willing to risk their popularity with the vast majority of the Japanese population (which is urban) in order to court farmers.[52] By 2002, farmers made up less than 8 percent of the voting public, or if one counts only full-time farmers, closer to 3 percent. Farmers have been ably represented by *Nokyo*, the nationwide agricultural cooperative organization that serves both as a lobby group and as the on-the-ground manager of the government's complicated system of agricultural sales and subsidies. With Nokyo's smaller membership, reduced political clout, and lower government price supports, a growing number of farmers are bypassing Nokyo to sell their products directly on the market.[53] The weakening of Nokyo's ability to mobilize votes was on full display in the Upper House election of 2004 when three out of ten Nokyo-backed candidates failed to win seats.[54]

After electoral reform, the LDP cut government subsidies to rural districts by 10–20 percent compared to the pre-1994 era.[55] The LDP had been under pressure from big business to reduce budget outlays to farmers for many years, and there had been some retrenchment in the early

[51]Occasionally, farmers would flex their electoral muscles through *de*mobilization. If they felt that the LDP, or some particular LDP incumbents, needed a reminder of farmers' importance, they would organize a collective abstention in an election.

[52]The new Lower House electoral rules reduced malapportionment but did not eliminate it altogether. Under current law, no electoral district may cross prefectural lines. Because Japan's population is so heavily concentrated in a handful of urban prefectures, this means that some depopulated rural prefectures will continue to be overrepresented, until the law is changed (the same is true of the district tier for the Upper House, in which each prefecture is a district). Among the numerous decentralizing reforms discussed during the Koizumi administration were plans to replace the current structure of forty-seven prefectures with a smaller number of larger subnational entities. Among other things, this would allow for reapportionment of the three hundred single-seat districts that would further dilute the remaining rural bias.

[53]Fewer farmers are attending Nokyo assemblies and public demonstrations. George Mulgan 2005: 264.

[54]George Mulgan 2005: 269.

[55]Horiuchi and Saito 2003.

1980s[56] and just before the 1989 Upper House election, but only after 1994 was the party free to cut back on rural subsidies in a big way. The LDP changed its emphasis from helping all farmers indiscriminately to helping full-time farmers become more productive. Fewer, more efficient farms could withstand increased agricultural imports, and Japan could eventually shed its pariah status as an agricultural protectionist.[57]

The agricultural lobby still exists, of course, and representatives from rural districts press for concessions as before. Koizumi's urban appeal notwithstanding, the LDP as a whole remains disproportionately strong in rural districts, as discussed in chapter 6.[58] The rural lobby also benefits from the fact that many Japanese city dwellers still identify with their agrarian roots; moreover, consumer cooperatives see the health risks of high levels of pesticides in the cheap agricultural imports from China as a more pressing problem than the high price of domestic produce.

The Fair Trade Agreements that the Japanese government has concluded with neighboring countries in recent years reflect the diminished-but-still-significant power of the Japanese agricultural lobby. The Koizumi administration took oblique aim at agricultural protection by entering into international negotiations in which Japanese farm supports were the principal stumbling block to liberalizing trade. The media were quick to join Japanese businesses in forming a Greek chorus against Japanese agricultural protection.[59] But even the redoubtable Koizumi compromised with the farmers. In the case of the Japan-Mexico Free Trade Agreement, Japan agreed to remove tariffs on 86 percent of imports from Mexico rather than 90 percent, and special protections would remain for certain commodities including pork, orange juice, beef, chicken, and fresh oranges.[60]

Japanese farmers remain politically powerful beyond their numbers because they are an interest group that can commit to voting on the basis of a single issue. Politicians have little uncertainty about what it takes to win farmers' votes, whereas ordinary voters whose income does not depend on policy protection can be fickle in their political preferences. The political clout of agriculture is a feature of single-issue interest groups

[56]Thies 1998.
[57]George Mulgan 2005: 275–276. See also Davis 2003 for a discussion of the impact of international negotiations, legal framework, and issue linkage on Japan's agricultural trade concessions.
[58]Scheiner 2006.
[59]*Nihon keizai shimbun*, November 12, 2004.
[60]George Mulgan 2005: 293.

anywhere, but Japanese farmers are now mere mortals without the talismanic powers that emanated from malapportionment and SNTV.

Small Businesses

Small business owners, like farmers, are famous in Japan as elsewhere for using political power to supplement economic strategies of survival. Defined as firms with fewer than three hundred workers, Japan's small and medium-sized firms employed three-quarters of the manufacturing workforce and an even larger proportion of the workforce in retail trade.[61] These workers could not all be counted on to vote for the LDP in exchange for favors to their employers, but counting only the owners of small businesses, the numbers were in the millions and large enough to represent a powerful voting bloc for the LDP.

Small businesses are a diverse group that includes subcontractors tied vertically to large corporations such as Toyota, niche market manufacturers, and mom-and-pop retailers. The LDP has a long tradition of supplying small businesses with low-interest loans, government budget subsidies, tax forbearance, and, for retailers, regulatory protection from big chains. Beginning in the early 1980s, the LDP began to lessen regulatory protection in response to persistent complaints from Japan's trading partners that the multilayered distribution system was slowing the flow of imports into Japan.[62] As in the case of agriculture, the LDP also began cutting budget subsidies in the 1980s to small businesses in order to ease the pressure on income taxes. But the introduction of competitive pressure was slow and minimal. By the 1990s, when air was whooshing out of Japan's hyperinflated economy, it was clear there were many small businesses that could survive only on life support.

Since the electoral reform, the LDP has responded to small businesses in ways reminiscent of its agricultural policy. The trend is to remove favors and allow bankruptcies or buyouts to solve structural problems. National franchises and big discount stores have driven out competition from many small shops that could afford little inventory.[63] Foreign retailers such as Costco and Toys "R" Us have established strong businesses throughout Japan.

[61]Smitka 2004.

[62]Upham 1993; Schoppa 1997.

[63]The Japanese retailer Ito Yokado bought 7-Eleven from the Southland Company in 1999. In 2005 the new Japanese holding company Seven and I Holdings became the parent company for Ito Yokado, 7-Eleven, and Denny's.

As with farmers, but to a lesser degree, bursts of political mobilization from the small business community still manage to elicit a response. Following the Big Bang, more competition in the banking sector forced banks to cut their loans to weak performers, particularly small, low-tech firms with limited access to the stock or bond markets. The LDP's small-firm constituency objected, and the LDP responded by nudging the Japan Development Bank and other government financial institutions to increase loans to small business. The LDP also ordered the Financial Services Authority to require banks to lend at least 10 percent of their loan portfolios to small and medium-sized enterprises.[64] These quotas were hortatory rather than mandatory, and the FSA's leverage was weak over banks that did not depend on it for help in dealing with nonperforming loans. Moreover, banks were free to fill their quotas with loans to high performance firms. All in all, the case suggests that the LDP's responsiveness to small firms as an organized group has attenuated but not disappeared.

Postal Deregulation

By the time Prime Minister Koizumi came into office in 2001, the LDP had already put financial deregulation on course. There was still, of course, much work to be done to implement the new policies. Koizumi assigned this task to his most trusted adviser on the economy, the economics professor Takenaka Heizo. As minister of state for economic and fiscal policy, Takenaka tussled with bankers about how much banks should be made to pay for their own nonperforming loans, and won more often than not.

With banking reform and fiscal tightening under way, Koizumi chose postal reform as the issue on which to stake his political career. Koizumi's choice was less quixotic than it might sound, because the postal system sat atop trillions of yen in savings deposits, which it passed along to government financial institutions for use in "industrial policy." It irked Koizumi that, within the LDP, there were still many old-guard politicians who relied on this and other spigots of government money to get elected, even though the new electoral rules made money-intensive strategies more expensive and inefficient than before. Moreover, commissioned postmasters were often leaders of the personal support networks (koenkai) of senior LDP politicians.[65] These politicians did battle with Koizumi at every turn to protect their pots of gold, and seemed to succeed when

[64]FSA directive, 2001.
[65]Maclachlan 2004.

the Diet diluted and then narrowly defeated Koizumi's postal privatization scheme in 2005.[66] But in a snap election following the Diet vote, Koizumi expelled the "postal rebels" and won an overwhelming electoral mandate to proceed with the reform. Although less drastic and more drawn out than Koizumi would have preferred, the reform divided the postal system into separate private companies for postal delivery, savings, and insurance. Most important for Koizumi, the savings system was no longer funneling money into the political system like an enormous intravenous tube.[67]

PENSIONS AND AGING

Japan's public spending on welfare has always been small as measured by percentage of the government budget allocated to social insurance costs such as pensions and health care. What has kept Japanese society relatively egalitarian is not European-style redistributive taxes and transfers, but, rather, stable employment and a distribution of assets that started on a relatively equal basis after World War II. Employment has remained high and stable in postwar Japan, both because of rapid economic growth in the manufacturing sector through the 1980s, and because less productive parts of the economy were kept afloat by the government's targeted favors to politically potent groups such as farmers and small business proprietors.

Now that politicians are less beholden to organized groups of the economically weak, they are cutting back the policy props and allowing unproductive firms to fail in droves. Unemployment fluctuates more with the business cycle than in the postwar years, and firms are more discriminating in the wage and tenure terms with which they engage their employees. The de facto welfare scheme of the postwar years is falling apart.[68]

Politicians, who now must appeal to the interests of the average voter

[66]Maclachlan 2007.

[67]In 2006 Prime Minister Abe Shinzo, less committed than Koizumi to deregulation, readmitted eleven of the postal rebels who had been reelected to the Diet as independents. The postal reform was not reversed, but Abe's action was a sign that the antireform dinosaurs are not yet extinct. On the other hand, public outrage at Abe's decision showed that business as usual was bad politics, and it sent Abe's popularity tumbling.

[68]Some economists, such as Iwai Katsuhito (2007), argue that Japan's traditional labor practices are more efficient than is shareholder capitalism, *particularly* in the postindustrial economy because of the growing importance of skilled labor in production and productivity. This assumes that protected labor is more productive, which is an open empirical question.

to win elections, are falling over each other to promise better public pensions and health care while maintaining fiscal health. But Japan faces one of the worst demographic nightmares among rich democracies, because of its extraordinarily low fertility rate. With fewer children to be tomorrow's workers and taxpayers, tomorrow's retirees wonder where the money will come from to fund their retirement pensions and pay for their healthcare costs.[69] Table 7.1 shows how Japan ranks among OECD countries in terms of fertility (last) and life expectancy (tops), and demographic situation.

To blame for Japan's low fertility, which sits at the bottom of the OECD rankings along with Korea and Italy, is the government's long-standing inattention to the way long-term labor contracts discriminated against women in the workforce. The government seems to have hoped that women who were discouraged from succeeding as career professionals would give up, go home, and have babies. Instead, more and more women opted out of motherhood altogether, or postponed it, and had just one child.[70]

Having relied for so long on unpaid welfare provision by housewives, the Japanese government now faces a catch-22 in building its welfare programs. The crumbling of old economic props makes government welfare provisions more vital than ever before to the lives of ordinary citizens. Demographically, the unfavorable ratio of the elderly to the young eliminates attractive ways to distribute the costs across taxpayers (see fig. 7.1).[71] Women represent the largest untapped (or undertapped) workforce who could contribute to the pension system, but paid employment might depress fertility further, as well as remove from the household the primary caregivers for Japan's seniors. The only conceivable solutions are new policies that would allow women to balance careers and motherhood, such as readily available child-care facilities, or large-scale immigration of workers. Eventually, both will likely be necessary.

---

[69]Kato and Rothstein (2006: 93) note that the LDP's belated attempts to spend its way out of the 1990s recession failed to stimulate the economy because of Japan's attenuated welfare state. This, in turn, "fortified public antipathy toward deficit finance."

[70]Schoppa 2006; Rosenbluth 2007.

[71]Samuelson (1958) argued that an unfunded social security program with a constant tax rate provides a positive rate of return that, in equilibrium, is equal to the rate of growth of the social security payroll tax base. As long as the payroll tax base of the social security system increases over time, pay-as-you-go systems can yield higher returns than can funded systems. We are grateful to Isabela Mares for this reference. Japan's problem is that its payroll tax base is not growing but shrinking, and very quickly.

TABLE 7.1
Japan's Place in World Rankings, 2008: Population and Aging

Median Age	Life Expectancy at Birth	Total Fertility Rate†	Infant Mortality Rate‡
Japan (44.2)	**3. Japan (82.12)**	108. Mexico (2.34)	220. Sweden (2.8)
Germany (43.8)	7. Australia (81.63)	117. Turkey (2.21)	**219. Japan (2.8)**
Italy (43.3)	8. Canada (81.23)	122. New Zealand (2.10)	216. Iceland (3.2)
Austria (42.2)	9. France (80.98)	125. USA (2.05)	215. France (3.3)
Finland (42.1)	10. Sweden (80.86)	132. France (1.98)	214. Finland (3.5)
Greece (41.8)	11. Switzerland (80.85)	143. Iceland (1.90)	212. Norway (3.6)
Belgium (41.7)	14. Iceland (80.67)	150. Ireland (1.85)	209. Czech Republic (3.8)
Sweden (41.5)	18. New Zealand (80.36)	158. China (1.79)	208. Germany (4.0)
Spain (41.1)	19. Italy (80.20)	159. Australia (1.78)	207. Switzerland (4.2)
Switzerland (41.0)	23. Spain (80.05)	160. Luxembourg (1.78)	206. Spain (4.2)
Denmark (40.5)	24. Norway (79.95)	161. Norway (1.78)	202. South Korea (4.3)
Netherlands (40.4)	26. Greece (79.66)	165. Denmark (1.74)	201. Denmark (4.3)
Canada (40.4)	27. Austria (79.50)	166. Finland (1.73)	200. Austria (4.4)
UK (40.2)	30. Netherlands (79.40)	174. Sweden (1.67)	199. Belgium (4.4)
Czech Republic (40.1)	31. Luxembourg (79.33)	175. Netherlands (1.66)	197. Luxembourg (4.6)
Hungary (39.4)	32. Germany (79.26)	176. UK (1.66)	194. Australia (4.8)
Portugal (39.4)	33. Belgium (79.22)	177. Belgium (1.65)	193. Portugal (4.8)
Norway (39.4)	36. UK (79.01)	182. Canada (1.58)	191. UK (4.9)
France (39.4)	37. Finland (78.97)	* EU (1.51)	190. New Zealand (4.9)

Luxembourg (39.2)	40. South Korea (78.72)	188. Portugal (1.49)	187. Canada (5.0)
Poland (37.9)	* EU (78.67)	189. Switzerland (1.45)	186. Ireland (5.1)
Australia (37.3)	45. Denmark (78.30)	195. Germany (1.41)	185. Greece (5.2)
South Korea (37.3)	46. Ireland (78.24)	197. Austria (1.39)	181. Italy (5.5)
Slovakia (36.9)	47. Portugal (78.21)	199. Greece (1.37)	* EU (5.7)
USA (36.7)	49. USA (78.11)	202. Hungary (1.35)	178. USA (6.3)
New Zealand (36.6)	61. Czech Republic (76.81)	203. Slovakia (1.35)	171. Poland (6.8)
Iceland (35.1)	72. Mexico (76.06)	205. Italy (1.31)	170. Slovakia (6.8)
Ireland (35.0)	75. Poland (75.63)	206. Spain (1.31)	162. Hungary (7.9)
China (34.1)	78. Slovakia (75.40)	208. Poland (1.28)	155. Netherlands (9.1)
Turkey (27.7)	105. China (73.47)	214. Czech Republic (1.24)	112. Mexico (18.4)
Mexico (26.3)	106. Hungary (73.44)	218. South Korea (1.21)	104. China (20.3)
EU (N/A)	122. Turkey (71.96)	217. Japan (1.21)	84. Turkey (25.8)

Source: Central Intelligence Agency. 2009. *The 2008 World Factbook.* https://www.cia.gov/library/publications/the-world-factbook/.

Note: The numerical rankings are for all countries of the world, but this lists include only the thirty OECD member countries, plus China and an entry for the European Union as a whole. There was no rank ordering available for the first column, median age. In all columns, the EU average is unranked.

[†]Total Fertility Rate (TFR) "gives a figure for the average number of children that would be born per woman if all women lived to the end of their childbearing years and bore children according to a given fertility rate at each age. TFR is a more direct measure of the level of fertility than the crude birth rate, since it refers to births per woman."

[‡]This entry gives the number of deaths of infants under one year old in a given year per 1,000 live births in the same year.

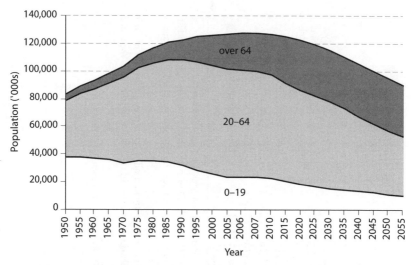

Figure 7.1. Japan's Shrinking and Aging Population, 1950–2055

Public Pensions

Japan's fertility rate of 1.21 children per woman of childbearing age is far below the "replacement level" (2.1) needed to stave off population decline. The effect on the working-age population is even more dramatic. When the government announced a social security pension scheme in 2001 to restore balance between projected income and expenditures, a population count published in 2002 showing fewer births than expected and greater longevity destroyed the validity of the projections. Japan's shrinking payroll base meant choosing between unpleasant alternatives: giving retirees less in benefits or making the young pay more in taxes.[72] The intergenerational conflict is a politically potent one because the elderly are likely to tether their votes to the pension issue, whereas young voters are an important swing constituency for both major parties.

The Japanese public pension is modest, forcing most Japanese to rely substantially on earnings-related employee pensions and on private savings. This is a problem, given the growing number of part-time workers in the Japanese economy, and firms' unwillingness to extend the Employment Pension Insurance scheme to cover them.[73] A third pension plan is reserved for public servants.

[72]By 2025, 1999 pension reform legislation will have reduced by 20 percent aggregate pension payouts (Takayama 2000: 2).

[73]Sakamoto, in a World Bank report, notes that "The government tried to extend the

Although firms and employees jointly pay the premiums for the Employment Pension Insurance, the government requires that the money for each of the three pension plans be vested with the government's Social Insurance Agency. In 1997, the agency streamlined the database for the three components of the pension system and assigned each individual a single reference number corresponding to records from any of the three accounts. Ten years later, in spring 2007, the pension issue was propelled to front-page headlines by the government's astonishing admission that the data transfer was botched for 50 million accounts. The number sounds preposterous, out of an entire population of 117 million, and the Japanese public reacted with understandable fury. A *Yomiuri* newspaper poll found that 76 percent of the public had lost faith in the pension system.[74]

In campaigning for Upper House elections of July 2007, the Democratic Party of Japan made full use of the government's embarrassment to turn the spotlight on the poverty of pensions. Try as he might to focus on Japan's national security environment, Prime Minister Abe was unable to draw public attention away from the depth and extent of Japan's pension problems. The DPJ gained popularity with the elderly for proposing a funded system, while it assuaged the young by promising to limit government spending on pensions to the revenue raised from the 5 percent consumption tax. The LDP parried with pledges to raise the government's share of the basic pension premium to one-half without specifying the tax source. When investigative reporters discovered that the Social Insurance Agency had paid ¥1.4 trillion over ten years to maintain its antiquated computer system and wasted another ¥1.1 trillion building vacation resorts, both parties pledged to abolish the agency.[75]

The DPJ's takeover of the Upper House in July 2007 not only cost Prime Minister Abe his job but also pointed to tougher bargaining over pension legislation in the direction of more tax-based funding.[76] The LDP's business-friendly proposal is to privatize the former Social Insurance Agency (SIA), breaking its operations into six units. The DPJ's counterproposal is

---

coverage of the EPI scheme to [part-time workers], but it could not obtain the agreement from the employers. It has decided to continue the discussion" (2005: 7). Employers and part-time workers, meanwhile, would like the government to raise the salary threshold for paying into the earnings-related pension scheme above the current ¥1.3 million (about $10,000). This is an issue about which women disagree among themselves, because women who work full-time object to the idea of subsidizing housewives or part-time workers (Kasza 2006: 87).

[74]Kwan 2007.
[75]Kwan 2007.
[76]*Nihon keizai shimbun*, June 16, 2007, 4.

to merge the SIA with the Tax Agency to create a body that would manage both tax collection and pension payments. Whatever the outcome of partisan bargaining, pensions in Japan have come under full public scrutiny, and no party in office can afford to slough off the plight of retired voters as the responsibility of employers or employees alone.

Health Care and Long-Term Care Insurance

Another issue that looms large in Japan's aging society is health insurance. By 2020, a third of Japan's population will be sixty-five or older. All health insurance plans in Japan are taxed to finance a national fund that covers all the health-care costs for the elderly.[77] The costs of providing health care to aging baby boomers will be even more burdensome in an economy struggling to escape a long-term economic slump.

Japan is justifiably proud of having one of the healthiest populations in the world at a cost—8 percent of GDP—just below the 8.83 percent OECD average and close to half of what the United States spends to lesser effect.[78] The LDP government managed to keep health-care costs in lockstep with GDP growth, thanks to periodic deals cut with doctors and hospitals, until 1990 when the bubble burst. Providers were unwilling to accept drastic real cuts for their services, and the government's effective subsidy of health insurance rose as a result.[79]

To get the health-care budget under control, the Koizumi government increased patients' copayments for drugs and medical services in 2002 from the previous 20 percent to 30 percent.[80] Koizumi sold this and other belt-tightening measures as a victory for taxpayers against runaway claims on government spending.[81]

[77]Rodwin 1993: 4.

[78]See http://www.oecd.org/dataoecd/20/51/37622205.xls. These figures aggregate public and private spending on health care The U.S. system, though largely privately provided, is by far the most expensive in the world, at 15.2 percent of GDP (Imai 2002).

[79]Ramseyer (2007) illustrates the extent of government-suppressed medical prices by showing that cosmetic surgeons, whose services are not covered by medical insurance and who therefore charge market prices, earn higher incomes than do other doctors, are more likely to have attended selective medical schools, and are more likely to be board certified.

[80]Imai 2002: 6; Kaiser Family Foundation 2007.

[81]The hike in copayments from 20 to 30 percent applied to working Japanese, not retirees. That is another reason this increase won't solve Japan's health-care financial challenge. Other unresolved issues in Japanese health care include big premium differentials for the same benefits across different employer insurance schemes; and regulations that limit competition among health-care providers (Imai 2002: 16).

The financial sustainability of Japan's health insurance system is by no means assured by a hike in patient costs, particularly given the growing number of elderly who will require more intensive care over the coming decades. In traditional Japanese society, multiple generations lived on the farmstead, enjoying built-in care courtesy of the women of the house. The Japanese welfare state was cheap because the government not only left pensions to employers, but also left child care and elderly care to families.[82] However heartwarming the image of the multigenerational family, women bore a heavy burden, and not only in terms of income forgone.[83]

In modern Japan, the same women who "voted with their feet" against traditional maternal roles, sending fertility rates downward, also balked at the prospect of being the default caretakers of the elderly.[84] In 2000 the LDP-Komeito government adopted a Long-Term Care Insurance Law to provide access to institutional care for people who can no longer function on their own. Early versions of the law mirrored the German law, under which each family would have the option of receiving a cash allowance to take care of the elderly at home. In a surprising shift, the Japanese government acceded to feminist pressure to make the benefit available *only* in the form of formal care services.[85]

Feminism is not a strong, organized force in Japan. There is no Japanese equivalent of the National Organization for Women. Women have made slow progress in areas such as sexual harassment in the workplace.[86] The mobilization of women's voices on the issue of Long-Term Care Insurance began as the work of one person, Higuchi Keiko, a feminist activist and professor of Tokyo Kasei University who was invited to serve on the National Advisory Council on the Health and Welfare of the Elderly.[87] She created a one-woman thunderstorm, promising to campaign nationwide against the exploitation of women in family-based care. Higuchi's call was taken up by others as well, but the speed of the government's

[82]This practice of "subsidiarity" is, of course, common among socially conservative welfare states. Gottfried and O'Reilly 2002.

[83]The psychological costs were also substantial, depicted in loving detail in soap operas.

[84]Schoppa 2006.

[85]Webb 2003: 47. The legal requirement would spare women from bargaining within their families from a position of weakness and appearing selfish in suggesting that an elderly family member move into assisted living arrangements.

[86]Because only 58 percent of working-age women work—far fewer if one excludes women in part-time or temporary work—the idea that women and men should have equal access to career success is not a hegemonic idea even among women.

[87]Webb 2003: 49; Ito 1999. For a glimpse of Higuchi's message, see http://www.sut-tv.com/terakoya/kousi/higuchki_keiko/kousi.htm.

response reveals striking political skittishness about alienating large swaths of the voting population under Japan's new electoral rules.

Administrative Decentralization

An additional policy reform, which goes to the institutional structure of politics itself, is the partial decentralization of administration to local governments. Historically, the Japanese government has reallocated large sums of money from richer, urban prefectures to poorer, rural ones, so that about a third of rural prefectural spending depended on transfers from the central government. But plans are under way to allow prefectures to raise more of their own revenues, and to force them to balance their own books.[88] Although the decentralizing trend appears incongruous with growing centralization of party leadership, closer inspection reveals that the motivation originates in the same place: changes in electoral incentives.

In 1995, soon after electoral reform, the Japanese legislature passed the Decentralization Promotion Law to begin studying possibilities for devolution of fiscal and administrative authority to local governments. This was followed by the Comprehensive Laws on Decentralization in 2000, the "Trinity" fiscal reforms in 2005, and the New Decentralization Promotion Law in 2007, all of which kept pushing in the direction of greater local fiscal and administrative autonomy.[89]

At first blush, the decentralizing move seems best explained by the dire fiscal straits of the central government, and the sense of urgency about stanching the overspending tendencies of local governments that expect to be bailed out when their own revenues run out.[90] But there is more to the story than that, because the central government has been in fiscal trouble before without resorting to decentralization. After all, giving local governments more control of their revenues and spending comes at considerable cost: the central government loses latitude to favor poorer rural prefectures at the expense of richer urban ones, removing one substantial mechanism for redistributing income to constituency groups of its choosing.

[88]Nishio 2007.
[89]Akaiwa 2003; Nomura 2008; Ministry of Internal Affairs and Communications 2006.
[90]Oates 1972; Rodden 2006. The bad incentives entailed in automatic bailouts have long been understood, but this is no guarantee that politicians avoid them.

The timing of the fiscal decentralization was no fluke, because the New Japanese Politics we have described in this chapter exposes government spending to a heightened level of taxpayer scrutiny, placing fiscal responsibility higher on the list of political priorities than in the past. More important, the reduction in rural overrepresentation that was accomplished by the change in electoral rules relocates the political middle to urban voters. Of course legislators who represent rural voters still clamor for more redistribution, but there are fewer of them, and their demands bear a higher price tag for the urban representatives who would incur the costs. It is possible that even the representatives of rural districts may see less benefit to the transfers under the new rules, because electoral competition has shifted from a personal to a partisan basis, putting the spotlight on policy differences rather than on disbursements of monetary favors.[91] That many municipalities are being forcibly merged, incorporating outlying rural townships into larger cities, is further evidence that politicians are shifting their attention to urban voters.[92] Taken together, these effects of electoral reform provide a more complete explanation for fiscal and administrative decentralization than does fiscal necessity alone.

CONCLUSIONS

Japan's electoral reform of 1994 shifted the political balance from economic interest groups toward ordinary voters for whom cartels represent a cost. Table 7.2 provides a summary of the major "before and after" differences discussed in this chapter. In the old political system, LDP politicians competed for office by specializing in the delivery of policy favors to particular types of firms or organized groups in exchange for votes and money. LDP politicians under SNTV differentiated themselves from each other in a multitude of ways, one of the most effective of which was to become members of different "policy tribes" (zoku) that dominated party committees in their respective areas of expertise. If one politician cultivated the agricultural vote, another would focus on the transportation industry, another on construction, and so on.[93] The result was a political

[91]Hirano (2006) shows that LDP incumbents were more likely to disburse intergovernmental transfers to favored constituents—those geographically concentrated around their hometowns—under the old electoral rules than under the new ones.

[92]"In Japan, the number of municipalities sharply declined...from 3,256 in January 2000 to 1,847 in April 2006" (Horiuchi and Saito 2009: 4).

[93]McCubbins and Rosenbluth 1995.

TABLE 7.2
Comparison of Japanese Political Economy before and after Reform

Variable	Before	After
Electoral Rule	SNTV Semiproportional Personalistic	MMM Majoritarian Partisan elections
Campaigns	Issue-free campaigns Product differentiation Niche (wholesale) politics Factions and money	Issue-based campaigns Median voter Public goods (retail politics) Factions irrelevant, money less important
Policy	Convoy financial system "No bank left behind" Rigid market segmentation Trade barriers / subsidies for inefficient farmers and SMEs	Big Bang (deregulation) Banks allowed to fail Universal banking Postal reform 10–20% cut in subsidies to rural areas FSA "requests" that 10% of bank loans go to SMEs

Outcomes

Main banks less important	Main bank relationships for many firms (albeit not for the most competitive ones)	Negative correlation b/w health of firm and reliance on main bank has increased
Cross-shareholding declining	Around 45% in 1987. Banks held about 15% of firm shares	Down to 27% in 2002 Bank-held shares down to 7.7%
Corporate finance changing†	Long-term debt-based finance; overlending and over-borrowing tolerated	More equity financing for strong, competitive firms Weaker firms still depend on bank loans
Employment changing; unemployment increasing	Lifetime employment for core workers	More merit-based promotion and pay. Regular workers hired after 1992 much less likely to stay with their firms for 10 yrs or more than those hired before 1992‡ Up to 2 million "Freeters"
FDI increasing, but still very low	Around 1% of GDP	More than doubled, to 2.4% (but still much lower than U.S. or W. Europe).
Foreign ownership of shares increasing	5.8% in 1980; 4.2% in 1989 ~ 0% of JASDAQ in 1980s	18.8% in 2000; 27.6% in 2007 Up to 23.5% in 2005
Inequality increasing	Gini coeff ~ .293 in 1989	Gini coeff ~.352 in 2004

†See Endo 1999: 323–328.

‡See Jackson 2007; Kambayashi and Kato 2009.

bias toward protectionist regulation for the sake of campaign contributions.

Under the new rules, a district-based politician attempting to patch together an electoral majority with money and votes from organized groups is vulnerable to a different (and much cheaper) campaign strategy focusing on ordinary voters as consumers and taxpayers. The new bar for winning a seat is a plurality of votes rather than the 15–20 percent of the votes needed in the old multimember districts, which makes a direct, general appeal to voters on the basis of public goods a considerably more efficient strategy. Because there is no longer a need to differentiate oneself from one's copartisans, cheaper strategies should trump more expensive ones. Politicians are more likely to win if they appeal directly to consumers and taxpayers who are cheated out of disposable income by the old-style regulatory and budgetary favors to special groups.

In this chapter, we recounted the effects of bank cartel dissolution on corporate governance and labor market practices. Without long-term bank loans as a prop, many firms have wound down cross-shareholding arrangements and reduced the percentage of workers to whom they offer lifetime contracts. As workers become more mobile and discount the possibility of riding up a slow corporate escalator until retirement, there is growing demand for professional training in fields such as law and business. Even in the wake of the 2008–2009 stock market tumble related to the global financial crisis, corporate finance has inexorably shifted away from bank loans toward greater dependence on stock and bond markets. As the labor market becomes more fluid, a growing number of workers find themselves without employment security or a guaranteed corporate pension that provided social insurance for many Japanese in lieu of a strong welfare state. In response to new competitive pressure for the median voter, the major parties have responded with plans to improve the general safety net.

Of course, well-organized groups continue to enjoy advantages under the new system. This is a truism of politics anywhere, rather than an example of continuity peculiar to Japanese politics. Because organized groups have more intense policy preferences than do ordinary voters, they are willing to work hard to put electoral competition in service of the issues they care most about. This matters even for district-based politicians who must weigh concerted efforts of mobilized groups against the shallower preferences of the electoral majority.

Their collective-action advantages notwithstanding, organized groups have systematically more or less influence over policy depending on the extent to which particular rules of political competition reward coordinating and mobilizing activities. Strong, majoritarian parties are best able to formulate and execute median voter policies, while weak majoritarian parties or parties in proportional electoral systems are more likely to favor organized groups. If this is right, policy making in Japan will come more to resemble that in the United Kingdom than that of either the United States or continental Europe. Because, like the United Kingdom, Japan is a parliamentary system with basically majoritarian electoral rules, the government can count on party discipline sufficiently strong to target, at the margin, swing districts and undecided voters rather than cater to safe districts and core voters. By contrast, in the United States, weak party discipline leaves more room for legislative bargaining, with the result that policy is more likely to favor core constituencies in majority districts.[94] In European countries governed by proportional representation electoral rules, the government logrolls the preferences of the core constituencies of coalition members. We expect that Japanese farmers and small business proprietors will become weaker in Japan than their counterparts in either the United States or continental Europe.

One salient difference between Japan and the United Kingdom is the persistence of small niche parties in Japan, thanks to the PR-list tier. Without a high likelihood of forming a majority government on its own, a large party must woo a coalition partner that could require policy concessions away from the center of gravity at the median. Although some of these parties represent narrow interest groups, the LDP finds the Komeito a desirable coalition partner precisely because it occupies political space near the middle of the political spectrum, particularly in cities. With its urban constituency, the Komeito has championed agricultural reform, environmental protection, and better social security.[95]

Our account has privileged electoral incentives over many other important factors, not because we think they constitute a monocausal explanation for relevant outcomes, but because they are an underacknowledged force behind old patterns and profound changes in Japan's political economy.[96] Japan's integration into the world economy began undermining the

[94]Also, because of gerrymandering, which is not a problem in Japan, there are exceedingly few competitive districts in U.S. House elections. Nearly all incumbents are safe, and free to pander to those core groups.

[95]The Komeito and the LDP disagree about the relative importance of the government's fiscal deficit and urban livelihood, with the LDP favoring a hike in the value-added tax to 8 percent and the Komeito favoring further fiscal stimulation to generate corporate profits and tax revenues more gradually. The coalition agreed to sequence the tax hike after economic recovery. *Asahi Shimbun*, December 24, 2008.

[96]This sets our account apart from, say, that of Pempel (1998), who analyzed the political upheaval along with the economic one, but did not draw causal links between the two, nor did he expect policy changes as far-reaching as those we have explained here. To be fair, we

viability of a model built around economic protectionism long before electoral rules were changed in 1994. But the old electoral rules created a bottleneck that motivated politicians to protect their personal support coalitions, even at growing cost.

We concluded our discussion in chapter 6 by noting that the new electoral rules are no panacea for the pathologies of Japanese politics. We are just as certain that they are not sufficient to cure all that ails the Japanese economy. If they were, Japan would not have languished in recession for most of the fifteen years since the electoral reform, and the government would have been swifter to cope with economic disasters of the sort visited on Japan following the global financial meltdown of 2008–2009.[97] We have already explained why the majoritarian turn has led to an increase in economic inequality.

The crash of 1990 and subsequent financial crisis could have provoked the Japanese government to turn inward, walling off its economy from the outside world. Low-productivity firms in agriculture and manufacturing would have gained a temporary stay of execution, but the long-run economic consequences would have been disastrous. And, in the years between the crash in 1990 and the electoral reform in 1994, the government did indeed seem to be circling the wagons. But the economic crash impacted politics as well, not least by encouraging politicians to engage in ever more egregious campaign finance improprieties, and by shortening the voters' patience with them. This, in turn, led to the LDP split and electoral reform, and although the new electoral rule may not have been chosen with economic policy reform principally in mind, it has had that effect. The new rules of electoral competition force politicians to devise plans for economic recovery that pass muster with average Japanese voters, so globally competitive firms and consumers are the winners in the New Japanese Political Economy, while the LDP's longtime special-interest clients are finding their access to pork and patronage significantly curtailed.

---

have had the benefit of an extra decade of change to examine, and the shape of the new system is much clearer now than it was in 1998.

[97]Partly as a result of the cleanup of the mountain of nonperforming loans in the 1990s, Japanese banks were less exposed to the pressures that led to the credit crisis (mostly mortgage-backed securities) than were their American and European counterparts. Still, the worldwide economic slowdown has clobbered the globalizing Japanese economy, as its export markets have shriveled and its own stock market has tumbled.

CHAPTER 8

Japan's Place in the World

INTRODUCTION

The theme of this book is that Japan's old policy equilibrium was upset in the 1980s and early 1990s by the forces of globalization. The political coalitions that sustained LDP power were split asunder when export markets were threatened with protectionism, and the interests of big business diverged from those of farmers and small firms in the nontradable sectors. The LDP did its best to shore up this coalition for a time, but ultimately required political reform and policy reform to construct a new support coalition.

The foreign policy challenges that Japan has faced since 1989, from the collapse of the Berlin Wall and the Gulf War, to the North Korean nuclear crisis and the rise of China, to the wars in Afghanistan and Iraq, were, of course, exogenous to the domestic politics of Japan. On the economic front, alarm bells went off in 2007 when Japan dropped below China for the first time on a list of countries ranked by international competitiveness by the International Institute for Management Development in Switzerland.[1] Japanese governments would have had to find some way to respond to these and other stimuli no matter what electoral rule governed how Japanese politicians attained office, and no matter the state of the Japanese economy. But we argue in this chapter that the particular ways the Japanese government has responded, and the implications of those responses for the future of Japanese foreign policy, cannot be fully understood without an appreciation of how the domestic politics of foreign policy making have changed over the period.

In 1993, the year heavyweight politician Ozawa Ichiro left the LDP to launch a new opposition party that later became the Democratic Party of Japan, he published a book urging Japan to become a "normal nation."[2] As the world's second-largest economy, wrote Ozawa, Japan should

---

This chapter draws heavily on Rosenbluth, Sato, and Zinn 2008.

[1] Japan fell to twenty-fourth, below China's fifteenth. "China Overtakes Japan in International Competitiveness." *Yomiuri Shimbun*, May 11, 2007.

[2] Ozawa 1993.

abandon its foreign policy minimalism that eschewed foreign entanglements while preying on the rest of the world with beggar-thy-neighbor economic protectionism. Among other things, Ozawa took frontal aim at Japan's "Peace Constitution," which had been imposed by the U.S. Occupation authorities but was now kept alive by an odd domestic coalition of pacifists on the left and capitalists on the right who, each for different reasons, preferred that the government limit defense expenditures and commitments.

Ozawa's foreign policy prescription, in the place of the LDP's post-Occupation inertia, was for Japan to accept the military burdens and open markets that accompany economic might. To Ozawa, Japan had been essentially bribing the U.S. government to tolerate chronic trade surpluses by making an enormous military contribution to the United States, including payment out of Japan's general account budget for the living costs of more than 100,000 American soldiers stationed on Japanese soil. If Japan were to deregulate its economy and open its markets to foreign products, Ozawa reasoned, Japan would be free to negotiate the U.S.-Japan security relationship on a more equal basis, in the way, say, NATO countries relate to the United States. Ozawa had been the architect of the 1992 UN International Peace Cooperation Law that authorized sending Japanese armed personnel abroad without resolving whether or not troop deployment was constitutional—in that instance, for Japanese soldiers to be deployed in noncombat roles in postwar Cambodia.[3]

One need not read into Ozawa's vision a veiled threat of nationalist and militarist revival. Ozawa's vision was avowedly realist, accepting the U.S.-Japan military alliance as the central and still irreplaceable feature of Japan's security policy. What Ozawa had in mind was not for Japan to attempt to bump the United States off its hegemonic pedestal, but to gain policy leverage by removing a constant irritant to the United States, namely, Japan's mercantilist trade policies. Japan could be a normal rather than an indebted ally once Japan's markets were open and Japan no longer had to buy U.S. goodwill on the economic front with favors in the defense realm. Furthermore, Ozawa cannot have failed to notice, the defense-for-trade deals seldom worked in Japan's favor because Congress often refused to play along with the administration and Department of Defense.

In the years after Ozawa wrote his book, Japan moved in the direction

---

[3]Although Japanese public support of the deployment wavered when two soldiers were killed early in their mission, the forces returned to Japan in 1993 to a hero's welcome. Japan subsequently sent troops to UN-sponsored peacekeeping operations in Mozambique in 1992, Zaire and Tanzania in 1994, the Golan Heights in 1996, and East Timor in 2002.

of his blueprint, if not in all of its particulars.[4] Importantly, the electoral rule change of 1994 brought foreign policy into public discussion in the same way that it has put the spotlight on domestic policy. Under the old electoral rule, politicians competed on their ability to provide pork and patronage, and there was no particularistic benefit attached to focusing on foreign policy matters. Now that politicians compete for office by taking positions on public policy issues that affect many voters, rather than building personal support networks on countless favors to donors and individual voters, public policy—foreign and domestic—has begun to figure more prominently in electoral campaigning.[5]

In this chapter, we explore how changes in Japan's electoral rules shifted the ground from under the foreign policy-making process, with the result that the Japanese public became more interested in taking an active role in world affairs. Japan's foreign policy during the postwar years had been a residual category of domestic politics,[6] often messy and inconsistent. Domestic politics of course continues to exert a profound influence on Japan's foreign policy, as it does in every country. But foreign policy in postwar Japan—and the central tenet of keeping ties with the United States on even keel—was squeezed into a small space that LDP leaders and bureaucrats of the Ministry of Foreign Affairs did their best to protect against LDP backbenchers' local spending and policy priorities. Under the changed electoral incentives after 1994, it became not only acceptable but imperative for politicians to have views about foreign affairs as well as other issues of national importance. Foreign policy has become the subject of public interest, scrutiny, and debate.

JAPAN'S POSTWAR FOREIGN POLICY

Japan's foreign policy was remarkably stable through the tumultuous years of the Cold War, the decline and reemergence of U.S. hegemony, and the rise of China as a regional and global power. Relying on the Security Treaty with the United States, the Japanese government hewed closely to the policy established by Prime Minister Yoshida Shigeru during the Occupation: concede to the United States as much as necessary,

---

[4]We do not mean to imply here that Ozawa himself was the driving force behind the policy changes, especially considering that he was a leader of various opposition parties throughout the period.

[5]Köllner 2007.

[6]Calder 1988.

but as little as possible. Yoshida managed to hide behind Article 9 to limit Japanese financial contributions to its own defense, and to keep open a small flow of economic exchange with China that was at variance with the American strategy to "contain" the spread of communism.[7]

During the Occupation, American officials had done their best to subdue the Left, purging thousands of Socialist and Communist politicians and union organizers from positions of responsibility and censoring their publications. When the Occupation was over, American diplomats continued to monitor the Left, as well as the activities of the merely sympathetic. An indication of jittery American nerves is revealed in a recently declassified secret note written to the State Department by Ralph J. Blake, the American consul general in Kobe in 1955, about a Japanese Methodist minister, Tanimoto Kiyoshi, who wanted to establish a peace memorial in Hiroshima. Besides the peace memorial project, Tanimoto's other visible activity was to conduct a speaking tour of American churches to raise money for twenty-five victims of the atomic bomb awaiting plastic surgery to remove their keloid scars. Blake warned, "The Reverend Tanimoto is pictured as one who appears to be anti-Communist and probably sincere in his efforts to assist the girls.... However, in his desire to enhance his own prestige and importance he might ignorantly, innocently, or purposefully lend himself to or pursue a leftist line."[8]

As it turned out, the mild-mannered Methodist minister was the least of the Americans' problems. The Socialist and Communist parties, capitalizing on the horrors of the Hiroshima and Nagasaki atomic bombs, put the peace movement to powerful political use. On the streets and in Diet proceedings, the Left protested energetically against a U.S.-Japan alliance that "stank of gunpowder" (*kinakusai kankei*). They warned of impending embroilment in America's foreign military adventures and sounded the alarm about the steady growth of American nuclear capability. It did not help the American image in Japan when several Japanese fishermen were irradiated by fallout from an even bigger atomic bomb tested at the Bikini Atoll in the South Pacific in 1954. Radiation sickness, which patients experience in increasingly gruesome phases for years or even decades, periodically provided fresh and eminently newsworthy ma-

---

[7]Secretary of State John Foster Dulles made it clear to Prime Minister Yoshida that a condition of the U.S.-Japan security alliance was that Japan recognize the Chiang Kai-shek government on Taiwan as the legitimate government of China, and eschew official relations with Mao's Communist China.

[8]Hersey 1989: 147.

terial for the Japanese media to broadcast to the dismayed public about the inhumane destructiveness of nuclear weapons.[9]

In 1960, when President Eisenhower and Prime Minister Kishi were to sign a revised bilateral Security Treaty, the political Left put up a spectacular display of opposition with the help of idealistic students and a public in full-blown allergic reaction to militarism. In fact, the revised treaty contained provisions more favorable to Japan, because for the first time the United States promised to come to Japan's aid in the event of attack rather than only using Japan as a forward staging base for American operations in Asia as the original treaty had stipulated. But it was not so much the terms of the treaty that many Japanese found objectionable, as the fact that Japan was subordinating its foreign policy to that of America's global strategy in a very general sense. An angry mob thronged the motorcade of Eisenhower's press secretary, James Haggerty, bouncing on his car and pounding angrily on his windows. Although Haggerty managed to beat a hasty retreat to the airport and flee the country unscathed, the Eisenhower administration was spooked by the incident and canceled the state visit. The treaty revision passed the LDP-controlled Diet anyway, but not without ferocious protests on the streets and a few fistfights on the floor of the legislature before it was all over.[10]

The anti-security-treaty clamor was dissipated as a result of the LDP's successful substitution of massive favor mongering for political debate.[11] Although the systemization of the LDP's electoral strategy took some years after the party's formation in 1955, by the mid- to late 1960s the LDP's electoral machine worked as beautifully to cultivate votes as an enormous network of sprinklers irrigates a parched landscape. Giving up on the viability of the Left as a policy anchor against the LDP, the right wing of the Socialist Party split off in 1960 to form the Democratic Socialist Party, and the Komeito formed as a new moderate party in 1964. Both parties went along with the Security Treaty, at least passively, giving the LDP enough votes in the Diet to pass subsequent revisions without effective opposition.

The LDP's electoral strategy required the creation of a complex set of

[9]Hersey 1989: 96, 136. The "Bravo" bomb was said to have thirteen hundred times the destructive force of the bomb that destroyed Hiroshima. A map of the boat's route and proximity at the time of the explosion can be viewed at http://www.pcf.city.hiroshima.jp/virtual/VirtualMuseum_e/exhibit_e/exh0503_e/exh05032_e.html.

[10]Scalapino and Masumi 1962; Packard 1966.

[11]This is not to say that the 1960 Security Treaty Crisis was the end of violent public protest in Japan. See Marotti 2009 for an excellent discussion of the rise and fall of protest politics over security issues.

personal loyalties allocated among copartisans, rather than the clear articulation of public policies that would paint all LDP politicians with the same brush. As surely as pigs to a trough, LDP politicians gravitated to committee assignments that would give them access to favors with which to attract money and votes. Party and Diet committees on defense and foreign affairs were among the least popular, and were typically filled by party seniors who had already secured safe seats, or by members of the Upper House whose election was assured by their location on party-controlled lists rather than by the cultivation of a personal following.

Japan's response to the Iraqi invasion of Kuwait in the summer of 1990 provides a window into postwar Japanese foreign policy making, characterized by Japan's supporting the United States as much as necessary to keep the alliance healthy, but as little as possible to preserve resources for domestic use. Because foreign policy was the province of LDP leaders, while backbenchers busied themselves cultivating local electoral support with policy favors, Japan's strategic interests were rarely the subject of national attention, and money for foreign ventures was always tight. In spite of the enormous importance of Kuwaiti oil to the Japanese economy, Japan did not join the coalition of thirty-four countries organized to enforce the United Nations Resolution 678, which set a withdrawal deadline for Iraqi armies. Nor did Japan rush to pledge financial support for the U.S.-led military operation to oust Iraqi forces from Kuwait.

By the end of the Gulf War six months later, however, Japan had provided $15 billion in support of the operation, far more than any other ally and over a fourth of the $54 billion of total aid the United States received from the coalition. And yet Japan endured a severe public relations beating from parts of the U.S. government and media for being a reluctant (and merely financial) contributor.[12] Absent domestic political incentives to grapple with foreign policy choices, however, the LDP government was a reluctant buyer of American foreign policy at prices largely dictated in Washington.

NEW RULES OF THE GAME

The electoral reform of 1994 worked in the direction of a more activist foreign policy in two ways. First, rank-and-file politicians now have more

---

[12]Niksch and Sutter 1991. Secretary of State James Baker chided the Japanese government, saying, "Your checkbook diplomacy, like our dollar diplomacy of an earlier era, is clearly too narrow." Ishizuka 2005: 67.

incentive to take a stand on foreign policy issues. To an odd degree for one of the world's largest economies, foreign policy and defense debates had been absent from national election campaigns between the 1960s and the 1990s.[13] Electoral competition under the new mixed-member system, by contrast, directs public attention to differences among parties in the place of differences among candidates of the same party. In the single-member districts, the one candidate who gains the most support wins the seat, placing a premium on candidates who can present voters with broadly appealing policy platforms. In the proportional representation tier, parties win seats according to how well they convince voters of the merits of their platforms for advancing Japan's security and welfare, broadly conceived.[14]

The second effect of the changed electoral rules on security policy was in concentrating more powers in the office of the prime minister, enabling him to speak more decisively on behalf of the governing party and the country. Because backbenchers benefit from a coherent party platform and a leader who can execute campaign promises, there is less inclination than before to constrain the party president (who is also the prime minister) with checks on his power. The LDP responded to the new incentives by revising the Cabinet Law in 2000, giving the prime minister greater authority to propose and draft policy from above rather than to await the bubbling up of initiatives and compromises from the ministries and the associated party committees. The cabinet secretary, as the chief administrative supporter of the prime minister, was given a larger staff and additional authority previously divided among the ministries of finance, foreign affairs, and defense. Legislation in 2003 equipped the cabinet secretary's Security Council, previously an advisory body with little independent information or authority, with new resources to cope with potential emergencies as they arose instead of moving through a complex array of ministerial and party committees as in the past.[15]

Prime Minister Koizumi's swift response in 2001 to support the U.S. military in Afghanistan and then Iraq, though unpopular in Japan, stood in stark contrast to Prime Minister Kaifu's prolonged hand-wringing over the Gulf War a decade earlier. In a historic departure from prior foreign

---

[13]Nagahisa 1994.

[14]Once aspirants to office had to woo voters on the basis of issues, internal party committees with jurisdiction over national policy took on more importance for politically ambitious politicians. Moreover, politicians began to feature foreign policy issues in their campaign material (and, now, on their Web pages) in a way that was almost completely absent under the old system.

[15]Estévez-Abe, Hikotani, and Nagahisa 2008.

policy, Japan sent a contingent of some six hundred soldiers to perform support and humanitarian roles in Iraq, the first foreign deployment of Japanese troops to a war zone since the end of World War II. There is no doubt that Koizumi's more decisive personality played a role, as did the 70 percent popularity rating that gave him a few points to burn in managing Japan's foreign relations. But another way to think about Koizumi's actions is that Japan's new electoral rules made the election of a strong leader like him more likely and gave him more room for maneuver against backbencher resistance. We argue that the ascension of Koizumi was an effect of the political reform, not an independent cause.

POLICY CHANGES AND JAPAN'S NEW NATIONALISM

Japan's postreform policy-making apparatus shapes the style and content of Japan's foreign policy in discernible ways, some of which have been taken to signal the frightening reappearance of militarist nationalism. Several "straws in the wind" have particularly worried neighboring countries who experienced Japan's wartime depredations. The Japanese Ministry of Education has permitted the publication of several history textbooks that whitewash Japan's actions in Asia in the 1930s and 1940s. LDP politicians continue to conduct official visits to Yasukuni Shrine to pay their respects to soldiers who died in World War II, including seven military and political leaders hanged by Occupation forces for war crimes. As if that were not enough, a majority of Japanese now support revising Article 9 of the constitution.[16] In this section, we sift through the evidence surrounding each of these issues for possible signs of rising Japanese nationalism.

The Textbook Controversy

Japan's Ministry of Education, Culture, Sports and Technology (MEXT) reviews and authorizes textbooks every four years for use in Japanese public- and private-school curricula. This is a role the government education bureaucracy has undertaken since the Meiji Restoration, and although the Japanese Supreme Court ruled in 1997 that the government ought to interfere as little as possible with the writers' views and school

---

[16]"52% Support Revision of Constitution," *Yomiuri Shimbun*, April 3, 2009, http://www.yomiuri.co.jp/dy/national/20090403TDY01305.htm.

boards' choices, they determined that the authorization process itself was not unconstitutional.[17] The government's oversight of school textbooks has been a lightning rod for Asian countries' ire at what they perceive as Japan's anemic remorse for the devastation and horrors wreaked on neighboring countries by the Japanese military before and during World War II. In 1982, a particularly rancorous exchange over Japanese textbooks led the Ministry of Education to include a provision in textbook guidelines that the sensitivity of Asian nations to wartime history be taken into account. But China and Korea in particular have often objected to textbook passages that understate the horrors of the war, including the Rape of Nanking, the testing of biological warfare on Chinese citizens, and the forcible recruitment of Asian women to service the sexual needs of Japanese soldiers.

Most recently, Asian feelings were inflamed by a "revisionist" textbook approved by the Japanese government in 2001 and again in 2005 that explicitly rejects a "masochistic view" of history and portrays Japan's war in Asia in largely defensive terms.[18] In 2005 the *China Daily* called the offending textbook "an unfit teaching tool," a "political provocation," and went on to comment that "without a consensus on the history issue and other disputes, the Asian peoples cannot place their trust in Japan's desire to play a bigger role in world affairs."[19] Undeterred, the LDP government approved legislation in April 2006 that would add "nurturing love of country" as an explicit aim of public education.[20]

Is Japan's textbook revisionism a harbinger of renewed nationalist fervor? Only eighteen of over forty thousand schools nationwide chose to adopt the particular textbook that provoked such a furor in 2001 and 2005, which means at most 0.04 percent of Japanese middle school students learn history through this lens. To the disappointment of the right-wing publishing company that produced the book, the vast majority of Japanese school boards chose textbooks that give a more full-bodied account of Japanese brutality in Asia. Even in most of the municipalities

[17]The Supreme Court ruling came down in response to one of the historian Ienaga Saburo's challenges against the government's censorship of his depiction of Japanese military brutality in the war against China from 1937 to 1945. The court was characteristically diplomatic, agreeing to the ministry's oversight role while urging forbearance.

[18]Ishiyama 2003. The principal author of this new textbook is a former leftist historian who rejected Japan's self-abnegating view of history during a sabbatical year in the United States. For more about this unapologetic textbook, see the publishing company's Web page at http://www.tsukurukai.com.

[19]*BBC News* 2005.

[20]*Taipei Times* 2006.

where the controversial textbook was adopted, groups of parents and concerned citizens petitioned against the book's use. Some LDP politicians and Japanese government officials were sympathetic to self-congratulatory history, to be sure, but opposition parties in the Diet challenged the government at every turn, and the textbook disputes do not appear to signal a rising tide of militarist nationalism among the Japanese public at large.

Yasukuni Shrine

If China and Korea take textbook revisionism as a sign of callous disregard for the feelings of Asian populations victimized by Japanese military expansion, they view official visits by Japanese politicians to Yasukuni Shrine as bald endorsements of Japan's militarist past at the highest levels of power. Built in 1869 to commemorate soldiers killed in the imperial campaign against the Tokugawa, Yasukuni Shrine became the center of the cult of the emperor promoted by the military in the 1930s.[21] Although Yasukuni became a private Shinto organization in 1947 when the postwar constitution mandated separation of church and state, the shrine contains the remains and tokens of Japan's war dead, and is viewed by opponents and supporters alike as a central shrine of state Shinto.[22]

In 1978, in deference to the Bereaved Families Association (*Nihon Izokukai*) and other conservative groups that had pressed for decades for the proper burial of General Tojo Hideki and six other military leaders who had been hanged for war crimes, the LDP quietly moved the remains of these men to Yasukuni.[23] The loud objections of opponents and victims of the war, both inside and outside Japan, have continued ever since.

LDP prime ministers have often visited Yasukuni Shrine, in a show of respect to the war dead required by the conservative flank of the party's electoral base. The Bereaved Families Association, which represented the families of the war dead, has claimed membership of about two million, but more important to the LDP was its high level of organization that could deliver votes with certainty. Although the association is losing po-

---

[21] In 1932, a group of Catholic students refused to take part in a school trip to Yasukuni Shrine on grounds of religious freedom. To skirt possible constitutional problems in requiring schoolchildren to participate in shrine rituals, the military government declared that Shinto shrines were nonreligious institutions whose purpose was to foster loyalty to the emperor. Weinstein 1983a.

[22] The holiest shrine is the Grand Shrine of Ise, dedicated to the sun goddess Amaterasu Omikami, who in Shinto belief is the mother of Japan's first emperor, Jimmu.

[23] Weinstein 1983b.

litical clout as "bereaved families" age and change priorities, Prime Minister Koizumi visited Yasukuni Shrine every year while he was in office, from 2001 to 2006.

The governments of China and Korea issued formal protests at each of Koizumi's official visits. In 2003, South Korean president Kim Dae Jung urged the Japanese government to move the Class A war criminals to another burial site, and though Koizumi set up a commission to study the possibility, he stuck with the status quo when the commission deadlocked. Koizumi continued to visit the shrine each year, and in 2005 Korea temporarily withdrew its ambassador to Japan to underscore its objection.[24] Koizumi's successor, Abe Shinzo, cooled diplomatic temperatures by eschewing a Yasukuni visit on August 15, 2007, but he remained an unsympathetic character in Asia for his emphasis on patriotism and for his misty-eyed references to Japan's traditional values.[25]

It may be, as some observers have noted, that the Chinese and Korean governments enjoy the popular support in their countries that Japanese insensitivity generates for them.[26] But at a minimum, official visits to Yasukuni Shrine seem to signify a government willingness to irritate neighboring countries that see themselves as war victims. The Yasukuni visits raise the broader question of whether the Japanese government was pandering to nationalist public opinion at home, or whether the LDP was trying to cook up a new batch of nationalism. If support for Yasukuni visits was already high, politicians could score easy points by braving foreign ire to make the trip.

One might imagine that Japan's prolonged economic malaise gave rise to spontaneous expressions of nationalism by economic losers who gain psychic satisfaction from belonging to a winning cause, or that politicians attempted to stoke nationalist opinion as a way to generate political support around nonmaterial issues. Perhaps the government sought to stoke nationalism as a way of distracting the public from economic woes, particularly those at the losing end of economic restructuring, if economic losers are more likely to identify with nationalist causes.[27]

The fact that Japanese public opinion, particularly among urban voters,

[24]*Yonhap News* 2006.

[25]Abe's decision to stay away might have been a calculation as much of the domestic response as of the international one. Abe spent most of his brief tenure prioritizing constitutional reform and a "strong Japan," and watched his popularity plummet as voters prioritized the perilous state of the economy.

[26]Shayo 2005.

[27]Shayo 2005.

has remained mildly negative over the years toward these official visits casts doubt on the broader claims about playing the nationalism card to a wide domestic audience.[28] Business leaders were also concerned about inciting the antagonism of neighboring trading partners, and in 2006 Okuda Hiroshi, a Toyota executive and head of the Japan Business Federation (*Keidanren*), officially expressed misgivings about prime ministers' official visits to Yasukuni Shrine. Hojo Kakutaro, chairman of the Japan Association of Corporate Executives (*Keizai Doyukai*) followed soon thereafter with a similar statement.

Rather than pandering to a latent-but-prevalent xenophobia, Koizumi appears to have been engaging in a strategic ploy to solidify his weak electoral flank vis-à-vis conservative, rural voters who would value symbolic gestures of this kind, while staying the course on his substantively pro-urban political and economic reforms. Before Koizumi won the LDP's presidential election in 2001, he was not among the group of Diet members vocally committed to visiting Yasukuni Shrine. By contrast, Hashimoto Ryutaro, his main opponent for the party presidency, was serving as head of the Bereaved Families Association, and Koizumi wanted to secure the core partisan vote in the LDP presidential election. Noteworthy also is that Koizumi was careful to avoid visiting Yasukuni immediately before the September 2005 general election. Unlike the election for the LDP presidency in which Koizumi was concerned principally with conservative voters, he needed support from centrist voters in the general election. The fact that Koizumi's successor, Abe Shinzo, took a drubbing in the 2007 Upper House elections, partly because of his hawkish foreign policy platform (and despite his avoidance of Yasukuni), suggests that the public was not leading the way and was unwilling even to follow.

The majority of LDP Diet members do not, in fact, visit Yasukuni Shrine, and such visits have decreased in recent years. It seems clear that LDP members are sensitive to the range of views within their constituencies about Yasukuni. Incumbents are not only supported by Shintoists, who are enthusiastic about increasing governmental involvement in Yasukuni, but also by other competing religious sects such as the Soka Gakkai that advocate establishment of a nonreligious commemorative facility for war casualties. The Soka Gakkai, as discussed in chapter 4, is the organizational cornerstone of Komeito, the LDP's junior coalition partner since 1998. In any given year, about a quarter of LDP legislators typically send

---

[28]"Public Opinion concerning Prime Ministers' Visit to Yasukuni Shrine," *Yomiuri Shimbun*, October 7, 1985; August 17, 2006.

a legislative secretary or some other proxy to the shrine rather than visit in person and incur the wrath of the Soka Gakkai on whom they may depend for vote mobilization.

Koizumi cultivated the U.S.-Japan alliance throughout his tenure, which bought him the security to snub the feelings of Asian neighbors. His championing of the interests of urban voters also bought him some freedom on symbolic issues such as Yasukuni that had deep and special meaning for rural voters. Although his successor, Abe, was a more genuine believer in what Harvey Mansfield would call "a manly history" of Japan,[29] voters rejected his vision, at least when it came at the expense of dealing with economic and social security issues that they felt were more pressing.

Article 9

Article 9 of the constitution of Japan is a product of institutional design that the American Occupiers soon came to rue. Entitled "Renunciation of War" it reads:

> Aspiring sincerely to an international peace based on justice and order, the Japanese people forever renounce war as a sovereign right of the nation and the threat or use of force as means of settling international disputes.
>
> In order to accomplish the aim of the preceding paragraph, land, sea, and air forces, as well as other war potential, will never be maintained. The right of belligerency of the state will not be recognized.

Although a peace pledge made sense in 1946 to the Allied victors seeking to avoid a resurgence of Japanese militarism, within a couple of years the United States had changed its priority to combating communism worldwide and would have preferred for Japan to put considerable resources into U.S.-directed military spending. But unlike other democratization measures, such as economic deconcentration, that were not difficult to reverse, constitutional entrenchment of the peace pledge made remilitarization difficult for the United States to demand. Prime Minister Yoshida Shigeru won his place in history using the U.S.-made constitution to rebuff American requests for Japanese remilitarization, saving the government budget for civilian rebuilding.[30]

The "Yoshida Doctrine," which called for spending as little as possible

[29]Mansfield 2006.
[30]Yoshitsu 1982.

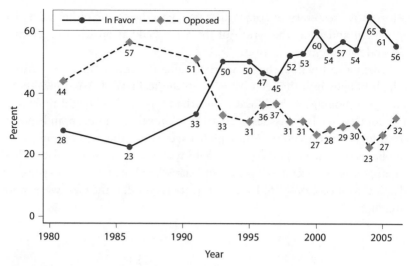

Figure 8.1. Public Opinion concerning Constitutional Revision
  Source: *Yomiuri Shimbun*, various issues.

on defense, while paying as much as necessary for the U.S. nuclear umbrella, allowed Japan to keep defense expenditures within more or less 1 percent of GNP for the entire postwar period. But as the Japanese economic miracle unfolded, 1 percent of Japan's GNP became a staggering amount of money. Today, Japan's defense expenditures are among the largest in the world. To be sure, Russia and China have far more military personnel under arms, and Japan lacks their offensive capability. But Japan has long ago ceased to be a defenseless country in any meaningful sense of the word.

Public opinion in favor of revising the constitution began to rise in the mid-1980s and finally tipped into majority position in the mid-1990s (see fig. 8.1). Coupled with this openness to constitutional revision is growing public approval for teaching about defense and foreign policy in schools. But mainstream opinion opposes nuclear armament or going it alone outside the U.S.-Japan Security Treaty framework.[31] Evidently, the Japanese public is willing to own up to a reality that is already here: Japan is an enormous, but defensive and status-quo-favoring military power, and Article 9 is a flagrant falsehood. The groups that favor going nuclear or preach the glories of military aggrandizement have never been more fringe than they are today, though their voices are heard in the public debate over foreign policy that had been absent for forty years.

[31]Hughes 2004.

PIECING TOGETHER THE EVIDENCE

The asymmetry in public opinion across different dimensions of foreign policy suggests that nationalism is not an insidious new force in Japan.[32] While Japanese show growing interest in an active foreign policy, proxied in figure 8.2 by the percentage of respondents who think Japan should be a permanent member of the UN Security Council, this is not matched by a growing national pride, or willingness to support the government's foreign policy, "right or wrong."

Japanese feelings of national pride have remained stable over recent decades and are not particularly high by international standards. According to opinion polls, in Japan a smaller percentage of the citizens take pride in their history than is true of the populations of most developed countries, far behind not only the United States and the United Kingdom but other World War II aggressors such as Germany and Italy as well. Japanese citizens are also lukewarm, by OECD standards, in support for their government "through thick and thin." While a third of Americans say they support their government even when they believe the government is wrong, only a quarter of the Japanese respondents expressed this kind of unconditional support. Moreover, this percentage has not increased in Japan between 1995 and 2003.[33]

The backdrop against which to view the rising public support in Japan for an active foreign policy is the shift in Japan's geopolitical position. Japanese increasingly view China's rise with alarm, because rising powers tend to be "revisionist," or inclined to change the status quo through territorial or economic expansionism. The Japanese interest in creating a balance of power with China is heightened by the growing tensions between the two countries, which have focused on competition for raw materials and markets, and for which Japanese textbooks and other signs of Japan's perceived lack of remorse are merely a lightning rod for Chinese competitiveness.[34]

Oddly enough, however, Japan's defense spending seems only weakly related to its geopolitical challenges. The LDP government has held Japan's

---

[32]Against the possible argument that pacifist passivity is simply wearing off as the people who experienced the war die off, support for an active foreign policy has been growing across age cohorts in Japan, and, indeed, older voters are somewhat more supportive of an active foreign policy than are younger voters.

[33]International Social Survey Programme (1998, 2003).

[34]"China's Economy Sways the World," *Yomiuri Shimbun*, March 21, 2007, p. 4; "China Challenges U.S. Hegemony," *Yomiuri Shimbun*, February 7, 2007.

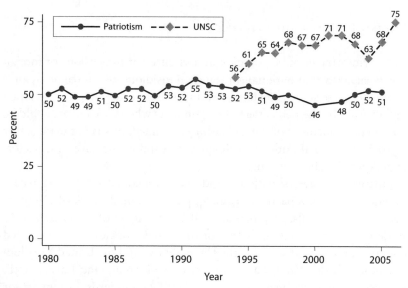

Figure 8.2. Strength of Patriotism.
The percentage of respondents who regard themselves as patriotic (dark line) and support Japan's permanent seat in the UN Security Council (gray line)
Source: Cabinet Office (http://www8.cao.go.jp/survey/index-sha.html).

military expenditures steady at 1 percent of GNP before and after the Cold War, and before and after China's debut on the international scene as a great power. This reveals the extent to which Japan relies on economic engagement and U.S. military might for its security. The LDP government has remained sufficiently confident of the U.S. defense commitment to avoid a military buildup on an even bigger scale that would only alarm its neighbors and fuel an explosive regional security dilemma. This fact, of course, serves to endorse rather than refute the Japanese government's realist calculations about the costs and benefits of going it alone, without the United States.[35] What realism cannot explain, however, is why the Japanese public has become more interested in these issues and is willing to take a more active part in foreign policy debates.[36] For that, we do well to abandon the realist fiction that the Japanese state simply

[35]Hughes 2004.

[36]For that matter, one might also ask why the Japanese public was not visibly worried about the Soviet threat during the Cold War. The Soviet shooting down of a Korean civilian aircraft near Japan in 1983 did not translate in Japanese opinion polls into a desire for a more active security policy.

maximized its national utility, and consider instead the changed domestic political incentives regarding public discussion of foreign policy issues.

Taken together, evidence from Japanese public opinion and elsewhere points to a public that supports an active role in world affairs, not out of an urge for dominion or escapism from domestic woes, but from an informed sense of Japan's options and international obligations. Japan's relationship with China remains on more or less even keel. It is true that recent revelations of tainted products from China, including poisonous milk powder and toxic toothpaste, dumplings, and bean paste, have made many Japanese uneasy about consuming Chinese goods.[37] Acid rain from China's coal furnaces is destroying some species of pine on Japan's northeast coast.[38] China's ambitious space programs and military expenditures, and China's unwillingness to push North Korea harder to release Japanese abductees, are other sources of Japanese uneasiness. On the other hand, Japanese prime ministers after Koizumi have been more tactful on the Yasukuni Shrine issue, and the two countries continue to benefit from enormous bilateral flows of goods and services.[39]

When it comes to Japan's role in the Middle East, the Japanese public has been critical of many aspects of the Iraq War and the American-led reconstruction of Iraq, but Japan remained the second-largest donor for postwar Iraq, behind only the United States. Japan's reconstruction efforts included training teachers, supporting the police, and restoring wetlands.[40] The LDP/Komeito government passed legislation authorizing Self Defense Forces to help refuel American ships in the Indian Ocean bound for Afghanistan, in the face of considerable criticism of Japanese involvement by the opposition DPJ.[41] The Japanese public divided on Japan's support for American foreign policy in the Middle East, but not deeply so, and on balance favored contributing to projects that were viewed by the international community as promoting peace and development.[42]

[37]"Sino-Japan Cooperation Vital over Gyoza Scandal," *Yomiuri Shimbun*, February 16, 2008; "Toxic Substances Found in Chinese Bean Paste," *Yomiuri Shimbun*, October 9, 2008.

[38]"Tinge of Green as China Becomes Top Polluter," *Japan Times*, October 6, 2008.

[39]"Fukuda, Hu Should Restore Diplomatic Balance," *Yomiuri Shimbun*, May 4, 2008; "Shirakaba Gas Field Key to 'Progress'; Japan, China Closer to Joint Development," *Yomiuri Shimbun*, May 9, 2008; "Japan, China Laud 'Successful' Summit," *Yomiuri Shimbun*, May 9, 2008; "Smoother Path between Rivals," *Japan Times*, May 9, 2008; "Japanese Banks Follow Manufacturers into China," *Japan Times*, December 30, 2005.

[40]"Kansai U.N. Offices Helping to Restore Iraq Marshlands," *Yomiuri Shimbun*, September 27, 2008.

[41]"Cabinet Extends MSDF Refuelling Duties," *Asahi News Service*, May 10, 2003.

[42]"SDF Still Looking for the Best Way to Make a Graceful Iraq Exit," *Asahi Shimbun*,

Neither xenophobia nor an aggressive foreign policy orientation is mounting in Japan. The public's views remain moderate, while showing a willingness to accept a larger responsibility for Japan's own defense in the face of growing international uncertainties. Japan's new domestic political climate, we suggest, has thrust these strategic issues to the forefront of electoral politics for the first time in decades. Japan's changed electoral rules motivate politicians to bring foreign policy issues into full public debate, and the public has responded by endorsing a realist foreign policy, but one that emerges from the shadows with greater transparency about its intentions and means.

Conclusions

The Japanese people's view of their role in the world reflects the calculations of a newly engaged citizenry about appropriate responses to Japan's changing international environment. Japan's geopolitical circumstances—particularly the rise of Chinese economic and military might and destabilizing shocks from North Korea—provide grist for domestic debate, but it is the new electoral environment at home that gives politicians an incentive to draw voters into this debate. As a result, voters have grown accustomed to thinking about Japan's foreign policy choices, and have expressed preferences for an open-eyed and self-conscious but clearly defense-oriented posture, for which the alliance with the United States remains the cornerstone.

What is novel about Japanese foreign policy making since the mid-1990s is not the outcomes, for even a rewrite of Article 9 would not open the floodgates of pent-up militarist longings. Opinion polls show neither signs of growing national pride nor an edgy discomfort with the geopolitical status quo that could spill over into support for a new round of military adventurism. Voter preferences are changing at the margin toward a more proactive role in foreign policy and in favor of changing Article 9 to fit with the realities of Japanese military power and roles. Support for the U.S.-Japan security alliance also remains strong, and for now, the public favors only incremental increases in defense spending along the lines of the old formula of keeping the United States happy.

Japan's neighbors count on the U.S.-Japan Security Treaty to rein in

March 20, 2006; "Japan Should Play a Larger Human Security Role," *Asahi News Service*, April 6, 2004; "Rebuilding Iraq Is the Path to a New World Order," *Asahi News Service*, March 20, 2004.

Japan's possible foreign policy aspirations, but it is likely that the bilateral nature of this treaty is partly responsible in the first place for Japan's insensitivity to its neighbors' concerns. In postwar Europe, where Germany was embedded in a multilateral NATO and an increasingly vibrant common market, sensitivity to the feelings of former war victims of German wartime aggression was mandated at the highest level of government and enforced down the chain to localities and private actors.[43] In Japan, where U.S. patronage could trump regional ill will on the strategic stage, the pressure to show remorse was weaker and came principally from Japanese business interests that were, in any case, powerless to stop the fulminations of right-wingers with megaphones.

Of course, politics is not only about cool calculations, and it is possible that Japan's "cool nationalism" could turn hot under some conditions. Although there are no signs yet of politicians stoking emotional fires under national identity, perhaps growing income inequality will tempt politicians to invoke nationalist symbolism to curry electoral favor. In addition, some worry that Japan's irritation with China's and Korea's constant harping could grow into full-blown fury. Nationalism in China and Korea, by comparison with that in Japan, is "hot" in the sense that it translates into intense national pride, and is easily mobilized for angry protests and denunciations of countries such as Japan. There is some danger, perhaps, that persistent anti-Japanese rhetoric could turn the Japanese public's current "apology fatigue" into virulent xenophobia.

There are, however, strong reasons to doubt the "hot nationalism" scenario. First, most voters appreciate that Japan's geopolitical situation is extremely constraining. Venting public rage at China's or Korea's opportunistic use of wartime history would not enhance Japan's security or livelihood. For now, and for the foreseeable future, Japanese recognize the limits of their room for maneuver even as they consider abandoning parchment pledges such as Article 9 that are out of line with the reality. Second, Japan's new electoral rules push the two largest parties to target their appeals to the middle of the political spectrum. Although there is a small minority of right-wing fanatics in Japan who want to relive the glory days of regional expansion, their voices are ridiculed in mainstream politics. Nationalist feelings, however intensely held by some groups on the right or opposed by those on the left, are massaged into something quite tame in the vast middle of the political spectrum.

[43]Lind 2008.

CHAPTER 9

Conclusions

INTRODUCTION

Deep changes are under way in Japan's political economy, prompted by a reorganization of the dominant economic interests in Japan and underwritten by new rules of political competition. But in another sense, Japan is the very embodiment of stability, for these changes have not called into question the legitimacy of democracy itself. In contrast to the violent coup that brought an end to Japanese legislative politics in 1932, it is now unthinkable that Japan would succumb to a military overthrow or that the LDP would react to electoral loss by bringing in the tanks. The fact that Japanese democracy routinely survives pitched battles over the costs and benefits of globalization illustrates the profound difference between regime stability and policy stasis.

Japan is a wealthy democracy that, like other countries with this happy combination, provides a window into the reasons capitalism and democracy often find themselves paired together. But the coupling can take many forms. Japan has experimented not only with democracy in different institutional configurations, but with various flavors of capitalism as well. Japan's peculiar SNTV electoral system since 1925 generated strong incentives to ply interest groups with policy favors, a pattern that was always inefficient, but became a serious problem only after Japan came under irresistible pressure to open its markets to foreign trade and finance. Majoritarian politics, more than many other forms of electoral competition, tends to generate relatively free markets, because productive economic sectors find natural allies in the average consumers and taxpayers who are politically privileged under majoritarian rules. By contrast, some rich democracies, such as those in continental Europe, allocate the costs and benefits of global economic integration across groups in a way that limits the growth of income inequality. In Japan in the 1990s, successful businesses resisted that blend of institutions and policies that they feared would perpetuate protection of the economy's least productive sectors. Although competition will inject dynamism into Japan's economy, Japan is likely to drop down in the league tables of the world's most equal nations.

The same post-1994 electoral rules that drew voters into partisan debates over economic policy have also sparked new public awareness of, and interest in, foreign policy. We do not believe that a more inclusive policy-making process will necessarily create a more peace-loving foreign policy (sometimes populism can turn aggressive, after all). At the same time, we also see little reason to worry that the Japanese public is in danger of being overcome by xenophobia. For its many flaws, one of the virtues of the majoritarian electoral system is that it tends to marginalize fringe impulses, including radical brands of nationalism. Japan's role in the world in the first part of the twenty-first century will be less passive than it has been since 1945, but still far more modest than the adventurism of the early twentieth century.

JAPANESE DEMOCRACY

Democracy is put to the test when a government is voted out of power. The incumbent government can pack its bags and leave in hopes of another chance at the polls, or it can barricade itself in office in defiance of the people's choice. After a decade of shifting coalitions before 1955, Japan's democracy did not face this test again for nearly four decades. But it passed the test in 1993, when disenchanted voters deprived the LDP of its legislative majority in the Diet, bringing in a coalition government of traditional opposition parties and LDP defectors.

Or did Japan, in fact, pass the test? In less than a year the LDP was back again.[1] How different is Japan from soft authoritarian regimes[2] that operate through dominant parties and retain office through extensive corruption?

Japan had functioning democratic institutions from 1945 onward, in the sense that parties competed in fairly contested elections in an environment of free speech and freedom of association. It is important to remember that even if the LDP's majority was rarely in doubt for decades, nearly all individual LDP incumbents were "running scared" at each and every election. Even relatively senior incumbents would lose an election, accept the outcome, and regroup to regain a seat the next time around.[3] The

[1]Although the Socialist Murayama Tomiichi was prime minister from June 1994 through January 1996, the LDP dominated that coalition government, and every prime minister since Murayama has come from the LDP.

[2]Johnson 1987.

[3]Most often, an incumbent LDP MP's election loss would be at the hands of a candidate backed by a rival faction, so Steven Reed (1994) has referred to this phenomenon quite aptly as a game of "musical chairs," in which one viable candidate was left standing when

LDP's dominance, through the party's control of electorally relevant resources, is an extreme case of soft power that exists along a continuum in democratic systems. In every democracy, ordinary voters who might wish to boot out an incumbent party face a collective action problem, but the problem is more severe in personalistic systems like postwar Japan's in which politicians used money and other favors to "buy" insurance against unfavorable party swings. Japan's multimember districts, which posed an inconvenience to majority-seeking parties by forcing them to field multiple candidates in direct competition with one another, also shifted electoral competition away from programmatic appeals to personal loyalty. Under those conditions, disenchanted voters' collective action problem was magnified by their inability to vote on the basis of party platforms; resources trumped all else. A conservative party such as the LDP, which could appeal to business interests and milk them for campaign financing, was the hands-down favorite to dominate such a system. Insofar as it was the party in power, the LDP's control over government resources also produced something of a virtuous cycle (or a vicious one from the Opposition's perspective) in a system based on clientelism.[4]

By the early 1990s, the LDP was being scissored by voters who had become more expensive to buy, on the one hand, and businesses that were less willing to provide the money, on the other. Urbanization increased the number of voters who cared more about clean air and disposable income, leaving fewer farmers to sustain the party on the basis of agricultural protection alone. Economic development increased the number of businesses that cared more about low taxes and fiscal responsibility than about special favors, while global economic integration undermined the ability of the unproductive sectors to compensate the LDP for the ever-increasing levels of protection that those backwater industries required. Although the LDP tried to add urban voters and competitive businesses to its coalition of protected sectors, the marriage of convenience to keep the LDP in power came at a high cost for Japanese society's rising groups: urbanites and competitive sectors.

Although the LDP's electoral margins had been shrinking for decades, more LDP politicians saw the writing on the wall when the bubble economy collapsed. The electoral rule change was a compromise between an LDP trying to make the best of a bad situation and an Opposition trying

---

the music stopped at the end of each round. We hasten to emphasize, however, that for the competitors themselves, it was less a game than it was a cutthroat competition.

[4] Reed and Bolland 1999; Scheiner 2006.

to engineer more turnover in government. By agreeing to the PR tier, which keeps the Opposition divided with the allure of small party survival, the LDP gave itself some breathing room. But the majoritarian pull of the single-seat districts was sufficiently strong to create (after a couple of attempts in the immediate postreform free-for-all) a large party competitor, and the LDP did its best to remake itself as a party of urban consumers and competitive businesses.

The LDP has survived so far as a powerful party, but only because it has begun to adapt to new conditions of electoral competition. It is no longer the case that the LDP's control of local clientelistic networks can trump all counterappeals to ordinary voters, forcing the LDP to play a catch-up game in popular electioneering. The party's 2005 Lower House triumph, run as a referendum on Koizumi's reform agenda, announced that this was not the LDP of the 1960s, 1970s, or 1980s.[5]

Unfortunately for reformers, Koizumi's successors, especially Prime Minister Aso Taro, responded to the 2007 setback by backpedaling to assuage rural voters, rather than by calling the DPJ's bluff as the new "pro-rural" party and continuing to push the reform agenda. This waffling, in addition to the government's seeming inability to cope with the financial crisis that began in 2008, led to the LDP's poor showing in the 2009 Lower House election (see the epilogue to this book). Another LDP split is certainly possible, as the Koizumian reformers who survived the 2009 election cut bait and leave the old guard a much-reduced rump party in opposition. Whether the LDP manages to hang together and learns its lesson, or whether it finally collapses, we are confident that any future ruling party or coalition will have to resume the reforms that the LDP started, and that the new logic of Japanese politics demands.

DEMOCRACY AND CAPITALISM

Much of the writing about Japanese politics is preoccupied, in turns, with the LDP's long-standing hegemony or its impending demise. While fascinating in its own right, the drama of the LDP's hold on power is dwarfed in substantive significance by the profound changes ongoing in Japan's

---

[5]We recognize that the LDP has continued to dominate rural districts (Scheiner 2006), but this is more by default than by design. At least until the DPJ's inroads in the 2007 *Upper House* election, no other party has challenged the LDP in rural areas since the reform. But evidence of the LDP's changed strategy is that the gist of the DPJ's successful rural appeal was to restore some of the subsidies the LDP cut under Koizumi.

political economy, and by the way the LDP has adapted in response. The LDP's mercantilist, steel-and-rice logroll between exporters and inefficient sectors of the economy began falling apart in the 1980s, eventually to be replaced by a coalition structured around globally efficient firms and ordinary consumers. In the modern world economy, efficient producers and consumers, in some combination, receive more of the policies they prefer in majoritarian electoral systems, and Japan is no exception. Whether it is the LDP or the Democratic Party of Japan that holds the reins of government, public policy will support open markets and modest welfare spending.

The transition to neoliberalism, Japanese-style, has been messy, and remains incomplete, and legislation in Japan as elsewhere favors corporate supplicants over the general electorate on issues that are of low salience to the average voter.[6] But Japan's transformation is so deep that it has not only brought about a new thrust in Japanese public policy; it has also forced an overhaul in the rules of political competition that underpin the policy-making process. The old electoral rules that had facilitated cross-sector compromises embedded in Japan's one-way internationalism were no longer compatible with the combustible chemistry of global economic integration, and were blown out like a cork stuck in a bottleneck.[7]

This was not supposed to happen. Japan's developmental strategy that encouraged exports but not imports was designed to please everybody (domestically) by giving Japanese manufacturers overseas outlets while protecting home players from foreign competition. Freedom to export, in fact, might have been a sufficient sop to globally competitive firms, even when they outgrew their need for government sponsorship, if it had not been for the growing costs that Japan's lagging sectors imposed on taxpayers, both corporate and individual. Conflicting market incentives cut right through the middle of the LDP's core support base, alienating successful exporters from the sectors of the economy, such as agriculture, construction, transportation, and retail, that needed ever-more-expensive protective regulation to survive.

The precise details of the LDP's struggle to reinvent itself around a new support base—and the attempts of the Democratic Party of Japan to do the same—are extremely complex and require a deep understanding of

---

[6]Stigler 1971.

[7]Thus we agree with Pempel (1999), who calls global economic pressures on Japan "structural gaiatsu"; with Hiwatari (2001: 8), who sees electoral reform as a way to usher in policies more consistent with global economic integration; and with Campbell (2002: 11), who thinks that globalization and other economic pressures will make protectionism difficult to maintain in Japan.

the Japanese particulars. In broad strokes, however, what happened in Japan is intelligible in any language. The wealth earned in world markets proved greater than all of the resources that domestic laggards could put together in a last-ditch effort to hold the castle walls. The old mercantilist structure crumbled, requiring even a different electoral system as the new foundation.

Japan's choice of a mostly majoritarian electoral system does not imply that all rich democracies are headed for plurality electoral systems because those rules best accommodate capitalist consumerism—we are not predicting global institutional convergence. Multiple institutional choices are compatible with global markets, and any given institutional arrangement allows for a range of policy responses. But as a general matter, majoritarian systems motivate politicians to target policies toward consumer interests, which are compatible with the free flow of goods and services that profit efficient firms. Single-member-district systems vary in the extent to which they favor consumers and taxpayers over interest groups, of course, depending on party discipline. Where partisan rather than personalistic competition is strong, as in the United Kingdom, competitive firms do not need to provide large donations to protect their freedom of movement, and politicians in any event do not need large campaign war chests. In the textbook case, electoral campaigning and neoliberal policies are mutually reinforcing because fluid asset flows are in the best interests of both the median voter and competitive firms. By contrast, where individual politicians have to supplement weak partisan brand-names with their own efforts to achieve name recognition, as in the United States, politicians have an incentive to sell regulatory and other favors in exchange for money, at least up to the point that the resulting policy skewness starts to cut into the party's overall popularity with voters. Japan has strong party discipline, because there, as in the United Kingdom and other parliamentary systems, legislative majorities face the possibility of new elections in the event of successful votes of no confidence. This gives us reason to expect that Japan's policy-making environment will look more British than American in the future.[8]

By contrast, in the proportional representation systems of continental

[8]One complicating factor is that, electoral rules notwithstanding, Japanese bicameralism is much more potent than the British variety. Indeed, Japan's current version of divided government (with the opposition in control of the Upper House) is extremely rare in parliamentary democracies (Druckman and Thies 2002), and could cause either policy stalemate or very broad-based policy logrolls (Heller 1997). Ultimately, if the opposition continues to use its Upper House control to stonewall, a constitutional crisis along the lines of the Australian one in 1975 (Lijphart 1984) is not out of the question.

Europe, where parties tend to be both strong and narrowly based, the granting of favors to interest groups is institutionalized in coalition bargains and long-term deals. Proportional electoral rules work in favor of well-organized groups, and against the wholesale embrace of an exporter-consumer coalition.[9] Countries with proportional representation typically cope with economic integration by compensating the losers from trade and finance with generous social insurance provisions.

Japan's compromise among the existing parties over the 1994 electoral rules settled on a system with majoritarian bias, but with a portion of the legislature reserved for proportional representation that would save a place for small parties. None of the small parties provides a particularly effective vehicle for mainstream labor unions or other economic groups. While it is at least hypothetically possible that disgruntled farmers and small business proprietors could form their own small parties in an attempt to anchor policy in friendlier waters, such parties would have to bid for the affections of whatever larger party is playing the role of coalition formateur (be it the LDP, the DPJ, or any other large party that emerges should one of those collapse). The LDP's principal coalition partner since 1998, the Komeito, is a well-organized group of urban voters more or less at the ideological median and disinclined to provide a back door to interest-group influence. As long as there are a number of small parties from which to choose coalition partners, that formateur will choose to ally with a small party that requires the smallest deviation from its own median-regarding strategy. This bodes better for a party like the Komeito than for a party of the protectionist rump.

Japan's politicians might have chosen instead a more European institutional solution, with very different results. Lifetime employment, corporate cross-shareholding, and other relationally based contracts would have been easier to preserve in that scenario. They did not choose proportionality in part because organized labor, already weak in postindustrial Japan, found itself excluded from the bargaining table where institutional choices were made.[10] Labor's weakness from the old electoral rules carried over into the genetic material of the new electoral rules. The economy's efficient businesses, which demanded little from government other than low taxes and secure property rights, preferred electoral rules that

---

[9]Bawn and Thies 2003; Bawn and Rosenbluth 2006.

[10]Recall from chapter 6 that when the Socialist Party torpedoed the original, much more proportional electoral law bill, the Hosokawa government chose to compromise with the LDP, rather than give in to Socialist pressure for even greater proportionality. This was in large part because Hosokawa and other reformist leaders wanted to build a large party alternative to the LDP, and needed more majoritarian rules to facilitate that goal.

would make it difficult for unproductive groups to make effective demands on government coffers.[11]

We have emphasized the changes under way in Japan, but it is important to add a significant caveat. Japan's capital and labor markets are not headed for the degree of laissez-faire that characterizes the markets in the United States and the United Kingdom, at least not immediately. As a matter of course, Japan's political economy encounters resistance to change from vested interests reluctant to give up old advantages. The manufacturing exporters that have been the engine of change in Japan have vast investments in plants and infrastructure. This distinguishes them from the service-sector firms in finance, insurance, software, and leisure that lead productivity growth in the United States and the United Kingdom. Toyota and Panasonic, compared to Citibank, Barclays, Microsoft, or McDonald's, have far more invested in actual physical plant and cannot shift as quickly to technology-intensive production processes. They will be more conservative in making use of existing production technology and equipment, and will continue to value a core set of workers with firm-specific skills and knowledge. Only when Japan moves aggressively into the services industry will there be the corporate support base for government policies that maximize asset mobility.[12]

In practical terms, this means that corporate Japan continues to be the principal conduit for social welfare provisions, since this is a way that firms compete for skilled labor, and this in turn means that welfare varies significantly by employment status. The trade-off of Japan's move toward neoliberalism, as in other majoritarian electoral systems, is that income disparities will grow larger. The two main parties hover around the political middle, and while they posture and pronounce on the merits of social insurance for the people the market inevitably leaves behind, neither party can win majorities around a strongly redistributive stance under these electoral rules.

Majoritarian systems create a bias toward free markets, but there is a

[11]On the many legislative matters in which voter interest and attention is weak, interest groups retain a structural advantage born of their collective action advantage. Moreover, as Japan's income disparity grows and weakens the Japanese consumer's sense of being a representative member of the middle class, the median voter might become a less compelling target in both practical and normative terms. Voters' material and social interests are becoming more diffuse, making it harder for politicians to appeal to their common interests. It stands to reason that this creates more room for legislative deals with groups that have intense preferences, away from those of the electoral median.

[12]Schaede (2006: 36–37) suggests that for risk-averse firms, today's more competitive environment "may lead to a smaller, more protective group, perhaps even with a more hierarchical organization and chain of command," whereas more aggressively competitive firms will more readily shed cross-shareholding as "an undesirable drag on profits."

range among and within majoritarian systems. For one thing, people seem more willing to have their tax dollars spent on the poor and unfortunate if they can imagine being in those shoes, a feat of empathy more easily accomplished when the welfare recipients are people like themselves and different only in life stage or luck.[13] Terrible economic shocks that bring down the mighty can alter voter preferences in favor of higher levels of social insurance, at least as long as that generation governs, as witnessed in post-Depression America or postwartime England. The economic calamity that began in 2008 could prove to be such an episode as well.

On the other hand, generosity to one's own kind could either preclude or fall victim to liberal immigration policies, translating into chariness toward people on the outside. The typical stance of big business toward immigration is favorable, but Japan's employers, particularly those that rely on team-production methods, have valued the disciplinary effects of a strong corporate culture more than the potentially lower wages from a larger labor pool. Resistance to immigration springs, then, from the same source as the attachment to lifetime employment of workers, and both will decline gradually as firms adopt more flexible personnel strategies in response to shorter and more fluid contracts in corporate finance.

Democratic Foreign Policy

The occasionally alarmist rhetoric from China and Korea notwithstanding, Japan does not pose a military threat to its neighbors. Threat implies ability and intent, neither of which the Japanese possess. Geopolitically, Japan's military power is dwarfed by America's, making the U.S.-Japan alliance still the least costly way for Japan to maintain its security. This fact is only amplified by the rise of China as a regional and global power, and by periodic needling from North Korea. Talk in Japan in the 1970s and 1980s about developing an independent foreign policy no longer makes sense now that Japan needs the United States as ballast against China.

Japan's victims from World War II worry that signs of rising Japanese nationalism portend an aggressive intent, however unwise it might be geopolitically. This fear is misplaced. For one thing, the "democratic peace" literature finds evidence that democracies are less likely to attack other democracies. Not only do democracies put foreign policy decisions in the hands of those who bear the costs of war[14] and often slow them-

---

[13]Gilens 1999.

[14]As (the nondemocratic) Prince John in the movie *Shrek* put it, "Many of you will have

selves down with checks and balances; they are also more likely to have interlocking interests through trade and agreements. Granted, democracies have a less peaceful record against nondemocracies, presumably because even self-governing publics are willing to bear the costs of wars that they believe they can win.[15] Nonetheless, it is harder to imagine a scenario in which the Japanese would be willing to take on China—which is both militarily formidable and a source of profit for many Japanese businesses—than to envision one involving a debilitating first strike against, say, North Korea.

The principal reason for our expectation of a peaceful Japanese foreign policy is that Japanese domestic politics, post electoral reform, has moderate tendencies. Majoritarian electoral rules pressure politicians to hew to positions in the most densely populated political middle. The fringe elements in Japan that noisily propagate unfulfilled imperialistic longings are chronically sidelined in mainstream political debate. Japan's anxious neighbors would find less reason to worry in public opinion polls, which show little change in national pride and aggressive intention, than in the right-wingers' sound trucks whose shrill appeals mostly fall on deaf ears. What matters is the pacifism of the median voter. The signs that the Japanese public has awakened to the possibilities of a more active global role for Japan should not be read as emerging hostile intent.[16] It is one thing to desire a seat on the UN Security Council, and quite another to want to change national borders. Electoral campaigning after the rule change of 1994 has drawn the public into foreign policy discussions and awakened a latent and natural interest in national security. Far from posturing at extreme positions, however, the major parties compete to appear moderate, reasonable, and competent.[17]

---

to die in this war, but it is a sacrifice I am willing to make." Kant (1991 [1794]), the father of the democratic peace proposition, has a large modern following. See Doyle 1986; Russett 1993; Bueno de Mesquita et al. 1999 and 2003; Reiter and Stam 2002.

[15]Ferejohn and Rosenbluth 2008.

[16]Hughes (2004: 58) argues that post–Cold War Japanese policy makers have pushed for a more "normal" (read: assertive) foreign policy, but he agrees that while public opinion "has by and large come to support, or at least acquiesce in the push for 'normalisation'... [it] is still highly cautious on security matters."

[17]A quite recent example of this was the 2007–2008 political battle to reauthorize the deployment of Maritime Self-Defense Force ships to resume a refueling mission in the Indian Ocean for U.S.-led antiterrorism operations. The ships were recalled when the opposition DPJ used its Upper House majority to kill the reauthorization, and were sent back only after the LDP used its two-thirds Lower House majority to override the Upper House veto. The irony of this brouhaha is that the DPJ leader was none other than Ozawa Ichiro, who, recall from chapter 8, called for a more "normal" Japanese foreign policy in his 1993 book but now argued the pacifist position that such a mission was a violation of Article 9 of the

CONCLUSIONS

Majoritarian rules of political competition have reoriented politicians' incentives in Japan. Logrolls still take place and targeted favors still exist as in politics anywhere, but they have given ground to policies aimed at the median voter. No longer able to count on geographically and functionally narrow personal support networks to carry an election, politicians now work to develop positions on a range of policy issues that appeal to the vast swath of voters in the political middle. This is not to say that policy muddiness vanishes, because the political middle can be torn between competing concerns for, say, low taxes and economic security. Politicians still have incentives to dissemble, hem, and haw, but their targets are now those fickle voters in the middle.

The power of electoral rules to reshape policy debates and to redraw the contours of economic regulation demonstrates the importance of political institutions. Dismantling protective regulation has cost formerly favored businesses billions of yen because politicians are now more compelled to lean toward the interests of consumers and taxpayers when forced to make a choice. Markets for money, labor, and the products they produce have changed substantially as a result. That the same voters and the same politicians could be channeled by a new set of electoral incentives to overhaul the economic rules of the game is as compelling a testament to the power of formal rules as one can find anywhere.

But to stop with the observation about the significance of institutional arrangements would be to understate the importance of the material forces that supported Japan's long-standing institutional arrangements in the first place, and their part in bringing down the old edifice. Dramatic shifts in economic interests and resources destroyed the political equilibrium, rendering the old electoral rules an anachronistic albatross by reducing to rubble the corporate interests that bankrolled the LDP's electoral machines in the old multimember districts. Although (or perhaps because) the LDP had lavished favors on its business supporters and protected them from economic competition, many of those firms failed to innovate and increase their productivity. The result was an economy with vast areas of dismal performance, masked by regulatory props. Japan's integration into the world economy undermined the feasibility of those props, including the zero interest rates that created the enormous asset

---

constitution. The lesson for us is that Ozawa, ever the tactician, obviously calculated that the passive pacifist position was still a politically popular one, whatever he actually believed was the right thing to do.

bubble of the 1980s. Once the air had gone out of the bubble, weak sectors of the economy were left without the resources to buy LDP elections in the traditional manner. The LDP had to find another way.

The substantive story of this book is of the LDP's efforts to reinvent itself as a party that pairs efficient businesses with taxpayers and consumers, a more affordable coalition to maintain in a globalized economy than the older one of backwater sectors and rural voters. When the unproductive businesses and farmers that underwrote the LDP's hegemony under the old electoral rules ultimately failed to adjust to economic openness, the LDP has tried to switch horses, to a new coalition of productive businesses, taxpayers, and consumers. To do this, they adopted majoritarian electoral rules that would weaken the political power of interest groups at the tails of the demographic distribution. The DPJ, though in opposition, locates itself not far away, pressed by the same electoral rules to aim for the same types of voters in the political middle. As the center-left party, the DPJ places more emphasis on social insurance, but it is exquisitely sensitive to the price that voters pay for that insurance.

The story takes place in the exotic setting of an enigmatic country, but the lessons about the causes and consequences of institutional rules are universal to politics. Global economic integration compels political parties in rich democracies everywhere to forge sustainable bases of support in the face of heightened economic competition, but the institutional starting point also matters. In the PR systems of continental Europe—although organized labor has been forced to internalize some of the costs of competition by agreeing to more flexible wages and terms of employment, incorporating women and immigrants as new members—labor's place at the bargaining table ensures that these changes take place with a commitment to employee welfare. There is no reason to believe that these countries will abandon PR rules as long as labor and business can continue to make the requisite adjustments. In Japan, labor was excluded from the bargaining table. Like their counterparts in other majoritarian systems, Japanese parties are now more responsive to the median voter, but income inequality will grow as well. Economic globalization forced a rewriting of the political rules of the game in Japan, but who got to rewrite the rules is of vast consequence.

The 2009 General Election and
the LDP's Fall from Power

On Sunday, August 30, 2009, the Democratic Party of Japan won a dramatic victory, capturing 308 of the 480 seats in the House of Representatives and leaving the LDP in the dust with 119 seats. For the first time in postwar history, a party other than the LDP holds a legislative majority in the House of Representatives. The media and political pundits, at home and abroad, competed with one another for appropriately grand phrasing: "electoral tsunami,"[1] "landslide,"[2] "historic,"[3] the "rise of a new era,"[4] "a seismic shift in Japanese political culture."[5]

The election certainly was historic and important. But if the 2009 election was a tsunami, the undersea earthquake that produced the big wave was the electoral rule change of 1994 (and, as we've argued, that earthquake was itself induced by the collapse of the postwar political economy). The new majoritarian electoral rules produced incentives for politicians to align themselves into two large, majority-seeking parties aimed at the large swath of voters in the political middle. There may have been eleven parties contesting the 2009 election, and eight that won seats, but as table E.1 shows, the DPJ and LDP between them captured 285 of 300 SMDs (95 percent), up from 271 of 300 in 2005. The average effective number of parties in 2009 was 2.26, and since the two large parties dominated the PR tier as well, the effective number of parties in the Lower

---

[1] *Foreign Policy*, August 30, 2009, http://www.foreignpolicy.com/articles/2009/08/30/japans_electoral_tsunami/.

[2] *New York Times*, August 30, 2009, http://www.nytimes.com/2009/08/31/world/asia/31japan.html; *Economist*, August 31, 2009, http://www.economist.com/world/asia/displaystory.cfm?story_id=14340843.

[3] *International Herald Tribune*, August 31, 2009, http://www.highbeam.com/doc/1P1-170215606.html.

[4] *Wall Street Journal*, August 31, 2009, http://online.wsj.com/article/SB125160894574169933.html; *Financial Times*, August 31, 2009, http://www.ft.com/cms/s/0/f1240a92-9659-11de-84d1-00144feabdc0,dwp_uuid=a386a928-5a6a-11de-8c14-00144feabdc0.html?nclick_check=1; *Guardian*, August 31, 2009, http://www.guardian.co.uk/world/2009/aug/31/japan-elections-yukio-hatoyama/.

[5] *Arab News*, September 1, 2009, www.arabnews.com/services/print/print.asp?artid=125968&d=1&m=9&y=2009.

Table E.1

House of Representatives Election Results, Comparing 2005 and 2009

Party	September 11, 2005			August 30, 2009		
	Total	SMD	PR	Total	SMD	PR
Democratic Party	113	52	61	308	221	87
Liberal Democratic Party	296	219	77	119	64	55
New Komeito	31	8	23	21	0	21
Japan Communist Party	9	0	9	9	0	9
Social Democratic Party	7	1	6	7	3	4
People's New Party	4	2	2	3	3	0
Your Party	—	—	—	5	2	3
New Party Nippon	1	0	1	1	1	0
Other/Independent	19	18	1	7	6	1
Total	480	300	180	480	300	180

Source: http://www.yomiuri.co.jp/election/.

House as a whole is only 2.1. For all intents and purposes, Japan has become a two-party system.[6]

The LDP's mobilizational advantage under the old SNTV electoral system involved using its incumbency to protect inefficient farmers, manufacturers, and retailers from competition. This was dealt a fatal blow by a new electoral game in which the party to pitch the most appealing platform to the most voters wins. Under majoritarian electoral rules, the attempt to lock down voter loyalty with regulatory or fiscal favors to a subset of voters comes at the cost of alienating the electoral majority that is stuck with the bill for those favors. Responsiveness to swing voters in the middle of the political spectrum rather than fidelity to electoral outliers is the winning strategy under Japan's new electoral rules.

The 2005 and 2009 elections have demonstrated the partisan and programmatic (as compared with clientelistic) logic of the new system quite clearly. The most volatile electoral districts are in urban areas, where voters are not organized by interest groups or individual candidates' campaign machines. They have tired of paying for pork-barrel subsidies to

---

[6]The DPJ included in its 2009 manifesto a pledge to reduce the number of PR-tier seats in the Lower House from 180 to 100. Unless they simultaneously move to a national district (instead of the 11 regional districts they use now), that change would likely disadvantage small parties even more.

© Chappatte in *International Herald Tribune*—www.globecartoon.com

inefficient sectors of the economy, are worried about life after retirement with inadequate social security, and are afraid of unemployment in a stagnant economy. The same urban districts that handed Koizumi and the LDP a landslide victory in 2005 swung uniformly for the DPJ in 2009. Of the 100 most urban districts, the LDP beat the DPJ 74 to 16 in 2005 (with the other 10 going to small parties or independents), but the DPJ returned the favor to the tune of 84 to 10 in 2009.[7]

One might interpret such an about-face by urban voters as evidence of fickleness. We do not. In our view, voters in urban Japan were consistent in their preferences, but changed their minds about which party was more likely to deliver the policy changes they desired. We discussed the Koizumi landslide of 2005 in chapter 6. Recall that that election was precipitated by the rebellion that caused the defeat of Koizumi's postal reform bills, and that the DPJ had opposed those bills as well. This allowed Koizumi to assume the mantle of reformer-in-chief and ask for a mandate to move forward, against the intransigence of conservatives within his own party and opportunists in the DPJ. Urban voters were convinced, and they plumped for LDP candidates in 2005 in order to give Koizumi his mandate. They were voting not for the LDP, but for Koizumi and "reform."

[7] Reed, Scheiner, and Thies 2009.

After Koizumi stepped down, his successors dithered and even back-tracked. Under Abe Shinzo, the government misread the public mood in prioritizing symbolic foreign policy issues, and revealed incompetence in the form of a scandal involving millions of lost pension records. After the DPJ won the 2007 Upper House election and used its position there to block the Fukuda Yasuo government's bills, the LDP was unable to get anything accomplished. The Aso Taro government that followed Fuku-da's was erratic and unpopular, setting record lows in public opinion polls. By the time Aso finally dissolved the Diet and called the election (only a few weeks before the constitutionally mandated deadline), voters had given up on the post-Koizumi LDP as a vehicle for policy reform. They were willing to give the DPJ a chance.

The DPJ also took advantage of voter discontent with the short-term costs of the liberalizing reforms that had been enacted during the post-bubble period. A centerpiece of the DPJ campaign was a call for a welfare safety net to respond to the increases in unemployment and inequality that liberalization entailed. The DPJ even made huge inroads in rural areas by promising rural voters compensation for the lost subsidies and protections, in the form of direct income supports.[8] Thus, while the 2005 contest was about who could more credibly promise to bring reform, the 2009 campaign included party competition over how to deal with the costs of reform.

The DPJ easily won this battle, sympathizing with the "victims" of liberalization, without really promising to roll back the reforms them-selves.[9] Straight income transfers are considerably less distortionary than price supports, market protection, or inefficient public works projects. As the prospects of continued LDP hegemony faded, the party's interest-group-based organized support all but vanished. Many prefectural agri-cultural cooperative associations eschewed endorsement of LDP candi-dates and declared free votes, as did the Japan Medical Association, long a stalwart LDP client. But this was not only a bandwagon effect. In fact,

---

[8]The LDP had shifted its policies toward urban interests by, for example, cutting subsi-dies to rural districts. By mandating the absorption of rural communities into urban mu-nicipalities beginning in the late 1990s, the LDP also undercut powerful rural political orga-nizations that had magnified the voices of an electoral minority. Once rural mobilization had transformed from an electoral asset into a liability, the LDP acted decisively to weaken it.

[9]Even the DPJ's partnership with the People's New Party, whose main issue appeal was to undo Koizumi's postal reform, seems unlikely to portend a real reversal. More likely, the privatization will be delayed while the DPJ-led government works on a way to soften the blow to rural communities, for which postal workers did much more than simply deliver mail and administer the postal savings system (Maclachlan 2009).

a closer examination of the 2005 results shows that in the midst of Koizumi's (and by association, the LDP's) triumph that year, the party actually lost seats and votes in rural Japan. In 2009, however, the demise of the rural organized vote combined with the disillusionment of urban voters who had believed that Koizumi really could "change the LDP in order to change Japan" to produce the DPJ tsunami.

This is not to say that the LDP is through as a political force. Nearly 30 percent of the DPJ's SMD wins were by margins of fewer than 10 percentage points,[10] and many of the defeated LDP incumbents, especially those who were first elected in 2005 on Koizumi's coattails, will spend the time before the next election distancing themselves from the failed post-Koizumi LDP leadership and repairing relationships within their districts. The untested DPJ surely will make mistakes and fail to fulfill its most ambitious pledges, and some of those who were wooed by its promises of hope and change will again be disillusioned. It will be clear to the next generation of LDP leaders that as goes urban Japan, so goes political power, so even though the current LDP is older and more rural than before the election (having lost nearly every urban constituency), the party will have to find a way to appeal again to urban voters. This might not happen in time for the next election, and the party that figures it out might not still be called the LDP, but it is certain to happen. No party can hope to take power in Japan on the backs of rural voters alone, and urban voters have already shown that they are willing to change their minds if offered a persuasive and appealing alternative to the DPJ. Under the new electoral system, the likelihood that half a century of LDP dominance will simply be replaced by a similarly long DPJ hegemony is exceedingly low.

Instead, the DPJ's hold on power will depend almost entirely on its policy performance, because while it was able to wrest 200 seats away from the LDP in 2009, those seats are inherently volatile. There is no reason to believe that many of the seats are safe, because there is no longer any meaningful "organized vote" to capture and ingratiate with permanent policy rents. If the DPJ stumbles, most voters will be receptive to LDP appeals for another chance, or if the remaining LDP incumbents hunker down in their rural cocoons (42 of the LDP's 64 SMD winners in 2009 represent rural districts) and refuse to learn the lessons of 2009, a new party will emerge to compete for power in urban and suburban Japan.

In addition to appeals to voters on claims of competence, the 2009

[10]Reed, Scheiner, and Thies 2009.

election hints at the emergence of the sort of left-right continuum that underpins political competition in most majoritarian systems around the world, but which was difficult to discern in postwar Japan.[11] Although the contours of party adaptation are still coming into focus, it is possible to see the DPJ developing coherence as a center-left party, promising to help Japanese citizens navigate the vagaries of an increasingly volatile labor market by expanding the size and role of government-provided social insurance of various kinds. The LDP (or its successor), by shedding commitments to weak sectors of the economy, has a future as a center-right party that emphasizes the benefits of free enterprise and market dynamism. The climate of the 2009 election played to the DPJ's strengths, because the LDP had failed either to invigorate market forces or to address widespread fears of job loss or postretirement poverty. But voters in the political middle have multiple and conflicting interests, giving majoritarian electoral systems the quality that voting patterns can change quite dramatically depending on which kinds of interests are of the most concern in any given electoral year. The DPJ's promise to improve social insurance will run up against voters' concerns about the attending tax burden, which will be the center-right line of critique. Given voters' crosscutting preferences for both economic security and disposable income, neither party is invulnerable to the other. The new electoral incentives disincline either party to stray far from pragmatic, centrist compromises between social insurance and fiscal discipline.

Foreign policy is forged in the same centrist cauldron, we have argued. The DPJ's musings about a more independent foreign policy notwithstanding, both parties are hemmed in by U.S. geopolitical dominance, Chinese dynamism, and a voting public that wants to stay out of trouble with either power. The Japanese electorate, more than the parchment self-abnegation of the constitution's Article 9, harnesses Japan to the international status quo.

Without question, the nature of Japanese democracy has changed since 1994 in some significant ways. Under the old electoral rules, the LDP catered to well-organized groups that, in exchange for policy favors, helped the party operate elaborate electoral machines in multimember districts. Under the current, majoritarian, rules, swing voters in the political middle hold the key to electoral success. Income inequality will continue to increase in Japan as old protectionist regulation is dismantled, while voters' dislike of taxes for benefits they do not receive puts a

[11]Proksch, Slapin, and Thies 2009.

limit on new social security expenditures. The DPJ will be unable to make a hard left turn, settling instead for incremental improvements in social services. When the LDP (or, again, its successor) returns to government, it will be as a center-right party without a mandate to dismantle social insurance schemes that are popular with the general public.

Majoritarian systems are particularly good at providing minimally acceptable solutions for many voters, but are less likely than proportional systems to solve the collective action problem of getting to an equilibrium of, say, higher social insurance at the price of higher taxes. It is worth noting, however, that Japan is more likely to resemble the United Kingdom, where parliamentary democracy affords party leaders more resources with which to corral legislators into strong-mindedly ideological positions, than the United States, where backbenchers hew closely to district preferences. Strong party majoritarianism will give Japanese voters a choice between two platforms that, while close to the political middle, will be identifiably different.

Japanese Electoral Systems, 1947–Present

TABLE A.1.1
Electoral Rules for Japan's Lower House, 1947–Present

	Time Period		
	1947–1994	*1994–Present*	
Number of seats, districts	511[†] / 129[†]	300 / 300	180[‡]/ 11
Election rule	SNTV	Plurality (First past the post)	Closed-list PR
District size	2-6 (mean, median = 4)	1	6-29 (mean = 16.4)
Period of office	4 yrs, but subject to early dissolution	4 yrs, but subject to early dissolution	4 yrs, but subject to early dissolution

[†]In the last SNTV election, there were 129 districts and 511 seats. These numbers changed over time, as occasional redistrictings added urban seats and expanded the size of the chamber.

[‡]In the 1996 MMM election, there were 200 PR seats. This was reduced to 180 before the 2000 election.

BALLOT STRUCTURE

- Under SNTV, each voter cast one vote for an individual candidate in a multi-seat district.
- Under MMM, each voter is allotted one vote for a candidate in a single-seat district *and* one vote for a party in mulitiseat district.

ALLOCATION RULE

- Under SNTV, each district elected M members. With a couple of exceptions, M was equal to 3, 4, or 5.
- Under MMM, the district tier uses plurality rule. The regional tier uses closed-list PR-d'Hondt.
- Under MMM, a district candidate may also appear on her party's PR list.

TABLE A.1.2
Electoral Rules for Japan's Upper House, 1947–Present

	Time Period		
	1947–1980	*1983–1998*	*2001–Present*
Number of seats, districts	152 prefectural, 100 national list	152 prefectural, 100 PR	146 prefectural, 96 PR
Election rule for prefectural districts	SNTV, M = 1 to 4	SNTV, M = 1 to 4	SNTV, M = 1 to 5
Election rule for national list	SNTV, M = 50	Closed-list PR, M = 50	Open-list PR, M = 48
Period of office	6 years (76 MPs elected every three years).	6 years (76 MPs elected every three years).	6 years (73 MPs elected every three years).

Election Results, House of Representatives, 1986–2005

TABLE A.2
Election Results, House of Representatives, 1986–2005

July 6, 1986 (SNTV)	Vote %	Seat %	Total Seats
LDP	49.4	58.6	300
JSP	17.2	16.6	85
CGP	9.4	10.9	56
DSP	6.4	5.1	26
JCP	8.8	5.1	26
NLC	1.8	1.2	6
SDL	0.8	0.8	4
Other/Indep	6.0	1.8	9
TOTAL	100.0	100.0	512

February 18, 1990 (SNTV)	Vote %	Seat %	Total Seats
LDP	46.1	53.7	275
JSP	24.4	26.6	136
CGP	8.0	8.8	45
JCP	8.0	3.1	16
DSP	4.8	2.7	14
USDP	0.9	0.8	4
PP	0.4	0.2	1
Other/Indep	7.4	4.1	21
TOTAL	100.0	100.0	512

July 18, 1993 (SNTV)

	Vote %	Seat %	Total Seats
LDP	36.6	43.6	223
JSP	15.4	13.7	70
JRP	10.1	10.8	55
CGP	8.1	10.0	51
JNP	8.1	6.8	35
DSP	3.5	2.9	15
JCP	7.7	2.9	15
NPH	2.6	2.5	13
USDP	0.7	0.8	4
Other/Indep	6.9	5.9	30
TOTAL	100.0	100.0	511

October 20, 1996 (MMM)

	% PR Votes	% PR Seats	PR Seats	% SMD Vote	% SMD Seats	SMD Seats	Total seats
LDP	38.6	35.0	70	38.8	56.3	169	239
NFP	28.0	30.0	60	28.0	32.0	96	156
DPJ	10.1	17.5	35	10.7	5.7	17	52
JCP	12.6	12.0	24	12.6	0.7	2	26
JSP	2.2	5.5	11	2.2	1.3	4	15
NPH	1.3	0.0	0	1.3	0.7	2	2
DRP	0.3	0.0	0	0.3	0.3	1	1
Other/Indep	4.4	0.0	0	6.1	3.0	9	9
TOTAL	100.0	100.0	200	100.0	100.0	300	500

Table A.2
(cont.)

June 25, 2000 (MMM)

(MMM)	% PR Votes	% PR Seats	PR Seats	% SMD Vote	% SMD Seats	SMD Seats	Total seats
LDP	28.3	31.1	56	41.0	59.0	177	233
DPJ	25.2	26.1	47	27.6	26.7	80	127
CGP	13.0	13.3	24	2.0	2.3	7	31
JCP	11.2	11.1	20	12.1	0.0	0	20
LP	11.0	10.0	18	3.4	1.3	4	22
SDP	9.4	8.3	15	3.8	1.3	4	19
NCP	0.4	0.0	0	2.0	2.3	7	7
Other/Indep	1.3	0.0	0	8.1	7.0	21	21
TOTAL	100.0	100.0	180	100.0	100.0	300	480

November 9, 2003 (MMM)

(MMM)	% PR Votes	% PR Seats	PR Seats	% SMD Vote	% SMD Seats	SMD Seats	Total seats
LDP	35.0	38.3	69	43.8	56.0	168	237
DPJ	37.4	40.0	72	36.9	35.0	105	177
CGP	14.8	13.9	25	1.5	3.0	9	34
JCP	7.8	5.0	9	8.1	0.0	0	9
NCP	—	—	0	1.3	1.3	4	4
SDP	5.1	2.8	5	2.9	0.3	1	6
LL	—	—	—	0.2	0.3	1	1
Other/Indep	—	—	—	5.3	4.0	12	12
TOTAL	100.0	100.0	180	100.0	100.0	300	480

September 11, 2005 (MMM)	% PR Votes	% PR Seats	PR Seats	% SMD Vote	% SMD Seats	SMD Seats	Total seats
LDP	38.2	42.8	77	47.7	73.0	219	296
DPJ	31.0	33.9	61	36.7	17.3	52	113
CGP	13.3	12.8	23	1.4	2.7	8	31
JCP	7.3	5.0	9	7.3	0.0	0	9
SDP	5.5	3.3	6	1.5	0.3	1	7
PNP	1.7	1.1	2	0.6	0.7	2	4
NPN	2.4	0.6	1	0.2	0.0	0	1
NPD	0.6	0.6	1	0.0	0.0	0	1
Other/Indep	—	—	—	4.6	6.0	18	18
TOTAL	100.0	100.0	180	100.0	100.0	300	480

Note: See appendix 3 for a key to party names.

Election Results, House of Councillors, 1986–2007

TABLE A.3
Election Results, House of Councillors, 1986–2007

July 6, 1986	PR Vote %	PR Seat %	PR Seats	District Vote %	District Seat %	District Seats	Total Seats
LDP	38.6	44.0	22	45.1	65.8	50	72
JSP	17.2	18.0	9	21.5	14.5	11	20
CGP	13	14.0	7	4.4	3.9	3	10
JCP	9.5	10.0	5	11.4	5.3	4	9
Other/Indep	14.9	8.0	4	13	7.9	6	19
TOTAL	—	100.0	50	—	100.0	76	126

July 23, 1989	PR Vote %	PR Seat %	PR Seats	District Vote %	District Seat %	District Seats	Total Seats
JSP	35.1	40.0	20	26.4	34.2	26	46
LDP	27.3	30.0	15	30.7	27.6	21	36
Rengo	—	—	—	6.8	14.5	11	11
CGP	10.9	12.0	6	5.1	5.3	4	10
JCP	7	8.0	4	8.8	1.3	1	5
DSP	4.9	4.0	2	3.6	1.3	1	3
Other/Indep	14.9	6.0	3	18.6	15.8	12	15
TOTAL	100	100.0	50	—	100.0	76	126

July 6, 1986	PR Vote %	PR Seat %	PR Seats	District Vote %	District Seat %	District Seats	Total Seats
LDP	38.6	44.0	22	45.1	65.8	50	72
JSP	17.2	18.0	9	21.5	14.5	11	20
CGP	13	14.0	7	4.4	3.9	3	10
JCP	9.5	10.0	5	11.4	5.3	4	9
Other/Indep	14.9	8.0	4	13	7.9	6	19
TOTAL	—	100.0	50	—	100.0	76	126

July 23, 1989	PR Vote %	PR Seat %	PR Seats	District Vote %	District Seat %	District Seats	Total Seats
JSP	35.1	40.0	20	26.4	34.2	26	46
LDP	27.3	30.0	15	30.7	27.6	21	36
Rengo	—	—	—	6.8	14.5	11	11
CGP	10.9	12.0	6	5.1	5.3	4	10
JCP	7	8.0	4	8.8	1.3	1	5
DSP	4.9	4.0	2	3.6	1.3	1	3
Other/Indep	14.9	6.0	3	18.6	15.8	12	15
TOTAL	100	100.0	50	—	100.0	76	126

TABLE A.3

(cont.)

July 26, 1992	PR Vote %	PR Seat %	PR Seats	District Vote %	District Seat %	District Seats	Total Seats
LDP	33.3	38.0	19	43.4	64.9	50	69
JSP	17.8	20.0	10	12.9	15.6	12	22
CGP	14.3	16.0	8	7.8	7.8	6	14
JCP	7.9	8.0	4	10.6	2.6	2	6
DSP	5	6.0	3	2.3	1.3	1	4
Rengo	—	—	—	9.7	0.0	0	0
JNP	8.1	8.0	4	—	—	—	4
Other/Indep	13.8	4.0	2	13.3	7.8	6	8
TOTAL	—	100.0	50	—	100.0	77	127

July 23, 1995	PR Vote %	PR Seat %	PR Seats	District Vote %	District Seat %	District Seats	Total Seats
LDP	27.3	30.0	15	25.4	40.8	31	46
JSP	16.9	18.0	9	11.8	9.2	7	16
JCP	9.5	10.0	5	10.4	3.9	3	8
NFP	30.8	36.0	18	26.5	28.9	22	40
NPH	3.6	4.0	2	2.5	1.3	1	3
Other/Indep	11.9	2.0	1	23.4	15.8	12	13
TOTAL	—	100.0	50	—	100.0	76	126

TABLE A.3
(cont.)

July 12, 1998	PR Vote %	PR Seat %	PR Seats	District Vote %	District Seat %	District Seats	Total Seats
LDP	25.2	28.0	14	30.8	40.8	31	45
DPJ	21.7	24.0	12	16.2	19.7	15	27
JSP	7.8	8.0	4	4.3	1.3	1	5
JCP	14.6	16.0	8	15.7	9.2	7	15
CGP	13.8	14.0	7	3.3	2.6	2	9
LP	9.3	10.0	5	1.8	1.3	1	6
NPH	1.4	0.0	0	—	—	—	0
Other/Indep	6.2	0.0	0	27.9	25.0	19	19
TOTAL	—	100.0	50	100	100.0	76	126

July 29, 2001	PR Vote %	PR Seat %	PR Seats	District Vote %	District Seat %	District Seats	Total Seats
LDP	38.6	41.7	20	41.0	61.6	45	65
DPJ	16.4	16.7	8	18.5	24.7	18	26
CGP	15.0	16.7	8	6.4	6.8	5	13
LP	7.7	8.3	4	5.5	2.7	2	6
JCP	7.9	8.3	4	9.9	1.4	1	5
JSP	6.6	6.3	3	3.4	0.0	0	3
CP	2.3	2.1	1	—	0.0	0	1
Other/Indep	5.5	0.0	0	15.2	2.7	2	2
TOTAL	100.0	100.0	48	100.0	100.0	73	121

Key to Party Names

CGP	Clean Government Party (*Komeito*)
DPJ	Democratic Party of Japan
DRP	Democratic Reform Party
DSP	Democratic Socialist Party
JCP	Japan Communist Party
JNP	Japan New Party
JRP	Japan Renewal Party
JSP	Japan Socialist Party (renamed the Social Democratic Party)
LDP	Liberal Democratic Party
LL	Liberal League
LP	Liberal Party
NCP	New Conservative Party
NFP	New Frontier Party
NLC	New Liberal Club
NPD	New Party Daichi
NPH	New Party Harbinger (*Sakigake*)
NPN	New Party Nippon
PNP	People's New Party
PP	Progressive Party
Rengo	Japan Trade Union Confederation
SDL	Social Democratic League
SDP	Social Democratic Party (previously the JSP)
USDP	United Socialist Democratic Party

Bibliography

Abe, Masahiro, and Takeo Hoshi. 2007. "Corporate Finance and Human Resource Management in Japan." In *Corporate Governance in Japan: Institutional Change and Organizational Diversity*, edited by Masahiko Aoki, Gregory Jackson, and Hideaki Miyajima, 257–281. Oxford: Oxford University Press.

Abegglen, James C. 1958. *The Japanese Factory: Aspects of Its Social Organization.* Glencoe, IL: Free Press.

———. 1985. *Kaisha: The Japanese Corporation.* New York: Basic Books.

Acemoglu, Daren, and James A. Robinson. 2002. "The Political Economy of the Kuznets Curve." *Review of Development Economics* 6, 2: 183–203.

———. 2006. "Persistence of Power, Elites and Institutions." CEPR Discussion Paper No. 5603.

Adolphson, Mikael. 2000. *The Gates of Power: Monks, Courtiers and Warriors in Premodern Japan.* Honolulu: University of Hawaii Press.

Adolphson, Mikael, and J. Mark Ramseyer. 2007. "Property Rights in Medieval Japan: The Role of Buddhist Temples and Monasteries." The Harvard John M. Olin Discussion Paper No. 584. http://www.law.harvard.edu/programs/olin_center.

Aguilera, Ruth, and Gregory Jackson. 2003. "The Cross National Diversity of Corporate Governance: Dimensions and Determinants." *Academy of Management Review* 28, 3: 447–465.

Akaiwa, Hirotomo. 2003. "Toward a Third Japanese Revolution: The Political Economy of Japanese Fiscal Decentralization." MA thesis, Stanford University.

Alchian, Armen A., and Harold Demsetz. 1972. "Production, Information Costs, and Economic Organization." *American Economic Review* 62, 5: 777–795.

Allen, Franklin, and Douglas Gale. 2002. "A Comparative Theory of Corporate Governance." Wharton School and NYU Department of Economics Working Paper.

Almond, Gabriel A., and Sydney Verba. 1965. *The Civic Culture: Political Attitudes and Democracy in Five Nations.* Boston: Little, Brown.

Amyx, Jennifer. 2004. *Japan's Financial Crisis: Institutional Rigidity and Reluctant Change.* Princeton, NJ: Princeton University Press.

Amyx, Jennifer, and Peter Drysdale, eds. 2003. *Japanese Governance: Beyond Japan Inc.* New York: Routledge Courzon.

Anderson, Benedict. 1983. *Imagined Communities: Reflections on the Origin and Spread of Nationalism.* London: Verso.

Aoki, Masahiko. 1988. *Information, Incentives, and Bargaining in the Japanese Economy*. New York: Cambridge University Press.

———. 2007. "Endogenizing Institutions and Institutional Changes." *Journal of Institutional Economics* 3, 1: 1–31.

Aristotle. 1998. *Politics*. Translated by Ernest Barker. Oxford: Oxford University Press.

Asahi Shimbun. Various issues.

Asakawa, Kan'ichi. 1911. "Notes on Village Government in Japan after 1600, II." *Journal of the American Oriental Society* 31, 2: 151–216.

Asano, Masahiko. 2006. *Shimin shakai ni okeru seido kaikaku: Senkyo seido to kohosha rikuruuto*. Tokyo: Keio Gijuku Daigaku Shuppankai.

Asao, Keiichiro. 2000. "Shinsei Ginko o 'kokuzoku' ni shita no wa dare da" [Who Turned the Shinsei Bank into a Traitor?]. *Bungei Shunju*, September.

Baerwald, Hans H. 1986. *Party Politics in Japan*. Boston: Allen & Unwin.

———. 2002. "Postwar Japan: A Reminiscence." Japan Policy Research Institute Occasional Paper No. 27 (July). http://www.jpri.org/publications/occasional papers/op27.html.

Bawn, Kathleen, and Frances Rosenbluth. 2006. "Short versus Long Coalitions: Electoral Accountability and the Size of the Public Sector." *American Journal of Political Science* 50, 2: 251–265.

Bawn, Kathleen, and Michael F. Thies. 2003. "A Comparative Theory of Electoral Incentives: Representing the Unorganized under PR, Plurality, and Mixed-Member Electoral Systems." *Journal of Theoretical Politics* 15, 1: 5–32.

BBC News. 2005. "Textbook Angers Chinese, Korean Press." April 6. http://news.bbc.co.uk/2/hi/world/asia-pacific/4416593.stm.

Beal, Tim, Yoshiko Nozaki, and Jian Yang. 2001. "Ghosts of the Past: The Japanese History Textbook Controversy." *New Zealand Journal of Asian Studies* 3, 2: 177–188.

Beason, Dick, and Dennis Patterson. 2004. *The Japan That Never Was: Explaining the Rise and Decline of a Misunderstood Country*. Albany: State University of New York Press.

Beason, Dick, and David E. Weinstein. 1996. "Growth, Economies of Scale, and Targeting in Japan (1955–1990)." *Review of Economics and Statistics* 78, 2: 286–295.

Becker, Gary S. 1983. "A Theory of Competition among Pressure Groups for Political Influence." *Quarterly Journal of Economics* 98, 3: 371–400.

Beckmann, George. 1957. *The Making of the Meiji Constitution: The Oligarchs and the Constitutional Development of Japan, 1868–1891*. Lawrence: University of Kansas Press.

Berle, Adolf A., and Gardner C. Means. 1932. *Modern Corporation and Private Property*. New York: Commerce Clearing House.

Berry, Mary Elizabeth. 1982. *Hideyoshi*. Cambridge: Harvard University Press.

————. 1994. *The Culture of War in Medieval Kyoto.* Berkeley and Los Angeles: University of California Press.

————. 2005. "Samurai Trouble: Thoughts on War and Loyalty." *Journal of Asian Studies* 64, 4 (November): 831–847.

Berton, Peter. 1992. "The Japan Communist Party." In *The Japanese Party System*, edited by Ronald J. Hrebenar, 116–147. Boulder, CO: Westview Press.

Black, Duncan. 1958. *The Theory of Committees and Elections.* New York: Cambridge University Press.

Blomström, Magnus, Byron Gangnes, and Sumner La Croix. 2001. *Japan's New Economy: Continuity and Change in the Twenty-First Century.* New York: Oxford University Press.

Boix, Carles, and Frances Rosenbluth. 2004. "The Bones of Contention: The Political Economy of Height Inequality." Unpublished paper, American Political Science Association Annual Meeting.

Boix, Carles, and Susan C. Stokes. 2003. "Endogenous Democratization." *World Politics* 55, 4: 517–549.

Bolitho, Harold. 1974. *Treasures among Men: The Fudai Daimyo in Tokugawa Japan.* New Haven: Yale University Press.

————. 1979. "The Echigo War, 1868." *Monumenta Nipponica* 34, 3: 259–277.

Borton, Hugh. 1967. "American Presurrender Planning for Postwar Japan." Occasional Papers of the East Asian Institute, Columbia University.

Boserup, Ester. 1970. *Woman's Role in Economic Development.* New York: St. Martin's Press.

Bowen, Roger W. 1980. *Rebellion and Democracy in Meiji Japan: A Study of Commoners in the Popular Rights Movement.* Berkeley and Los Angeles: University of California Press.

Bremner, Brian. 2005. "Japan's Shinsei: Midsize Bank, Supersize Ambitions." *Business Week*, June 13.

Brewer, Elijah, Hesna Genay, William Hunter, and George Kaufman. 2002. "The Value of Banking Relationships during a Financial Crisis: Evidence from Failures of Japanese Banks." Federal Reserve Bank of Chicago Working Paper.

Brinton, Mary C. 2001. *Women's Working Lives in East Asia.* Stanford: Stanford University Press.

Brown, Philip C. 1993. *Central Authority and Local Autonomy in the Formation of Early Modern Japan: The Case of Kaga Domain.* Stanford: Stanford University Press.

Bueno de Mesquita, Bruce, James D. Morrow, Randolph M. Siverson, and Alastair Smith. 1999. "An Institutional Explanation of the Democratic Peace." *American Political Science Review* 93, 4: 791–807.

————. 2003. *The Logic of Political Survival.* Cambridge: MIT Press.

Burstein, Daniel. 1988. *YEN! Japan's New Financial Empire and Its Threat to America.* New York: Simon and Schuster.

Cain, Bruce E., John A. Ferejohn, and Morris P. Fiorina. 1987. *The Personal Vote: Constituency Service and Electoral Independence.* Cambridge: Harvard University Press.

Calder, Kent E. 1988. *Crisis and Compensation: Public Policy and Political Stability in Japan.* Princeton, NJ: Princeton University Press.

———. 1993. *Strategic Capitalism: Private Business and Public Purpose in Japanese Industrial Finance.* Princeton, NJ: Princeton University Press.

———. 1997. *Asia's Deadly Triangle: How Arms, Energy, and Growth Threaten to Destabilize Asia-Pacific.* London: Nicholas Brealey.

Campbell, John Creighton. 1997. "Initiating Public Long Term Care Insurance in Japan." *Journal of the International Institute,* 5, 1 http://hdl.handle.net/2027/spo.4750978.0005.104.

———. 2002. "Japanese Social Policy in Comparative Perspective." World Bank Working Paper 37197.

Campbell, John Creighton, and Naoki Ikegami. 1998. *The Art of Balance in Health Policy: Maintaining Japan's Low-Cost, Egalitarian System.* New York: Cambridge University Press.

Carey, John M., and Matthew Soberg Shugart. 1995. "Incentives to Cultivate a Personal Vote: A Rank Ordering of Electoral Formulas." *Electoral Studies* 14, 4: 417–439.

Choate, Pat. 1990. *Agents of Influence.* New York: A. A. Knopf.

Chopel, Alison, Nozomu Kuno, and Sven Steinmo. 2005. "Social Security, Taxation, and Redistribution in Japan." *Public Budgeting and Finance* (Winter): 20–42.

Christensen, Raymond. 1994. "Electoral Reforms in Japan: How It Was Enacted and Changes It May Bring." *Asian Survey* 34, 7: 589–605.

Chua, Amy. 2003. *World on Fire: How Exporting Free Market Democracy Breeds Ethnic Hatred and Global Instability.* New York: Doubleday.

Clark, Robert L., and Olivia S. Mitchell. 2002. "Strengthening Employment-Based Pensions in Japan." Pension Research Council Working Paper.

Colegrove, Kenneth. 1934. "Powers and Functions of the Japanese Diet." *American Political Science Review* 28, 1: 23–39.

Conlan, Thomas. 2004. *State of War: The Violent Order of Fourteenth-Century Japan.* Ann Arbor: Center for Japanese Studies, University of Michigan.

Cowhey, Peter F., and Mathew D. McCubbins, eds. 1995. *Structure and Policy in Japan and the United States.* New York: Cambridge University Press.

Cox, Gary W. 1990. "Centripetal and Centrifugal Incentives in Electoral Systems." *American Journal of Political Science* 34, 4: 903–935.

———. 1997. *Making Votes Count.* New York: Cambridge University Press.

Cox, Gary W., and Mathew D. McCubbins. 1986. "Electoral Politics as a Redistributive Game." *Journal of Politics* 48, 2: 370–389.

Cox, Gary, Frances McCall Rosenbluth, and Michael F. Thies. 1999. "Electoral

Reform and the Fate of Factions: The Case of Japan's Liberal Democratic Party." *British Journal of Political Science* 29: 33–56.

———. 2000. "Electoral Rules, Career Ambitions, and Party Structure: Comparing Factions in Japan's Lower and Upper Houses." *American Journal of Political Science* 44, 1: 115–122.

Cox, Gary, and Michael F. Thies. 1998. "The Cost of Intraparty Competition: The Single, Nontransferable Vote and Money Politics in Japan." *Comparative Political Studies* 31, 3: 267–291.

Craig, Gordon. 1951. "Portrait of a Political General: Edwin von Manteuffel and the Constitutional Conflict in Prussia." *Political Science Quarterly* 66, 1: 1–36.

Crichton, Michael. 1992. *Rising Sun*. New York: Ballantine Books.

Crystal, Jonathan. 2003. *Unwanted Company: Foreign Investment in American Industries*. Ithaca, NY: Cornell University Press.

Dahlberg, Frances, ed. 1981. *Woman the Gatherer*. New Haven: Yale University Press.

Daniels, Gordon. 1968. "The British Role in the Meiji Restoration: A Reinterpretive Note." *Modern Asian Studies* 2, 1: 291–313.

Davis, Christina L. 2003. *Food Fights over Free Trade: How International Institutions Provide Agricultural Trade Liberalization*. Princeton, NJ: Princeton University Press.

Dekle, Robert. 2005. *Understanding Japanese Savings: Does Population Aging Matter?* New York: Routledge.

Denzau, Arthur T., and Michael C. Munger. 1986. "Legislators and Interest Groups: How Unorganized Interests Get Represented." *American Political Science Review* 80: 89–106.

Divale, William Tulio, and Marvin Harris. 1976. "Population, Warfare, and the Male Supremacist Complex." *American Anthropologist* 78, 3: 521–538

Dixit, Avinash, and John Londregan. 1996. "The Determinants of Success of Special Interests in Redistributive Politics." *Journal of Politics* 58, 4: 1132–1155.

Dower, John W. 1986. *War without Mercy: Race and Power in the Pacific War*. New York: Pantheon Books.

———. 1999. *Embracing Defeat: Japan in the Wake of World War II*. New York: W. W. Norton.

Downs, Anthony. 1957. *An Economic Theory of Democracy*. New York: Harper & Row.

Doyle, Michael W. 1986. "Liberalism and World Politics." *American Political Science Review* 80, 4: 1151–1169.

Druckman, James N., and Michael F. Thies. 2002. "The Importance of Concurrence: The Impact of Bicameralism on Government Formation and Duration." *American Journal of Political Science* 46, 4: 760–771.

Duus, Peter. 1968. *Party Rivalry and Political Change in Taisho Japan.* Cambridge: Harvard University Press.

———. 1976. *The Rise of Modern Japan.* Boston: Houghton Mifflin.

Duverger, Maurice. 1954. *Political Parties.* New York: Wiley.

Edwards, Walter. 2000. "Contested Access: The Imperial Tombs in the Postwar Period." *Journal of Japanese Studies* 26, 2: 371–392.

Ehrhardt, George. 2009. "Rethinking the Komeito Voter." *Japanese Journal of Political Science* 10, 1: 1–20.

Endo, Yukihiko. 1999. "Can the 'Big Bang' Cure the Ills of Japan's Financial System?" In *East Asia's Financial Systems: Evolution and Crisis,* edited by Seiichi Masuyama, Donna Vandenbrink, and Chia Siow Yue, 314–346. Tokyo: NRI Nomura Research Institute.

Esping-Andersen, Gøsta. 1990. *The Three Worlds of Welfare Capitalism.* Cambridge, UK: Polity Press.

———. 1999. *Social Foundation of Post Industrial Society.* Oxford: Oxford University Press.

Estévez-Abe, Margarita. 2006. "Gendering the Varieties of Capitalism: A Study of Occupational Segregation by Sex in Advanced Industrial Societies." *World Politics* 59: 142.

———. 2007. "Gendering the Varieties of Capitalism: Gender Bias in Skills and Social Policies." In *The Political Economy of Japan's Low Fertility,* edited by Frances Rosenbluth, 63–86. Stanford: Stanford University Press.

———. 2008. *Welfare and Capitalism in Postwar Japan.* New York: Cambridge University Press.

Estévez-Abe, Margarita, Takako Hikotani, and Toshio Nagahisa. 2008. "Japan's New Executive Leadership: How Electoral Rules Make Japanese Security Policy." In *Japan and the World,* edited by Masaru Kohno and Frances Rosenbluth, 251–288. New Haven: CEAS, Yale University.

Estévez-Abe, Margarita, Torben Iversen, and David Soskice. 2001. "Social Protection and the Formation of Skills: A Reinterpretation of the Welfare State." In *Varieties of Capitalism: The Institutional Foundations of Comparative Advantage,* edited by Peter Hall and David Soskice, 145–183. London: Oxford University Press.

Fallows, James. 1989. "Containing Japan." *Atlantic Monthly,* May.

Farris, William Wayne. 2006. *Japan's Medieval Population: Famine, Fertility, and Warfare in a Transformative Age.* Honolulu: University of Hawaii Press.

Feldstein, Martin. 1997. "Transition to a Fully Funded Pension System: Five Economic Issues." NBER Working Paper 6149.

Ferejohn, John, and Frances Rosenbluth. 2008. "Warlike Democracies." *Journal of Conflict Resolution* 52, 1: 3–38.

Ferejohn, John, and Debra Satz. 2001. "Rational Choice Theory and Folk Psychology." Working Paper, Stanford University.

Foucault, Michel. 1977. *Discipline and Punish: The Birth of the Prison*. New York: Pantheon Books.

Francks, Penelope. 1987. "Review, *Agricultural Development and Tenancy Disputes in Japan* by Richard Smethurst." *Journal of Japanese Studies* 13, 2: 474–481.

Frieden, Jeffry. 1994. "International Investment and Colonial Control: A New Interpretation." *International Organization* 48, 4: 559–593.

Friedman, George, and Meredith LeBard. 1991. *The Coming War with Japan*. New York: St. Martin's Press.

Fujita, Tsugio. 1959. "Review of George Beckmann, *The Making of the Meiji Constitution: The Oligarchs and the Constitutional Development of Japan, 1868– 1891*, University of Kansas Press, 1957." *Monumenta Nipponica* 15, 3/4: 451–456.

Fukuda, Kosei. 1997. "An Empirical Analysis of US and Japanese Health Insurance Using Age-Period-Cohort Decomposition." *Health Economics* 16: 475–489.

"Gaijin at the Gates." 2007. *Economist*, August 16.

Gao, Bai. 1994. "Arisawa Hiromi and His Theory for a Managed Economy." *Journal of Japanese Studies* 20, 1: 115–153.

Garon, Sheldon. 1997. *Molding Japanese Minds: The State in Everyday Life*. Princeton, NJ: Princeton University Press.

Geanakoplos, John, Olivia Mitchell, and Stephen Zeldes. 2000. "Social Security Money's Worth," Cowles Foundation Paper No. 1005.

Gellner, Ernest. 1997. *Nationalism*. London: Weidenfeld and Nicholson.

George Mulgan, Aurelia. 2005. "Where Tradition Meets Change: Japan's Agricultural Politics in Transition." *Journal of Japanese Studies* 31, 2: 261–298.

Gerschenkron, Alexander. 1966. *Economic Backwardness in Historical Perspective*. Cambridge: Belknap Press, Harvard University Press.

Giannetti, Daniela, and Michael F. Thies. 2008. "Factional Politics in Italy and Japan." Paper presented at the Conference on the Long-Term Consequences of Electoral Rules Change: Comparing Italy and Japan. Bologna, Italy, November 28–29.

Gilbert, Martin. 2000. *Churchill: A Life*. London: Pimlico.

Gilens, Martin. 1999. *Why Americans Hate Welfare: Race, Media, and the Politics of Antipoverty Policy*. Chicago: University of Chicago Press.

Gluck, Carol. 1985. *Japan's Modern Myths: Ideology in the Late Meiji Period*. Princeton, NJ: Princeton University Press.

———. 1998. "House of Mirrors: American History-Writing on Japan." In *Imagined Histories: American Historians Interpret the Past*, edited by Anthony Molho and Gordon S. Wood, 434–454. Princeton, NJ: Princeton University Press.

Golden, Miriam A., and Lucio Picci. 2008. "Pork Barrel Politics in Postwar Italy, 1953–1994." *American Journal of Political Science* 52, 2 (April): 268–289.

Gordon, Andrew D. 2002. *A Modern History of Japan: From Tokugawa Times to the Present*. Oxford: Oxford University Press.

Gordon, Beate Sirota. 1997. *The Only Woman in the Room: A Memoir*. Tokyo: Kodansha.

Gottfried, Heidi, and Jacqueline O'Reilly. 2002. "Regulating Breadwinner Models in Socially Conservative Welfare Systems: Comparing Germany and Japan." *Social Politics* 9, 1: 29–59.

Gourevitch, Peter A. 2003. "The Politics of Corporate Governance Regulation." *Yale Law Journal* 112, 7: 1829–1880.

Gourevitch, Peter, and James Shinn. 2002. *How Shareholder Reforms Can Pay Foreign Policy Dividends*. New York: Council on Foreign Relations.

———. 2005. *Political Power and Corporate Control: The New Global Politics of Corporate Governance*. Princeton, NJ: Princeton University Press.

Gramsci, Antonio. 1994. *Letters from Prison*. Edited by Frank Rosengarten. New York: Columbia University Press.

Green, Michael J. 2001. *Japan's Reluctant Realism: Foreign Policy Challenges in an Era of Uncertain Power*. New York: Palgrave.

Grew, Joseph. 1944. *Ten Years in Japan*. New York: Simon and Schuster.

Hadley, Eleanor. 1949. "Japan: Competition or Private Collectivism?" *Far Eastern Survey* 18, 25: 289–295.

Hadley, Eleanor, with Patricia Hagan Kuwayama. 2003. *Memoir of a Trustbuster: A Lifelong Adventure with Japan*. Honolulu: University of Hawaii Press.

Hagen, William. 2002. *Ordinary Prussians: Brandenburg Junkers and Villagers, 1500–1840*. New York: Cambridge University Press.

Hall, John Whitney. 1966. *Government and Local Power in Japan, 500–1700: A Study Based on Bizen Province*. Princeton, NJ: Princeton University Press.

———. 1968. "A Monarch for Modern Japan." In *Political Development in Modern Japan*, edited by Robert Ward, 11–64. Princeton, NJ: Princeton University Press.

———. 1995. "The Muromachi Bakufu." In *Warrior Rule in Japan*, edited by Marius Jansen, 91–146. New York: Cambridge University Press.

Hall, John Whitney, and Jeffrey Mass, eds. 1974. *Medieval Japan: Essays in Institutional History*. New Haven: Yale University Press.

Hane, Mikiso. 1982. *Peasant, Rebels, and Outcastes: The Underside of Modern Japan*. New York: Pantheon.

Hayao, Kenji. 1993. *The Japanese Prime Minister and Public Policy*. Pittsburgh: University of Pittsburgh Press.

Hechter, Michael. 2000. *Containing Nationalism*. New York: Oxford University Press.

Hein, Laura. 2004. *Reasonable Men, Powerful Words: Political Culture and Expertise in Twentieth-Century Japan*. Berkeley and Los Angeles: University of California Press.

Heller, William B. 1997. "Bicameralism and Budget Deficits: The Effect of Parliamentary Structure on Government Spending." *Legislative Studies Quarterly* 22, 4 (November): 485–516.

Hersey, John. 1989. *Hiroshima*. New York: Vintage.

Herz, John. 1950. "Idealist Internationalism and the Security Dilemma." *World Politics* 20, 2: 157–180.

Hirano, Shigeo. 2006. "Electoral Institutions, Hometowns and Favored Minorities: Evidence from Japanese Electoral Reforms." *World Politics* 59, 1: 51–82.

Hirose, Michisada. 1989. *Seiji to kane*. Tokyo: Iwanami.

Hiwatari, Nobuhiro. 2001. "Why Electoral Reform and Party System Reorganization? The Impact of Global Capital Mobility on the Consensus Democratic Institutions of Italy and Japan." University of Tokyo Institute of Social Sciences Working Paper.

Hobson, John A. 1902. *Imperialism: A Study*. New York: James Pott and Co.

Horiuchi, Yusaku, and Jun Saito. 2003. "Reapportionment and Redistribution: Consequences of Electoral Reform in Japan." *American Journal of Political Science* 47, 4: 669–682.

———. 2009. "Removing Boundaries to Lose Connections: Political Consequences of Local Reform in Japan." Unpublished manuscript.

Horiuchi, Yusaku, and Jingru Wang. 2006. "Friendship during the Crisis: Chinese University Students' Attitudes towards Japan." ANU manuscript.

Hoshi, Takeo, and Anil Kashyap. 2001. *Corporate Financing and Governance in Japan: The Road to the Future*. Cambridge: MIT Press.

Hoshi, Takeo, Anil Kashyap, and David Scharfstein. 1990. "The Role of Banks in Reducing the Costs of Financial Distress in Japan." *Journal of Financial Economics* 27: 67–88.

Hoshi, Takeo, and Hugh Patrick, eds. 2000. *Crisis and Change in the Japanese Financial System*. Boston, MA: Kluwer Academic Publishers.

Hrdy, Sarah Blaffer. 1999. *Mother Nature: A History of Mothers, Infants, and Natural Selection*. New York: Pantheon Books.

Hrebenar, Ronald J., ed. 1986. *The Japanese Party System: From One-Party Rule to Coalition Government*. Boulder, CO: Westview Press.

———, ed. 1992. *The Japanese Party System*. 2nd ed. Boulder, CO: Westview Press.

Hudson, Mark. 1999. *Ruins of Identity: Ethnogenesis in the Japanese Islands*. Honolulu: University of Hawaii Press.

Hughes, Christopher W. 2004. *Japan's Re-emergence as a 'Normal' Military Power*. Oxford: International Institute for Strategic Studies.

Hume, David. 2001. *An Enquiry concerning Human Understanding*. Edited by Tom Beauchamp. New York: Oxford University Press.

Huntington, Samuel P. 1987. "The Goals of Development." In *Understanding Political Development*, edited by Myron Weiner and Samuel Huntington, 3–32. Glenview, IL: Scott Foresman/Little Brown.

Ienaga, Saburo. 1963. *History of Japan*. Tokyo: Toppan Printing Company.

Ike, Nobutaka. 1965. "The Fundamental Strength of Early Democratic Forces." In *Democracy in Prewar Japan: Groundwork or Façade?*, edited by George O. Totten, 27–35. Lexington, MA: D. C. Heath and Company.

Ike, Susumu. Forthcoming. "Competence over Loyalty: Lords and Retainers in Medieval Japan." In *War and Statebuilding in Medieval Japan*, edited by John Ferejohn and Frances Rosenbluth. Palo Alto, CA: Stanford University Press.

Ikegami, Naoki. 1991. "Japanese Health Care: Low Cost through Regulated Fees." *Health Affairs* 10, 3: 87–109.

Ikegami, Naoki, and John Campbell. 1997. "Health Care Reform in Japan: The Virtues of Muddling Through." *Health Affairs* 18, 3: 56–75.

Imai, Kazutoshi. 1994. "The Employment System and Human Resource Management." In *Business Enterprise in Japan: Views of Leading Japanese Economists*, edited by Kenichi Imai and Ryutaro Komiya, 225–260. Cambridge: MIT Press.

Imai, Kenichi, and Ryutaro Komiya. 1994. "Characteristics of Japanese Firms." In *Business Enterprise in Japan: Views of Leading Japanese Economists*, edited by Kenichi Imai and Ryutaro Komiya, 19–38. Cambridge: MIT Press.

Imai, Yutaka. 2002. "Health Care Reform in Japan." OECD Economics Department Working Paper No. 321.

Imamura, Keiji. 1996. *Prehistoric Japan: New Perspectives on Insular East Asia*. Honolulu: University of Hawaii Press.

———. 1997. *Sengoku kanayama densetsu o horu: Kai Kurokawa kanayamashu no sokuseki*. Tokyo: Heibonsha.

Inaba, Tsuguharu. Forthcoming. "Community Vitality in Medieval Japan." In *War and Statebuilding in Medieval Japan*, edited by John Ferejohn and Frances Rosenbluth. Palo Alto, CA: Stanford University Press.

Inoguchi, Takashi, and Tomoaki Iwai. 1987. *Zoku giin no kenkyu* [Research on Zoku Politicians]. Tokyo: Nihon keizai shimbunsha.

Inoue, Motohiko. 2002. *Hijoji no otoko: Ichimada Hisato no ketsudan ryoku* [A Man for Extraordinary Times: The Decisiveness of Ichimnda Hisato]. Tokyo: Zaikai kenkyujo.

International Social Survey Program (ISSP). 1998. *International Social Survey Program: National Identity, 1995*. [Computer file]. ICPSR release. Cologne, Germany: Zentralarchiv für Empirische Sozialforschung [producer]. Cologne, Germany: Zentralarchiv für Empirische Sozialforschung/Ann Arbor, MI: Interuniversity Consortium for Political and Social Research.

International Social Survey Program (ISSP). 2003. *International Social Survey Program: National Identity II, 2003*. http://www.gesis.org/en/services/data/survey-data/issp/modules-study-overview/national-identity/2003/.

Iriye, Akira. 1972. *Pacific Estrangement: Japanese and American Expansion, 1897–1911*. Cambridge: Harvard University Press.

Ishida, Takeshi. 1971. *Japanese Society*. New York: Random House.

Ishii, Susumu. 1995. "The Decline of the Kamakura Bakufu." In *Warrior Rule in Japan*, edited by Marius Jansen, 44–90. New York: Cambridge University Press.

Ishiyama, Hisao. 2003. "Japanese Textbooks Aren't Getting Much Better." Translated by Richard Minear from *Shukan Kinyobi* for *Japan Focus*. http://hnn.us/articles/1639.html.

Ishizuka, Katsumi. 2005. "Japan's Policy towards UN Peacekeeping Operations." *International Peacekeeping* 12, 1: 67–86.

Itagaki, Morimasa, ed. 1933. *Itagaki Taisuke zenshu*. Tokyo: Shunjusha.

Ito, Shuhei. 1999. "Kaigo hoken Seiko no jendaa mondai" [The Gender Problem of Long-Term Health Insurance]. *Josei Rodo Kenkyu* 36: 26–31.

Ito, Yukio. 2004. *Seito seiji to tenno* [Party Politics and the Emperor]. Tokyo: Kodansha.

Iversen, Torben, and Frances Rosenbluth. 2010. *The Political Economy of Gender*. New Haven, CT: Yale University Press.

Iwai, Katsuhito. 2007. "What Is a Corporation?: The Corporate Personality Controversy and Comparative Corporate Governance." In *Legal Orderings and Economic Institutions*, edited by Fabrizio Cafaggi, Antonio Nicita, and Ugo Pagano, 243–267. London: Routledge.

Iwai, Tomoaki. 1990. *Seiji shikin no kenkyu* [Research on Political Campaign Financing]. Tokyo: Nihon keizai shimbunsha.

Iwata, Masakazu. 1983. "Okubo Toshimichi." *Kodansha Encyclopedia of Japan*, 6:94. Tokyo: Kodansha International.

Jackson, Gregory. 2001. "The Origins of Nonliberal Corporate Governance in Germany and Japan." In *The Origins of Nonliberal Capitalism: Germany and Japan in Comparison*, edited by Wolfgang Streeck and Kozo Yamamura, 121–170. Ithaca, NY: Cornell University Press.

———. 2007. "Employment Adjustment and Distributional Conflict in Japanese Firms." In *Corporate Governance in Japan: Institutional Change and Organizational Diversity*, edited by Masahiko Aoki, Gregory Jackson, and Hideaki Miyajima, 282–309. Oxford: Oxford University Press.

Jackson, Gregory, and Hideaki Miyajima. 2007. "Introduction: The Diversity and Change of Corporate Governance in Japan." In *Corporate Governance in Japan: Institutional Change and Organizational Diversity*, edited by Masahiko Aoki, Gregory Jackson, and Hideaki Miyajima, 1–47. New York: Oxford University Press.

Japan Center for International Finance. 2004. "Assessment and Strategies of Foreign Financial Institutions in Japan regarding the Tokyo Financial/Capital Market." Tokyo: JCIF.

Jervis, Robert. 1976. *Perception and Misperception in International Relations*. Princeton, NJ: Princeton University Press.

Johnson, Chalmers. 1982. *MITI and the Economic Miracle*. Berkeley and Los Angeles: University of California Press.

———. 1987. "Political Institutions and Economic Performance: The Government-Business Relationship in Japan, South Korea, and Taiwan." In *The Political Economy of the New Asian Industrialism*, edited by Frederic C. Deyo, 136–165. Ithaca, NY: Cornell University Press.

Johnson, Chalmers. 1990. Public lecture at the Japan Society in New York City in 1990.

Kagono, Tadao, and Takao Kobayashi. 1994. "The Provision of Resources and Barriers to Exit." In *Business Enterprise in Japan: Views of Leading Japanese Economists*, edited by Kenichi Imai and Ryutaro Komiya, 89–104. Cambridge: MIT Press.

Kaiser Family Foundation. January 2007. *Health Care Spending in the U.S. and OECD*. http://www.kff.org/insurance/snapshot/chcm010307oth.cfm.

Kambayashi, Ryo, and Takai Kato. 2009. "The Japanese Employment System after the Bubble Burst: New Evidence." Center for Japanese Economy and Business Working Paper No. 268. Columbia Business School. www.gsb.columbia.edu/cjeb/research/ac.

Kanda, Hideki. 2000. "The Role of the Board in Overseeing Financial Reporting and Disclosure." OECD/ADB/World Bank Second Asian Roundtable on Corporate Governance. May 31–June 2.

Kant, Emmanuel. 1991 [1794]. *Political Writings*. Cambridge: Cambridge University Press.

Kase, Kazutoshi. 2004. "Unemployment Policy in Prewar Japan: How Progressive Was Japanese Social Policy?" *Social Science Japan Journal* 7, 2: 199–221.

Kasza, Gregory J. 2006. *The One World of Welfare: Japan in Comparative Perspective*. Ithaca, NY: Cornell University Press.

Kato, Junko, and Bo Rothstein. 2006. "Government Partisanship and Managing the Economy: Japan and Sweden in Comparative Perspective." *Governance: An International Journal of Policy, Administration, and Institutions* 19, 1: 75–97.

Katz, Richard. 1998. *Japan, the System That Soured: The Rise and Fall of the Japanese Economic Miracle*. Armonk, NY: M. E. Sharpe.

———. 2003. *Japanese Phoenix: The Long Road to Economic Revival*. Armonk, NY: M. E. Sharpe.

Katz, Richard. 2005. "Why the Corporate Defensiveness: Stable Shareholding Down, Foreign Ownership Up." *Oriental Economist*, June 2.

Kawada, Minoru. 1998. *Hara Takashi to Yamagata Aritomo*. Tokyo: Chuo koron shinsha.

Kennan, George. 1947. "The Sources of Soviet Conduct." *Foreign Affairs* 25: 466.

Kennedy, Paul. 1989. *The Rise and Fall of the Great Powers: Economic Change and Military Conflict from 1500 to 2000*. New York: Vintage Books.

Khoon, Chan Chee. 2006. "Renegotiating the Social Contract: Challenges to Health and Social Policy in Japan." *Japanese Economy* 33, 4: 128–145.

Kindleberger, C. P. 1972. "The Benefits of International Money." *Journal of International Economics* 2, 3: 425.

Kirkland, Russell. 1997. "The Sun and the Throne: The Origins of the Royal Descent Myth in Ancient Times." *Numen* 44, 2: 109–152.

Kishiro, Yasuyuki. 1985. *Jiminto zeisei chosakai* [The LDP Tax Committee]. Tokyo: Toyo Keizai Shimposha.

Kobayashi, Yoshinori. 1998. *Shin Gomanizumu Sengen: Sensoron*. Tokyo: Gentosha.

Kohno, Masaru. 1997. *Japan's Postwar Party Politics*. Princeton, NJ: Princeton University Press.

Köllner, Patrick. 2007. "Campaigning for the Japanese Lower House: From Mobilising to Chasing Voter?" GIGA Working Paper. http://www.giga-hamburg.de/workingpapers.

Komamura, Kohei, and Atsuhiro Yamada. 2004. "Who Bears the Burden of Social Insruance? Evidence from Japanese Health and Long-Term Care Insurance Data." *Journal of Japanese and International Economics* 18: 565–581.

Krauss, Ellis S., and Robert Pekkanen. 2004. "Explaining Party Adaptation to Electoral Reform: The Discreet Charm of the LDP?" *Journal of Japanese Studies* 30,1:1–34.

Kuhn, Steven L., and Mary C. Stiner. 2006. "What's a Mother to Do? The Division of Labor among Neanderthals and Modern Humans in Eurasia." *Current Anthropology* 47, 6: 953–980.

Kwan, Weng Kin. 2007. "Abe's Pension Pledge Fails to Sway Japanese." *Straits Times*, http://www.straitstimes.com, June 25, 2007.

Laakso, Markku, and Taagepera, Rein. 1979. "Effective Number of Parties: A Measure with Application to West Europe." *Comparative Political Studies* 12: 3–27.

La Porta, Rafael, Florence Lopez-de-Silanes, Andrei Shleifer, and Robert W. Vishny. 1997. "Legal Determinants of External Finance." *Journal of Finance* 52, 3:1131–1150.

Leduc, Benoit. 2003/2004. "The Anatomy of the Welfare-Zoku: The Institutional Complementarity of the Party Commissions and the National Reform Councils in the LDP Decision Making." *Pacific Affairs* 76, 4: 569–592.

Lee, Won deog. 2001. "A Normal State without Remorse: The Textbook Controversy and Korea-Japan Relations." *East Asian Review* 13, 3: 21–40.

Lee, Yih-Jiunn, and Yeun-wen Ku. 2007. "East Asian Welfare Regimes: Testing the Hypothesis of the Developmental Welfare State." *Social Policy and Administration* 41, 2: 197–212.

Leiserson, Michael. 1968. "Factions and Coalitions in One-Party Japan: An Interpretation Based on the Theory of Games." *American Political Science Review* 66: 770–87.

Lenin, Vladimir. 1916. Imperialism: The Highest Stage of Capitalism. Available on the Lenin Internet Archive. http://www.marxists.org/archive/lenin/works/1916.

Levitt, Steven D., and James M. Snyder. 1995. "Political Parties and the Distribution of Outlays." *American Journal of Political Science* 39, 4: 958–980.

Lewin, Bruno. 1988. "Review: Yet Another Array of Opinions on 'nihongo no kigen'." *Journal of the Association of Teachers of Japanese* 22, 1: 97–104.

Lijphart, Arend. 1984. *Democracies: Patterns of Majoritarian and Consensus Government in Twenty-one Countries.* New Haven: Yale University Press.

———. 1994. *Electoral Systems and Party Systems.* New York: Oxford University Press.

Lind, Jennifer M. 2004. "Pacifism or Passing the Buck? Testing Theories of Japanese Security Policy." *International Security* 29, 1: 92–121.

———. 2005. "Think Again: Japanese Textbooks." *Foreign Policy* web exclusive. http://www.foreignpolicy.com.

———. 2008. *Sorry States: Apologies in International Politics.* Ithaca, NY: Cornell University Press.

Lindbeck, Assar, and Jörgen W. Weibull. 1987. "Balanced-Budget Redistribution as the Outcome of Political Competition." *Public Choice* 52, 3: 273–297.

Lipscy, Philip. 2005. "Japan's Quest for Leadership in the Bretton Woods Institutions: Conceptualizing International Institutions as Cooperative Standards." Paper presented at the annual meeting of the International Studies Association, Hilton Hawaiian Village, Honolulu, HI.

Lipset, Seymour Martin. 1959. "Some Social Requisites of Democracy: Economic Development and Political Legitimacy." *American Political Science Review* 53, 1: 69–105.

Maas, Jeffrey. 1995. "The Kamakura Bakufu," In *Warrior Rule in Japan*, edited by Marius Jansen, 1–43. New York: Cambridge University Press.

Maclachlan, Patricia. 2002. *Consumer Politics in Postwar Japan: The Institutional Boundaries of Citizen Activism.* New York: Columbia University Press.

———. 2004. "Post Office Politics in Modern Japan: The Postmasters, Iron Triangles, and the Limits of Reform." *Journal of Japanese Studies* 30, 2: 281–313.

———. 2007. "Two Steps Forward, One Step Back: Japanese Postal Privatization as a Window on Political and Policymaking Change." Paper presented at a Conference on Japanese Politics, Stanford University, June 11–12.

———. 2009. "The Politics of Structural Reform in the Post-Koizumi Era: The Case of Postal Privatization." Unpublished manuscript prepared for the UCLA Workshop on Japan's Post-Bubble Political Economy, September 11–12, 2009.

Manow, Philip. 2001. "Business Coordination, Wage Bargaining, and the Welfare State: Germany and Japan in Comparative Historical Perspective." In *Comparing Welfare Capitalism: Social Policy and Political Economy in Europe, Japan, and the U.S.A.*, edited by Bernard Ebbinghaus and Philip Manow, 27–51. London: Routledge.

Mansfield, Harvey Clafin. 2006. *Manliness*. New Haven, CT: Yale University Press.

Marotti, William. 2009. "Japan 1968: The Performance of Violence and the Theater of Protest." *American Historical Review* 114, 1: 97–135.

Marquand, Robert. 2005. "Tokyo Teacher Embattled over War History." *Christian Science Monitor*, November 22.

Maruyama, Masao. 1946. "Chokokkashugi no ronri to shinri" [The Theory and Psychology of Hypernationalism]." *Sekai*.

———. 1958. *History of Political Thought in Japan*. Tokyo: University of Tokyo Press.

Masalski, Kathleen Woods. 2001. "Examining the Japanese History Textbook Controversies." National Clearinghouse for U.S.-Japan Studies, Indiana University.

McCormack, Gavan. 2001. "Introduction." In *Multicultural Japan: Paleolithic to Postmodern*, edited by Donald Denoon, Gavan McCormack, Mark Hudson, and Tessa Morris-Suzuki, 1–15. New York: Cambridge University Press.

McCubbins, Mathew D. 1991. "Party Politics, Divided Government, and Budget Deficits." In *Parallel Politics: Economic Policymaking in Japan and the United States*, edited by Samuel Kernell, 83–118. Washington, DC: Brookings Institution.

McCubbins, Mathew D., and Frances M. Rosenbluth. 1995. "Party Provision for Personal Politics: Dividing the Vote in Japan." In *Structure and Policy in Japan and the United States*, edited by Peter F. Cowhey and Mathew D. McCubbins, 35–55. New York: Cambridge University Press.

McCubbins, Mathew, and Michael Thies. 1997. "As a Matter of Factions: The Budgetary Implications of Shifting Factional Control in Japan's LDP." *Legislative Studies Quarterly* 22, 3: 293–328.

McElwain, Kenneth Mori. 2009. "How Long Are Koizumi's Coattails? Party-Leader Visits in the 2005 Election." In *Political Change in Japan: Electoral Behavior, Party Realignment, and the Koizumi Reforms*, edited by Steven R. Reed, Kenneth M. McElwain, and Kaoru Shimizu, 133–156. Palo Alto, CA: Walter H. Shorenstein Asia-Pacific Research Center.

McGillivray, Fiona. 2004. *Privileging Industry: The Comparative Politics of Trade and Industrial Policy*. Princeton, NJ: Princeton University Press.

McKean, Margaret A. 1981. *Environmental Protests and Citizen Politics in Japan*. Berkeley and Los Angeles: University of California Press.

McKean, Margaret A., and Ethan Scheiner. 2000. "Japan's New Electoral System: La plus ça change. . . ." *Electoral Studies* 19: 447–477.

Mikuriya, Takashi. 2007. "Sengo Hoshu Seijika-tachi no Shiso-teki Keifu." *Chuo Koron*. February.

Milanovic, Branko. 2005. "Half a World: Regional Inequality in Five Great Federations." *Journal of the Asia Pacific Economy* 10, 4: 408–445.

Milgrom, Paul, and John Roberts. 1994. "Complementarities and Systems: Understanding Japanese Economic Organization." Stanford University GSB Working Paper.

Milhaupt, Curtis J. 2003. "Nonprofit Organizations as Investor Protection: Economic Theory, and Evidence from East Asia." *Yale Journal of International Law* 29: 169.

————. 2006. "A Lost Decade for Japanese Corporate Governance Reform? What's Changed, What Hasn't, and Why." In *Institutional Change in Japan*, edited by Magnus Blomström and Sumner La Croix, 97–119. New York: Routledge.

Mincer, Jacob. 1968. "The Distribution of Labor Incomes: A Survey with Special Reference to the Human Capital Approach." *Journal of Economic Literature* 8, 1: 1–26.

Ministry of Internal Affairs and Communications. 2006. *The Local Government System in Japan.*

Mitsubayashi, Takeshi. 1975. *Tokushima han no shiteki kozo* [The Historical Construction of the Tokushima Domain]. Tokyo: Meicho Shuppan.

Miwa, Yoshiro, and J. Mark Ramseyer. 2006. *The Fable of the Keiretsu: Urban Legends of the Japanese Economy.* Chicago: University of Chicago Press.

Miyajima, Hideaki, and Fumiaki Kuroki. 2007. "The Unwinding of Cross-shareholding in Japan: Causes, Effects, and Implications." In *Corporate Governance in Japan: Institutional Change and Organizational Diversity*, edited by Masahiko Aoki, Gregory Jackson, and Hideaki Miyajima, 79–124. New York: Oxford University Press.

Miyajima, Hideaki, and Yishay Yafeh. 2003. "Japan's Banking Crisis: Who Has the Most to Lose?" Waseda University Working Paper.

Moore, Barrington. 1966. *Social Origins of Dictatorship and Democracy: Lord and Peasant in the Making of the Modern World.* Boston: Beacon Press.

Moriguchi, Chiaki, and Hiroshi Ono. 2006. "Japanese Lifetime Employment: A Century's Perspective." In *Institutional Change in Japan*, edited by Magnus Blomström and Sumner La Croix, 152–176. New York: Routledge.

Nagahisa, Toshio. 1994. "The Source of Japanese Opposition to Increasing Defense Commitments: The Influence of Electoral Systems." Ph.D. diss., UCLA.

————. 2007. "Reasons That Activated Japan in Security Commitments." Paper presented at the Conference on Japan and the World, Yale University, March 9–10.

Najita, Tetsuo. 1967. *Hara Kei in the Politics of Compromise, 1905–1915.* Cambridge: Harvard University Press.

————. 1968. "Inukai Tsuyoshi: Some Dilemmas in Party Development in Pre–World War II Japan." *American Historical Review* 74, 2: 492–510.

Nakane, Chie. 1970. *Japanese Society.* Berkeley and Los Angeles: University of California Press.

Nakanishi, Terumasa. 2006. *Nihon Bunmei no Kohai* [The Destruction of Japan's Civilization]. Kyoto: PHP.

Nakano, Minoru. 2002. *New Japanese Political Economy and Political Reform.* Florence, Italy: European Press Academic Publishing.

National Institute of Population and Social Security Research. 2002. "Chapter 2: Pensions." www.ipss.go.jp/s-info/e/Jasos2002/c_2.html.

Niksch, Larry, and Robert Sutter. 1991. "Japan's Response to the Persian Gulf Crisis: Implications for U.S.-Japan Relations." May 23. Congressional Research Service. http://digital.library.unt.edu/govdocs/crs/data/1991/meta-crs-8-tkl.

Nishio, Masaru. 2007. "Chihou Bunken Kaikaku" [Decentralization Reform]. Working Paper on Public Administration 5, University of Tokyo.

Nitobe, Inazo. 1905. *Bushido: The Soul of Japan.* Rutland: C. E. Tuttle Co.

Noble, Gregory W. 1989. "The Japanese Industrial Policy Debate." In *Pacific Dynamics*, edited by Stephan Haggard and Chung-In Moon, 53–96. Boulder, CO: Westview Press.

———. 2009. "The Decline of Particularism in Japanese Politics." Paper presented at the Annual Meeting of the Association of Asian Studies, Chicago, IL, March 26–29.

Nomura, Tomohiro, 2008. "The Effects and Incentive System of Decentralization in Japan." Working Paper, East Asian Studies, Yale University.

Norman, E. H. 1940. *Japan's Emergence as a Modern State: Political and Economic Problems of the Meiji Period.* New York: Institute of Pacific Relations.

North, Douglass C. 1990. *Institutions, Institutional Change, and Economic Performance.* New York: Cambridge University Press.

Oates, Wallace. 1972. *Fiscal Federalism.* New York: Harcourt Brace Jovanovich.

Ogishima, Seiji, and Takao Kobayashi. 2002. "Cross-Shareholdings and Equity Valuation in Japan." Nomura Securities Working Paper. March.

Ohnuki-Tierney, Emiko. 2002. *Kamikaze, Cherry Blossoms, and Nationalism: The Militarization of Aesthetics in Japanese History.* Chicago: University of Chicago Press.

Okazaki, Tetsuji. 2007. "Economic Development, Income Inequality, and Social Stability in Prewar Japan: A Prefectural Analysis." Center for International Research on the Japanese Economy, Discussion Paper F-500. June.

Ono, Hiroshi. 2003. "Foreign Ownership and Earnings in the Japanese Labor Market." Stockholm School of Economics Working Paper.

Ozawa, Ichiro. 1993. *Nihon Kaizo Keikaku.* Tokyo: Kodansha.

Packard, George. 1966. *Protest in Tokyo: The Security Treaty Crisis of 1960.* Princeton, NJ: Princeton University Press.

Pagano, Marco, and Paolo Volpin. 2005. "The Political Economy of Corporate Governance." *American Economic Review* 95, 4: 1005–1030.

Palmer, Robert.1959. *The Age of the Democratic Revolution: A Political History of Europe and the United States.* Princeton, NJ: Princeton University Press.

Patrick, Hugh. 2006. "Japan's Economy: Finally Finding Its Way to Full Employment and Sustained Growth." Center on Japanese Economy and Business Working Paper No. 249, Columbia Business School. November.

Patrick, Hugh, and Henry Rosovsky, eds. 1976. *Asia's New Giant*. Washington, DC: Brookings Institution.

Patterson, Samuel C., and Anthony Mughan, eds. 1999. *Senates: Bicameralism in the Contemporary World*. Columbus: Ohio State University Press.

Peek, Joe, and Eric S. Rosengren. 2000. "Collateral Damage: Effects of the Japanese Bank Crisis on Real Activity in the United States." *American Economic Review* 90, 1: 35–40.

———. 2001. "Determinants of the Japanese Premium: Actions Speak Louder Than Words." *Journal of International Economics* 53, 2 (April): 283–305.

Pempel, T. J. 1998. *Regime Shift: Comparative Dynamics of the Japanese Political Economy*. Ithaca, NY: Cornell University Press.

———. 1999. "Structural Gaiatsu: International Finance and Political Change in Japan." *Comparative Political Studies* 32, 8: 907–932.

———. 2005. *Remapping East Asia: The Construction of a Region*. Ithaca, NY: Cornell University Press.

Pempel, T. J., and Keichi Tsunekawa. 1979. "Corporatism without Labor? The Japanese Anomaly." In *Trends Towards Corporatist Intermediation*, edited by Philippe Schmitter and Gerhard Lehmbruch, 231–270. Beverly Hills, CA: Sage.

Peng, Ito. 2000. "A Fresh Look at the Japanese Welfare State." *Social Policy and Administration* 34, 1: 87–114.

Piggott, Joan. 1997. *The Emergence of Japanese Kingship*. Stanford: Stanford University Press.

Pohl, Nicole. 2002. "Foreign Penetration of Japan's Investment-Banking Market: Will Japan Experience the 'Wimbledon Effect'?" Stanford University APARC Working Paper.

Polachek, Solomon W. 1978. "Sex Differences in College Major." *Industrial and Labor Relations Review* 31, 4: 498–508.

Prestowitz, Clyde V., Jr. 1988. *Trading Places: How We Allowed Japan to Take the Lead*. New York: Basic Books.

Proksch, Sven-Oliver, Jon Slapin, and Michael F. Thies. 2009. "The Dynamics of the Party System in Postwar Japan: A Quantitative Content Analysis of Electoral Pledges." Paper prepared for the Annual Meetings of the American Political Science Association, Toronto, Canada, September 2–5, 2009.

Przeworski, Adam, and Fernando Limongi. 1993. "Political Regimes and Economic Growth." *Journal of Economic Perspectives* 7, 3: 51–69.

Quigley, Harold S. 1932. *Japanese Government and Politics: An Introductory Study. The Failure of the First Attempt*. Berkeley and Los Angeles: University of California Press. Excerpts reprinted in, *Democracy in Prewar Japan: Groundwork or Façade?* edited by George Totten. Lexington, MA: D. C. Heath and Company.

———. 1947. "Japan's Constitutions: 1890 and 1947." *American Political Science Review* 41, 5: 865–874.

Rae, Douglas. 1971. *The Political Consequences of Electoral Laws*. Rev. ed. New Haven: Yale University Press.

Rajan, Raghuram, and Luigi Zingales. 2003. "The Great Reversals: The Politics of Financial Development in the Twentieth Century." *Journal of Financial Economics* 61, 1: 5–50.

Ramseyer, J. Mark. 1994. "The Puzzling (In)Dependence of Courts: A Comparative Approach." *Journal of Legal Studies* 23, 2: 721–747.

———. 2007. "Talent and Expertise under Universal Health Insurance: The Case of Cosmetic Surgery in Japan." Working Paper, John Olin Center for Law, Economics, and Business, Harvard University.

Ramseyer, J. Mark, and Frances McCall Rosenbluth. 1993. *Japan's Political Marketplace*. Cambridge: Harvard University Press.

———. 1995. *The Politics of Oligarchy*. New York: Cambridge University Press.

Ravina, Mark. 1999. *Land and Lordship in Early Modern Japan*. Stanford: Stanford University Press.

Reed, Steven R. 1981. "Environmental Politics: Some Reflections Based on the Japanese Case." *Comparative Politics* 14, 2: 253–270.

———. 1990. "Structure and Behaviour: Extending Duverger's Law to the Japanese Case." *British Journal of Political Science* 29: 335–356.

———. 1994. "The Incumbency Advantage in Japan." In *The Victorious Incumbent: A Threat to Democracy?*, edited by Albert Somit et al., 278–303. Aldershot, UK: Dartmouth Publishing Company.

Reed, Steven R., and John M. Bolland. 1999. "The Fragmentation Effect of SNTV in Japan." In *Elections in Japan, Korea, and Taiwan under the Single Non-Transferable Vote*, edited by Bernard Grofman, Sung-Chull Lee, Edwin A Winckler, and Brian Woodall, 211–226. Ann Arbor: University of Michigan Press.

Reed, Steven R., Ethan Scheiner, and Michael F. Thies. 2009. "New Ballgame in Politics: Party-Centered, More Volatile." *Oriental Economist*, October.

Reed, Steven R., and Michael F. Thies. 2001a. "The Causes of Electoral Reform in Japan." In *Mixed-Member Electoral Systems: The Best of Both Worlds?*, edited by Matthew Soberg Shugart and Martin P. Wattenberg, 152–172. New York: Oxford University Press.

———. 2001b. "The Consequences of Electoral Reform in Japan." In *Mixed-Member Electoral Systems: The Best of Both Worlds?*, edited by Matthew Soberg Shugart and Martin P. Wattenberg, 380–403. New York: Oxford University Press.

Reischauer, Edwin. 1946. *Japan: Past and Present*. New York: Alfred Knopf.

Reiter, Dan, and Allen C. Stam. 2002. *Democracies at War*. Princeton: Princeton University Press.

Roberts, Luke. 1998. *Mercantilism in a Japanese Domain: The Merchant Origins of Economic Nationalism in 18th Century Tosa*. New York: Cambridge University Press.

Rodden, Jonathan. 2006. *Hamilton's Paradox: The Promise and Peril of Fiscal Federalism.* New York: Cambridge University Press.

Rodwin, V. G. 1993. "Health Insurance and Health Policy, American and Japanese Style: Lessons of Comparative Experience." NYU Wagner School of Public Service.

Rogowski, Ronald, and Mark Andreas Kayser. 2002. "Majoritarian Electoral Systems and Consumer Power: Price-Level Evidence from the OECD Countries." *American Journal of Political Science* 46, 3 (July): 526–539.

Rosenbluth, Frances McCall. 1989. *Financial Politics in Contemporary Japan.* Ithaca, NY: Cornell University Press.

———. 2007. *The Political Economy of Japan's Low Fertility.* Stanford: Stanford University Press.

Rosenbluth, Frances, Jun Saito, and Annalisa Zinn. 2008. "Japan's New Nationalism: The International and Domestic Politics of an Assertive Foreign Policy." In *Japan and the World: Japan's Contemporary Geopolitical Challenges,* edited by Masaru Kohno and Frances Rosenbluth, 229–250. New Haven, CT: Council on East Asian Studies, Yale University.

Rosenbluth, Frances, and Ross Schaap. 2003. "The Domestic Politics of Banking Regulation." *International Organization* 57 (Spring): 307–336.

Rosenbluth, Frances M., and Michael F. Thies. 2002. "The Political Economy of Japanese Pollution Regulation," *American Asian Review* 20, 1:1–32.

Rowley, Ian. 2004. "A Mortgage of Her Own." *Business Week,* July 12.

Russett, Bruce. 1993. *Grasping the Democratic Peace: Principles for a Post–Cold War World.* Princeton, NJ: Princeton University Press.

Sakairi, Nagataro. 1988. *Taisho Showa shoki zaiseishi* [A Financial History of the Taisho and Early Showa Periods]. Tokyo: Saki Shoten.

Sakamoto, Junichi. 2005. "Japan's Pension Reform." The World Bank Special Protection Discussion Paper No. 0541, December.

Samuelson, Paul Anthony. 1958. *Economics: An Introductory Analysis.* 4th ed. New York: McGraw-Hill.

Sasaki, Takeshi, et al., eds. 1999. *Daigishi to kane: Seiji shikin zenkoku chosa hokoku* [Diet Members and Money: A National Investigative Report on Political Financing]. Tokyo: Asahi sensho.

Sato, Seizaburo, and Tetsuhisa Matsuzaki. 1986. *Jiminto Seiken* [The LDP Administration]. Tokyo: Chuo koron sha.

Satow, Ernest. 1983. *A Diplomat in Japan: An Inner History of the Japanese Reformation.* Tokyo: Tuttle.

Scalapino, Robert. 1953. *Democracy and the Party Movement in Prewar Japan.* Berkeley and Los Angeles: University of California Press.

———. 1968. "Elections and Political Modernization in Prewar Japan." In *Political Development in Modern Japan,* edited by Robert E. Ward, 149–191. Princeton, NJ: Princeton University Press.

Scalapino, Robert A., and Junnosuke Masumi. 1962. *Parties and Politics in Contemporary Japan*. Berkeley and Los Angeles: University of California Press.

SCAP Public Health and Welfare Section. 1946. "Report on the Japanese Social Insurance Programs by the Labor Advisory Committee." Allied Operational and Occupation Headquarters, World War II. RG 331. National Archives, College Park, MD.

Schaap, Ross. 2002. "Institutions and Policy: Financial Regulatory Reform in Japan." Ph.D. diss., UCLA.

Schaede, Ulrike. 2006. "The Strategic Logic of Japanese Keiretsu, Main Banks and Cross Shareholdings, Revisited." Center on Japanese Economy and Business Working Paper No. 247, Columbia Business School. October.

Scheiner, Ethan. 2006. *Democracy without Competition in Japan: Opposition Failure in a One-Party Dominant State*. New York: Cambridge University Press.

Scher, Mark. 2001. "Bank Firm Cross Shareholding in Japan: What Is It, Why Does It Matter, Is It Winding Down?" United Nations Economic and Social Affairs SESA Discussion Paper No. 15.

Schirokauer, Conrad. 1993. *A Brief History of Japanese Civilization*. Fort Worth, TX: Harcourt Brace Jovanovich.

Schoppa, Leonard. 1997. *Bargaining with Japan: What American Pressure Can and Cannot Do*. New York: Columbia University Press.

———. 2006. *Race for the Exits: The Unraveling of Japan's System of Social Protection*. Ithaca, NY: Cornell University Press.

Scott, James. 1990. *Domination and the Art of Resistance*. New Haven: Yale University Press.

Shayo, Moses. 2005. "Nation, Class, and Redistribution: Applying Social Identity Research to Political Economy." Unpublished manuscript.

Sheingate, Adam D., and Takakazu Yamagishi. 2006. "Occupation Politics: American Interests and the Struggle over Health Insurance in Postwar Japan." *Social Science History* 30, 1: 137–164.

Shikibu, Murasaki. 1990. *The Tale of Genji*. Translated by Edward G. Seidensticker. New York: Vintage Books.

Shillony, Ben-Ami. 1981. *Politics and Culture in Wartime Japan*. New York: Oxford University Press.

Shimazu, Naoko, ed., 2006. *Nationalisms in Japan*. London: Routledge.

Shiozaki, Yasuhisa. 2002. "Can Japan's Ailing Banking System Be Cured?" Speech to the Japan Society in New York, May 2.

Shishido, Zenichi. 2006. "The Turnaround of 1997: Changes in Japanese Corporate Law and Governance." Seikei University Working Paper.

Shively, Donald. 1964–1965. "Sumptuary Regulation and Status in Early Tokugawa Japan." *Harvard Journal of Asiatic Studies* 25: 123–164.

Sims, Richard. 1998. "French Policy towards the Bakufu and Meiji Japan 1854–95." *Monumenta Nipponica* 54, 1: 126–127.

...er. 2000. "Why a Funded Pension System Is Useful and Why It ...eful." *International Tax and Public Finance* 7: 389–410.

...rst, Richard J. 1986. *Agricultural Development and Tenancy Disputes in Japan, 1870–1940*. Princeton, NJ: Princeton University Press.

Smith, Anthony. 1999. *Myths and Memories of the Nation*. Oxford: Oxford University Press.

Smitka, Michael. 2004. "Japan's Macroeconomic Dilemmas: The Implications of Demographics for Growth and Stability." Working Paper. Williams School of Commerce, Washington and Lee University.

Smits, Gregory. 2000. "Ambiguous Boundaries: Redefining Royal Authority in the Kingdom of Ryukyu." *Harvard Journal of Asiatic Studies* 60, 1: 89–123.

Soma, Masao. 1986. *Nihon Senkyo Seidoshi* [A History of the Japanese Electoral System]. Fukuoka: University of Kyushu Press.

Soskice, David. 1990. "Reinterpreting Corporatism and Explaining Unemployment: Coordinated and Uncoordinated Market Economies." In *Labour Relations and Economic Performances*, edited by C. Dell'Aringa and R. Brunetta, 170–211. Basingstoke: Macmillan in association with the International Economic Association.

———. 1999. "Divergent Production Regimes: Coordinated and Uncoordinated Market Economies in the 1980s and 1990s." In *Continuity and Change in Contemporary Capitalism*, edited by Herbert Kitschelt et al., 101–134. New York: Cambridge University Press.

Souyri, Pierre. 2001. *The World Turned Upside Down: Medieval Japanese Society*. New York: Columbia University Press.

Steslicke, William. 1973. *Doctors in Politics: The Political Life of the Japan Medical Association*. New York: Praeger Publishers.

Stigler, George J. 1971. "The Theory of Economic Regulation." *Bell Journal of Economics and Management Science* 2: 3–21.

Streeck, Wolfgang. 2001. *High Equality, Low Activity: The Contribution of the Social Welfare System to the Stability of the German Collective Bargaining Regime*. San Domenico di Fiesole, Italy: European University Institute.

Sugita, Yoneyuki. 2003. *Pitfall or Panacea: The Irony of US Power in Occupied Japan, 1945–1952*. New York: Routledge.

Sugiyama Lebra, Takie. 1976. *Japanese Patterns of Behavior*. Honolulu: University of Hawaii Press.

Swenson, Peter. 2002. *Capitalists against Markets: The Making of Labor Markets and Welfare States in the United States and Sweden*. New York: Oxford University Press.

———. 2007. "Good Distribution, Bad Delivery, and Ugly Politics: The Traumatic Beginnings of Germany's Health Care System." Yale University Working Paper.

Taipei Times. 2006. "Japanese Cabinet Approves "Patriotic Education" Legislation." April 29. http://www.taipeitimes.com/News/front/archives/2006/04/29/2003305142.

Takagiwa, Seijiro. 1969. *Ritsuryo jidai no nomin seikatsu* [Agrarian Life in the Ritsuryo Period]. Tokyo: Toko shoin.

Takahashi, Tetsuya. 2005. *Yasukuni Mondai*. Tokyo: Chikuma Shobo.

Takayama, Noriyuki. 2000. "Pension Reform in Japan at the Turn of the Century." Hitotsubashi University Department of Economics Working Paper. March.

Takayanagi, Shun'ichi. 1975. "Review, Nihon shinwa no hikaku kenkyu" [Comparative Research on Japanese Mythology]. *Monumenta Nipponica* 30, 3: 335–339.

Takigawa, Seijiro. 1969. *Ritsuryo jidai no nomin seikatsu*. Tokyo: Toko Shoin.

Tamamoto, Masaru. 2001. "A Land without Patriots: The Yasukuni Controversy and Japanese Nationalism." *World Policy Journal* (Fall): 33–40.

Tatebayashi, Masahiko. 2004. *Giin koudou no seijikaeizigaku: Jimintou shihai no seido bunseki* [The Logic of Legislators' Activities: Institutional Analysis of LDP Dominance in Japan]. Tokyo: Yuhikaku.

Thelen, Kathleen, and Ikuo Kume. 2001. "The Rise of Nonliberal Training Regimes: Germany and Japan Compared." In *The Origins of Nonliberal Capitalism: Germany and Japan in Comparison*, edited by Wolfgang Streeck and Kozo Yamamura, 200–228. Ithaca, NY: Cornell University Press.

———. 2006. "Coordination as a Political Problem in Coordinated Market Economies." *Governance: An International Journal of Policy, Administration, and Institutions* 19, 1: 11–42.

Thies, Michael F. 1998. "When Will Pork Leave the Farm? Institutional Bias in Japan and the United States." *Legislative Studies Quarterly* 23, 4: 467–492

———. 2002. "Changing How the Japanese Vote: The Promise and Pitfalls of the 1994 Electoral Reform." In *How Asia Votes*, edited by John Fuh-sheng Hsieh and David Newman, 92–117. New York: Chatham House.

Tiedemann, Arthur. 1971. "Big Business and Politics in Prewar Japan." In *Dilemmas of Growth in Prewar Japan*, edited by James Morley, 267–316. Princeton, NJ: Princeton University Press.

Toby, Ronald. 2001. "Review: Rescuing the Nation from History: The State of the State in Early Modern Japan." *Momumenta Nipponica* 56, 2: 197–237.

Tokyo Stock Exchange. 2008. *2007 Shareownership Survey*, p. 5. http://www.tse .or.jp/english/market/data/shareownership/index.html.

Totman, Conrad. 1967. *Politics in the Tokugawa Bakufu 1600–1843*. Cambridge: Harvard University Press.

———. 1975. "Fudai Daimyo and the Collapse of the Tokugawa Bakufu." *Journal of Asian Studies* 34, 3: 581–591.

———. 1981. *Japan before Perry: A Short History*. Berkeley and Los Angeles: University of California Press.

———. 1982. "From Reformism to Transformism: Bakufu Policy, 1853–1868." In *Conflict in Modern Japanese History: The Neglected Tradition*, edited by Tetsuo Najita and J. Victor Koschmann, 62–80. Princeton, NJ: Princeton University Press.

———. 1988. *Politics in the Tokugawa Bakufu*. Berkeley and Los Angeles: University of California Press.

———. 1993. *Early Modern Japan*. Berkeley and Los Angeles: University of California Press.

Totten, George. 1965. *Democracy in Prewar Japan: Groundwork or Façade?* Lexington, MA: D. C. Heath and Company.

Toya, Tetsuro. 2006. *The Political Economy of the Japanese Financial Big Bang*. Oxford: Oxford University Press.

Tsang, Carol. 2007. *War and Faith: Ikko Ikki in Late Muromachi Japan*. Cambridge: Harvard University Press.

Tsebelis, George, and Jeannette Money. 1997. *Bicameralism*. New York: Cambridge University Press.

Turner, David. 2007. "Jasdaq Foreign Ownership Soars." *Financial Times*, June 25. http://www.ft.com.

Unger, J. Marshall. 2000. "Reconciling Comparative and Internal Reconstruction: The Case of Old Japanese /ti, ri, ni/." *Language* 76, 3: 655–681.

Upham, Frank. 1993. "Privatizing Regulation: The Implementation of the Large-Scale Retail Stores Law." In *Political Dynamics in Contemporary Japan*, edited by Gary D. Allinson and Yasunori Sone, 264–294. Ithaca: Cornell University Press.

Uriu, Robert M. 1996. *Troubled Industries: Confronting Economic Change in Japan*. Ithaca, NY: Cornell University Press

U.S. Office of the Secretary of Defense. 2007. *Annual Report to Congress: Military Power of the People's Republic of China*.

Varley, H. Paul. 1973. *Japanese Culture: A Short History*. New York: Praeger.

———. 1994. *Warriors of Japan as Portrayed in the War Tales*. Honolulu: University of Hawaii Press.

Vogel, Ezra. 1979. *Japan as Number One: Lessons for America*. Cambridge: Harvard University Press.

Vogel, Steven K. 2006. *Japan Remodeled: How Government and Industry Are Reforming Japanese Capitalism*. Ithaca, NY: Cornell University Press.

von Wolferen, Karel. 1990. *The Enigma of Japanese Power: People and Politics in a Stateless Nation*. New York: Vintage.

Vovin, Alexander. 1994. "Is Japanese Related to Austronesian?" *Oceanic Linguistics* 33, 2: 369–390.

Waltz, Kenneth. 1979. *Theory of International Politics*. New York: McGraw Hill.

———. 1993. "The Emerging Structure of International Politics." *International Security* 18, 2: 44–79.

Webb, Philippa. 2003. "Legislating for Care: A Comparative Analysis of Long-Term Care Insurance Laws in Japan and Germany." *Social Science Japan Journal* 6, 1: 39–56.

Weber, Max. 1946. "National Character and the Junkers." In *From Max Weber:*

Essays in Sociology, edited by Hans H. Gerth and C. Wright Mills, 386–395. New York: Oxford University Press.

Weingast, Barry R. 1997. "The Political Foundations of Democracy and the Rule of Law." *American Political Science Review* 91 (June): 245–63.

Weinstein, David E., and Yishay Yafeh. 1998. *On the Costs of a Bank Centered Financial System: Evidence from the Changing Main Bank Relations in Japan.* Cambridge: Harvard Institute of Economic Research.

Weinstein, Stanley. 1983a. "State Shinto," *Kodansha Encyclopedia of Japan.* 7:245. Tokyo: Kodansha International.

Weinstein, Stanley. 1983b. "Yasukuni Shrine," *Kodansha Encyclopedia of Japan.* 8:319. Tokyo: Kodansha International.

Whittaker, D. H. 1997. *Small Firms in the Japanese Economy.* New York: Cambridge University Press.

Widome, Daniel. 2006. "Why Japan's Neighbors Secretly Love the Yasukuni Shrine." *New Republic Online*, August 30.

Williams, Justin. 1979. *Japan's Political Revolution under MacArthur: A Participant's Account.* Athens: University of Georgia Press.

Wood, Christopher. 1992. *The Bubble Economy: Japan's Extraordinary Speculative Boom of the '80s and the Dramatic Bust of the '90s.* New York: Atlantic Monthly Press.

Yamaguchi, Jiro. 2004. *Sengo Seiji no Hokai: Demokurashi wa dokoe Yuku ka.* Tokyo: Iwanami Shoten.

Yamamura, Kozo. 1974. "The Decline of the Ritsuryo System: Hypotheses on Economic and Institutional Change." *Journal of Japanese Studies* 1, 1: 3–37.

Yamano, Sharin. 2005. *Kenkanryu.* Tokyo: Shinyusha.

Yashiro, Naohiro, and Takuro Morinaga. 2007. "What's to Blame for the Growth in Inequality?" *Japan Echo* 34, 3: 10–15.

Yomiuri Shimbun. Various issues.

Yonhap News. 2006. "Seoul-Tokyo Summit to Test Diplomatic Relations." October 4. http://english.yonhapnews.co.kr/Engnews/20061004/61000000002006 1004141017E8.html.

Yoshitake, S. 1930. "Etymology of the Japanese Word 'fude'." *Bulletin of the School of Oriental Studies*, University of London, 6, 1: 45–53.

Yoshitsu, Mike. 1982. *Japan and the San Francisco Peace Settlement.* New York: Columbia University Press.

Index